Saint Peter's University Library
Withdrawn

AMERICAN EDUCATION

Its Men

Ideas

and

Institutions

Advisory Editor

Lawrence A. Cremin
Frederick A. P. Barnard Professor of Education
Teachers College, Columbia University

The Principles,
Origin and Establishment
of the
Catholic School System
in the United States

Rev. James A. Burns

ARNO PRESS & THE NEW YORK TIMES
*New York * 1969*

Reprint edition 1969 by Arno Press, Inc.

*

Library of Congress Catalog Card No. 74-89155

*

This edition is published by arrangement with
the Holy Cross Fathers

*

Reprinted from a copy in Teachers College Library

*

Manufactured in the United States of America

LC
501
B7
1969

Editorial Note

AMERICAN EDUCATION: *Its Men, Institutions and Ideas* presents selected works of thought and scholarship that have long been out of print or otherwise unavailable. Inevitably, such works will include particular ideas and doctrines that have been outmoded or superseded by more recent research. Nevertheless, all retain their place in the literature, having influenced educational thought and practice in their own time and having provided the basis for subsequent scholarship.

Lawrence A. Cremin
Teachers College

The Principles,
Origin and Establishment
of the
Catholic School System
in the United States

THE PRINCIPLES,
ORIGIN AND ESTABLISHMENT

OF THE

CATHOLIC SCHOOL SYSTEM

IN THE UNITED STATES

BY

REV. J. A. BURNS, C.S.C., Ph.D.

President of Holy Cross College, Washington, D. C.
Author of " The Growth and Development of the Catholic School System
in the United States."

New York, Cincinnati, Chicago

BENZIGER BROTHERS

PRINTERS TO THE | PUBLISHERS OF
HOLY APOSTOLIC SEE | BENZIGER'S MAGAZINE

1912

Permissu Superiorum.

Nihil Obstat.

REMY LAFORT,
Censor Librorum.

Imprimatur.

✠JOHN M. FARLEY,
Archbishop of New York.

NEW YORK, APRIL 15, 1908.

COPYRIGHT, 1908, BY BENZIGER BROTHERS.

PREFACE

IT HAS been the aim of the author in the present volume to exhibit a coherent view of the Catholic school movement in the United States from the earliest times down to the great immigration period, which began about the year 1840. The characteristic feature of the movement during all this time was the steady effort to build and equip schools, provide teachers, and overcome fundamental difficulties both from within and from without. It was the period of the establishment of the schools. There was comparatively little in the way of academic progress. This came later on, when the influx of religious Orders from Europe and their rapid growth provided a greater supply of teachers, and thus made it possible to give to the teacher a better training. It is the intention to present a study of this second period, that of the development of the schools, in another volume. The educational work of Bishop Hughes obviously belongs to the first of these two periods rather than to the second, and for this reason, notwithstanding some disturbance of the chronological order, it is dealt with in the present volume.

The first four chapters of the work, together with the Introduction, appeared in successive numbers of "The Catholic University Bulletin" during 1906-7. Of these, the Introduction and the chapter on Colonial schools in Pennsylvania were reprinted from the "Bulletin" pages and published by the Reverend Superintendent of Catholic Schools, Philadelphia, in the series of quarterly "Educational Briefs," the former appearing in July, 1907, and the latter in January, 1908. The first five chapters and the Introduction were, in 1906, presented by the author to the Faculty of Philosophy of the Catholic University of America, in part fulfilment of the requirements for the degree of Doctor of Philosophy.

To the Reverend Doctors E. A. Pace, Thomas E. Shields, and Thomas J. Shahan, of the Catholic University; Rev. J. Devitt, S.J., Georgetown University; Rev. Philip R. McDevitt, Superintendent of Schools, Philadelphia; to the Ursuline Sisters, New Orleans, the Visitation Sisters, Georgetown, the Sisters of Charity, Emmittsburg, and the Sisters of Loretto, Ky.; to Mr. Martin I. J. Griffin, editor of the "American Catholic Historical Researches," Philadelphia; to Mr. George H. Schaefer, Chief Clerk in the Land Office, Annapolis, and to the Librarian of the Bureau of Education, Washington, the author feels a particular indebtedness, and wishes to express his acknowledgment of the important service they rendered him, either in connection with the gathering of the materials for this work or in the revision of particular sections of it.

JAMES A. BURNS.

HOLY CROSS COLLEGE,
WASHINGTON, D. C.
MARCH 19, 1908

CONTENTS

Contents

CHAPTER VII

The Early Teaching Communities

CHAPTER VIII

Influence of the Hierarchy

10 *Contents*

CHAPTER IX

BISHOP HUGHES AND THE SCHOOL QUESTION

The Educational Trend. Catholic Schools and the State. Origin of the School Controversy. First Petition to

APPENDIX

INTRODUCTION

A GENERAL VIEW

To UNDERSTAND a great movement in the world of thought or action, it is usually necessary to approach it on its historic side. It is difficult to grasp its inner spirit and purpose, or gauge aright its possibilities and power, except one bring to the study of its present condition a thorough knowledge of its past. The larger and more complex the movement is, the more important the study of its past becomes. Only in its history are we able to discern, in clear perspective, the principles that gave it birth, presided over its development, and form the mainspring of its present activity. Only in its past development, as Newman has pointed out, do we find the key to a correct understanding of what it is essentially at present, and what it is likely in the future to become.

The Catholic parish school system in the United States represents a great religious and educational world-movement. "The greatest religious fact in the United States to-day," says Bishop Spalding, "is the Catholic school system, maintained without any aid except from the people who love it." Its magnitude and complexity make it difficult to understand. Most non-Catholics who treat of it fail to apprehend either its purpose or its power. A school system which comprises 1,000,000 pupils, over 20,000 professional teachers, more than $100,000,000 worth of property, with an annual expenditure in the neighborhood of $15,000,000; which combines absolute unity and fixity of essential purpose with a flexibility of program as great as that which obtains in the public school system; which is national in its organization, and, at the same time, diocesan; which unites in the administration of each school three widely separated elements of authority, the bishop, the parish priest, and the nun—a system that does all this and does it effectively, without jar or noise, must be a very large and complex thing. It could not be the creation of a day. It must have come about gradually, as the result of a process of development. And to be understood it must be studied as such.

RELATION TO THE CHURCH

As a matter of fact, the foundation of the Catholic parish school system in the United States dates from the early years of the Maryland Colony. It represents, therefore, a development covering a period of over two hundred and fifty years. Broadly speaking, we can distinguish two great periods in its development, the first, extending down to the time of the Revolution, and the second, from that epoch-making event to our own day. The salient feature of its growth throughout the whole time is its dependence upon the growth of the Church in general. A direct relation existed between the development of the Church and the development of Catholic schools. We see the proof of the existence of this relation during the first period in the fact that, whenever Catholic settlements were formed and Catholic life reached any degree of maturity, Catholic schools were set up and a corresponding educational development took place. In settlements where Catholic life was weak or short-lived, either no schools were established, or those that were had only a short or desultory existence. In the post-Revolutionary period, the relation is even more clearly illustrated. The growth of Catholic parish schools and their organization into a great system has kept an even pace, in a remarkable way, with the rapid and extraordinary growth of the Church. The main factors in the Church's development—immigration and migration, the hierarchy, parish and diocesan organization, the religious Orders, the Councils—have constituted also the main factors in the growth of the schools. And the influences that were at work to retard the Church's progress have had a correspondingly hampering effect upon the schools. The relation between Church and school has been, in fact, so close that it is impossible to disassociate the history of the one from that of the other. The parish school has been from the very beginning an agency of the Church. It is really a part of the Church's wider organization, and both in principles and in practical working it belongs to the Church's system.

GENESIS AND PRINCIPLES

The fact of this relation is itself sufficient to fix the place of the Catholic parish school system in educational history, and to exhibit its connection with the general world-movement for religious education, even if this connection were not made plain by the religious and educational antecedents of the men and women who founded our early parish schools. In point of fact, however, there is a direct historic connection between the Catholic school system in this country and the Catholic school systems of various countries of Europe. The first Catholic schools here were offshoots of the existing school systems there. The founders and first teachers of our schools were products of the Catholic schools and colleges of Europe, and the institutions they established here were reproductions, to a great extent, of those in which they had been trained, or with which they were familiar in the Old World. All through the history of the Catholic school system in this country, this European influence is traceable through immigration, the religious Orders, and other agencies. It has been a potent factor in the making of our schools and colleges and in the molding of their character.

We should expect to find, therefore, that the religious principles for which our parish school stands are the same as those for which the distinctively Christian school has stood in every age and under every variety of conditions. Those principles sprang from certain definite views about man and God, and the relationship of man with God— views that are as unchangeable as Christianity itself, and are indeed of its very essence—that man is a moral being; that the voice of conscience is a reflection of the eternal moral law; that God has made a revelation of truth through Christ, outside of the natural order of things; that man is destined for another and a more perfect life beyond the grave, for which his life on earth has been ordained as a preparation—these are concepts that lie at the

root of Christian education. Out of these ideas
have developed several well-defined principles with
respect to education, its end and scope and appropriate accompanying circumstances, which are traceable all through the history of religious schools.
These principles have, in substance, been held inflexibly by Catholics as well as by many Protestants,
and they are likely to be held inflexibly, at least by
Catholics, whatever may be the development or condition of religious education in the future. Let us
try to define clearly just what these principles are,
as we see them unfolded in the gradual evolution
and organization of Christian education, and more
particularly as we see them expressed in the development of the parish school system in the United
States.

FIRST PRINCIPLE—WILL-TRAINING

Looking at the matter historically, then, we may
say that moral training, or the education of the will,
is one of the fundamental things the Christian
school stands for. It is generally admitted that
moral character counts for more than mere knowledge in the struggle of life, and that moral training
is an important duty of the school. So far practically all educators agree. But lines of cleavage in
this commonly held view begin to disclose themselves when we ask, what is the ideal? Fundamen-
tally, moral character is based upon the distinction
between good and bad, right and wrong, virtue and
vice. But again, what is the ideal of good, and
right, and virtue? Is it to be found simply in the
natural order of things—in the dicta of a reason

and conscience rightly informed by a knowledge of the laws of the outer and inner worlds? Is the ideal that of the natural virtues, and no more? Here the position of the Christian school is plain and fixed. It necessarily rejects as insufficient the ideal which is based upon the natural virtues alone. For the Christian, the ideal of character is that set up by Christ—an ideal which finds its sanction in conscience, too, but which commends itself to conscience as clearer, fuller, loftier, and more perfect than that which reason, unaided, is able to propose. In a word, it is the development of *Christian* character, based upon the supernatural virtues and teachings of Christ, not distinct from the natural virtues, but including them and much more besides, which the Christian school places first among its duties, as the thing of most fundamental importance to the child.

The ideal of character to be striven for thus constitutes a note of radical difference between the Christian school and the school in which religion is not taught, or in which the religion taught is not Christian. The ideal being different, the view as to the means to be made use of in moral training is different also. The Christian school looks to a knowledge of the higher moral law which has come to us through Christ, joined to the practice of the moral and the Christian virtues, as the means to be made use of for the training of character. It stands squarely opposed, therefore, to that doctrine of Herbart, which seems to be finding an ever wider acceptance in our day, that "school discipline and instruction in the common branches, if illumined by the fundamental moral ideas, may be the adequate means for developing moral character."[1] The doctrine is debatable enough, if we take the ideal of moral character to be simply that of the natural man. But surely it can not be maintained, and it was doubtless not the mind of Herbart to maintain, that "school discipline and instruction in the common branches" is an adequate means for the development of *Christian* character. The two systems are irreconcilably opposed in point of ideal and purpose.

SECOND PRINCIPLE—RELIGIOUS KNOWLEDGE EDUCATIVE

In the second place, the Christian school stands for the principle that religious knowledge possesses a direct and important educative value for the pupil, apart from its influence in the formation of moral character, and its function as a dogmatic basis for the primary precepts of morality. Broadly speaking, all truth is educative, but all truth can not be comprehended in the school curriculum. A selection has to be made. What shall be the basis for the selection? Manifestly, the intrinsic educative power of the subjects to be taught, under the given circumstances, and their importance for the pupil's after-life. In both these respects, it is maintained, religious knowledge possesses a very high degree of value for the growing mind.

INTRINSIC EDUCATIVE POWER

The mind develops through knowledge, and knowledge is gained and assimilated through the

[1]De Garmo, Herbart and the Herbartians, p. 56.

relationship of idea to idea. When the child enters
the school for the first time, his mind has reached
a certain stage of development, and is in possession
of certain ideas. The work of the teacher is to develop these ideas still further, or rather to aid in
their self-development. For this purpose, the principles of identity, of equality, of likeness, of causal-
ity, of the esthetic, and the like, which the mind
of the child has already learned through experience
to employ, are brought into play, and made to serve
as apparatus for the apprehension of new ideas, as
well as for the better assimilation and structural
disposition of the existing content of the mind.
Now, the apprehension and assimilation of religious
knowledge is based upon these same organic mental
processes. In the realm of religious truth, idea is
related to idea, just as in the realm of secular
knowledge. The two realms, in fact, have many
points of contact. At bottom, all religious truth
bears upon the relation of man and the universe
to God, and the apprehension of this relation involves the exercise by the mind of those same structural mental principles of equality, likeness, causal-
ity, and the rest, which form the subjective basis
of instruction in secular knowledge. From this
point of view, therefore, the teaching of religion
does not necessarily involve the introduction of any
foreign principle into the methods of instruction.

Moreover, the mind of the child has already a
substratum of religious knowledge. It is gifted
with a certain religious sense, inclining it toward
religion, and causing it eagerly to reach out to
apprehend new religious ideas. It is only necessary to suppose, then, that the religious truths

presented in the catechetical instruction or otherwise are made sufficiently simple and concrete, in order to have present all the conditions requisite for their easy and effective apperception in the pupil's mind.

But the apperceiving ideas are not confined to the purely religious content of the pupil's mind. They include other elements also, to a greater or lesser extent. They include purely secular as well as religious elements. For when the work of religious instruction is rationally done, the religious truths imparted to the child are presented linked in the closest relationship to truths of the natural order. The doctrine of the Incarnation, for instance, is presented in a setting of historical, geographical, moral, and esthetic facts, and the ideas which rise up in the pupil's mind to embrace the complex image will correspond to the setting of truths in the natural order enveloping the religious doctrine, as well as to the religious doctrine itself. This is a very important point, for it is in this precisely that the chief educative value of religious teaching for the growing intelligence lies. It is just here that religious instruction in the school possesses an intellectual and practical value which religious instruction in the Sunday-school or the church can never have. For as the religious doctrine is gradually unfolded, in the course of time, the setting of historical, geographical, moral, and esthetic elements is made continually to expand. In this way, an ever wider and more intimate correlation is established in the pupil's mind between the doctrines of faith and the facts and principles derived from the study of the common branches.

SAINT PETER'S COLLEGE LIBRARY
JERSEY CITY, NEW JERSEY 07306

The supreme relation of man and the universe to God, the Creator of all things, is thus apperceived in connection with the relations of man and the other component elements of the universe to each other. A continuous process of co-ordination and synthesis is set up between the pupil's outer experience and his secular studies on the one hand, and his inner experience and the doctrines of faith on the other. A tendency is created to see truth in the whole, to see particular truths as all converging toward a common center, rather than as separated fragments, or as divergent series that never meet. In an embryonic way, the process may be likened to the work of the great medieval schoolmen, who attempted to synthesize, in their theological *Summas,* the truths of philosophy and of the natural sciences with the dogmas of faith and their corollaries as embodied in the Christian revelation.

AN OBJECTION

The process is, in the main, synthetic, but if the work is intelligently done the analytical and critical faculty of the pupil's mind is also brought into play. Assimilation and co-ordination necessarily involve analysis and comparison. The objection, that the principle of religious instruction is authority, while that of secular knowledge is demonstration and verification, and that these principles are so different that, under the same conditions of instruction, they are mutually incompatible,[1] is based upon a twofold misconception. It supposes, in the first place, that the authority

[1]Hon. W. T. Harris, Proceedings National Ed. Ass'n, 1903.

invoked by the teacher in religious instruction is essentially different from that which is appealed to in the imparting of secular knowledge. The authority is indeed different, but, in its practical aspect, it is merely a difference of degree of imperativeness. The objection supposes, secondly, that the "principle of demonstration and verification" is inapplicable in religious instruction. It must be remembered, however, that, for the immature mind of the child, the all-important thing is not method so much as matter, not truth in its relation to its sources so much as truth in its relation to the existing content of the mind. The study of truth in its relation to its demonstrable sources is properly the work of maturer years. It is the work of the high school, the college, and the university. The supreme law of psychological change during the first years of school life, like the law of physiological change during the same period, is expansion. The mind of the child is an embryonic miniature of the whole world of knowledge. It hungers for knowledge of every kind which is capable of being correlated with the vague, general ideas it already possesses. It is the business of the teacher to satisfy this wholesome craving for knowledge and to develop it still more, in accordance with the laws of psychological growth and the actual and future environment of the pupil. This is the main work in the beginning. And yet, while doing this, the teacher should endeavor also to develop gradually the spirit of inductive inquiry and demonstration. The objection is right in supposing that this is, partially at least, the duty of the elementary school. It is wrong, however, in supposing that this may not or should not be done in the case of religious instruction. The objection here rests, in fact, upon a false psychological premise, in taking for granted the absence of such religious knowledge in the pupil as would enable him to bring the religious truths taught within the range of his powers of personal experience and verification. But does this apply to religion any more than to the other subjects of the curriculum? The teaching, for instance, that all things come from God, and that all things, if rightly looked at, give evidence of this relationship with God—is the mind of the pupil less able to grasp this truth, and to apply it in his observation of the internal and external phenomena he has experience of, than to understand the great principles of history and geography, and to submit their lessons to the probabilities of his personal experience? The objection would indeed be valid, if religious instruction in the school were simply a drill in abstract ideas. But it would hold equally against the teaching of geography and history in an abstract and uninteresting way.

IMPORTANCE FOR AFTER-LIFE

The tendency toward the synthesis of secular and religious knowledge, which is set up in the school by the teaching of religion in connection with the common school subjects, does not stop with the termination of the school period. It is carried over into the after-life of the pupil. From this point of view also, the teaching of religious truth in the school possesses a supreme educative value, not only as regards conduct and character, but also in respect of thought and feeling. What a knowledge of the elementary truths of faith does for the child, in helping him to harmonize his immature experiences of the outer order of things with the inner experiences of his soul and his religious sense, this the deeper and fuller development of the same truths, which comes with growing maturity of mind, does for the boy and the man, in the presence of the universe, and the infinity of complex relations which it involves. A man can not think rightly or profoundly about any single fact or thing without being led back by it, step by step, to the great central religious truth, from which all else proceeds. A life can not be regarded as rightly ordered which leaves out of account the Supreme Life, in the knowledge of which the end and purpose of all other life is to be sought.

Take the doctrine of the Incarnation, for instance, with all that it imports in respect of man's life and destiny. What a light this doctrine throws upon the idea of God, and upon the relations of all other beings to God, as well as to each other! Even in the sphere of purely mundane things, there is no single truth or group of truths which, in their deeper aspect, it does not touch and color. There is no mystery along life's pathway which it does not, to some extent, illumine. If the doctrine of the Incarnation represent a real truth, therefore, it is a matter of vital consequence for the after-life of the pupil that he be made acquainted with this truth as soon, as fully, and as effectively as possible. The exclusion of such a doctrine from the circle of subjects which are to be made the basis of the child's instruction in school could be justified only

on the ground that it does not represent a real truth,
or one that is certain.   And in the Christian mind
there is no place for this alternative.

THIRD PRINCIPLE—RELIGIOUS ATMOSPHERE

A third fundamental thing the Christian school
stands for is a religious atmosphere. By the atmosphere of the school is meant the sum of all the
educative influences of the schoolroom, outside of
the formal instruction.   Study and recitation, lesson and lecture, represent only a part of the educational forces of the school.   They constitute the
formal process.   But there are other and not less
powerful agencies at work, though they are less
obvious and direct in their operation.   There is the
influence of the teacher, outside of the teaching
proper, an influence which is positive even though
not perceived, which springs from the teacher's
character, personality, and general manner of life.
There is the influence of the pupils upon each other,
the interacting effect of their personal views, characters, conduct, manners, as well as, in a remoter
degree, of their respective home surroundings.
There is the influence of the appointments and ornaments of the schoolroom itself, which may be made
to speak lessons of order, neatness, virtue, and
religion day by day, silently, but none the less effectively, through appeal to the eye and the esthetic
sense.

It is the aim of the Christian school to turn all
such things to account for the attainment of its
specific end.   If the teaching of religion is a thing
of supreme importance in the work of the school,

than the training of the intellect; that the school must be surrounded by an atmosphere of religion and piety; that the teaching of religious truth is of vital consequence for the right education of the child; and that religious instruction, to be effective, must be begun in the elementary grades, and be co-ordinated with instruction in the common branches.

METHODS OF TEACHING RELIGION

The interest of the Church in the schools has always centered about these fundamental principles. In the teaching of the purely secular branches she has had no direct interest. She took the curriculum of secular studies such as she found it, and left its development to the operation of the ordinary laws of educational growth. Outside of the matter of religion, there has been no attempt to differentiate Catholic parish schools from other denominational schools or from the public schools. The tendency has been rather the other way.

While Catholics, however, have clung faithfully to the historic ideals of the Christian school, it needs but a slight acquaintance with the history of Catholic schools in the United States to make one realize that the working out in practice of the principles outlined above is a matter which opens up grave difficulties and problems. If we compare, for instance, the teaching of religion in the parish schools to-day with the teaching of it a few generations ago, it will be seen that great changes have taken place. Religion had a larger place formerly in the curriculum than it has now. The catechetical drill was more thorough, and took up more time. More importance was attached to it. The value to the growing mind of a knowledge of the truths of faith, simply as *knowledge,* was better evidenced in practice formerly. Not that the principle itself, perhaps, that religious truth, when properly taught, has a high educative value, is any less accepted now. But conditions in the school have changed. Secular studies have been multiplied. To make room for them, the time given to religious instruction has been cut down. There are some compensations, of course, for this. Methods of teaching religion have improved. The ill-prepared teachers of the early days, often with little or no religious training themselves, have been replaced by teachers who are devoted to the service of religion by profession. The more distinctly religious atmosphere of the school is relied on to-day to do much of what was formerly done by direct instruction and drill.

Not only have there been great changes in the extent and methods of religious teaching in our schools in the past, but great differences in both these respects exist to-day. Parish schools are sometimes found within a few blocks of each other in which the teaching of religion is about as different as it could be, the dogmatic content remaining the same. In some schools, the sum total of the religious influences at work hardly extends beyond the bare half hour of catechism-teaching. In others, religion is kept in the foreground all the time. In some instances, the desire to rival the rich and varied program of the neighboring public schools has caused a paring down of the religious work of the school to such an extent that anything like a religious atmosphere is scarcely possible. On the other hand, we see schools whose standard in secular studies is quite as broad and as high as that of the best public schools of their class, which are still able to include in their program various exercises of piety as well as classes in religious instruction.

Here and there throughout the country, the effort is being made to bring the methods of catechetical instruction more fully into accord with sound psychological principles. In a number of our best schools, catechism is now being taught by employing the same methods as prevail in the teaching of the other common branches. In these schools direct religious instruction is accompanied by object lessons, blackboard and chart illustrations, songs, and devotional exercises—in a word, the senses, the imagination, the emotions, the will and the affections are all appealed to, as well as the intelligence, in the endeavor to bring down the religious truths that are taught from the region of the abstract and the metaphysical, and to render them easily assimilable for the mind of the child. Several catechisms, too, have recently made their appearance which embody these methods in a practical and attractive form. It must be admitted, however, that in the great majority of our schools, in many even which are thoroughly modern in methods of teaching in respect of other subjects, the catechetical instruction is still given after the fashion of a century ago. It is a dry, hard drill in abstract, theological formulæ, and little more. There is no appeal to the senses, and little, if any, to the imagination, the heart, and the will. The cate-chisms in more common use, so far as pedagogical principles and methods are concerned, offer not the slightest improvement over those of a century ago. If anything, they are worse; they are longer, more technical, and more abstract. The question might well be raised as to why the question-and-answer manner of teaching should be considered the *ne plus ultra* of method in religious instruction, since it has long been discarded in the teaching of other branches; but even apart from this, the make-up of our common catechisms is such as to leave them open to the gravest objections, in point of both prin-ciple and method.

It is evident, in fact, that, on the religious side, the parish school of to-day is very far from having reached the term of its complete development. It is still in a partly embryonic condition. The ad-justment of means to end and principles has to be-come much closer and to proceed much farther before anything approaching a satisfactory condi-tion as regards religious training can be said to be attained. In point of religious teaching, the de-velopment of our schools is, on the whole, far be-hind their development in respect to secular studies. This is a strange fact, and it would be a grave men-ace to the future of our schools, did not a considera-tion of the causes that have brought about this condition, in the light of the past history of the schools, warrant the hope of a fuller development in the future on the religious side. The need of greater unification, or at least simplification, of the school curriculum, is now widely recognized, and the fuller realization of this need, together with the growing movement for more effective religious instruction in the school, will doubtless lead our educators and teachers in time to give to the teaching of religion the place of supreme importance it deserves.

DEVELOPMENT OF OTHER FEATURES

Outside of the matter of religion, there are a number of features about the development of the Catholic parish school system in the United States which merit the special study of the student of education. On the economic side, what has been accomplished, taken together with the manner of its accomplishment, is altogether unique in the history of education. In respect of organization and administration, there are features of even greater interest. Just as the Church, under the new conditions confronting Catholic life in America, has developed an organization and a spirit adapted to the successful carrying on of her work under those conditions, so her school system has, under the pressure of adverse circumstances at certain points and the enlargement of opportunities at others, grown into a form and structure which is greatly different from our public school system on the one hand, and, on the other, from the existing systems of Catholic schools in other lands. As an illustration of this, it is sufficient to point to the fact that the parish school system, owing to the nature of its organization, is altogether exempt from some of the crying abuses to which our public schools are subjected, such as, for instance, the manipulation of school interests for personal ends. It is noteworthy, too, that Catholics

in other lands have become interested in the parish
school system here, and are studying its organization and methods.

The development of the schools on the academic
side is a feature also that is full of interest. How
the old rigid "Three R" curriculum of the poverty-stricken Catholic schools in colonial days has
expanded gradually, with the growth of educational thought, until to-day it is practically indis-
tinguishable, in point of content, from the broad
and bountiful curriculum of the State-endowed public schools; how the few, poor, and ill-prepared
lay teachers of the early days have come to be replaced by the great communities of trained religious
teachers who carry on the work of the parish
schools to-day; how the more or less crude and un-
scientific methods that obtained during the first
period of our parish school history have gradually
given way to the vastly improved methods of teaching that are in use now—all this and much more
that pertains to the academic development of the
schools calls for the attention and careful study of
the student of education, whether interested in the
religious problem or not.

Yet the parish schools have received but scant attention at the hands of our educational historians.
Those features of our school system which distinguish it from the public school system in respect
of organization and administration have been almost altogether neglected. In some educational histories, the very existence of the parish school system
has been practically ignored. It is hoped that, in
the following pages, through the account that will
be given of the origin and establishment of our

schools, justice may be done, in some measure, to the work of Catholic educators; but the subject is large enough to afford room for more detailed and searching study at every important point.

PLAN AND SOURCES

In setting forth the facts which have been gathered relative to the parish schools, it has been borne in mind that their development is intimately interwoven with that of the Church, and also that practically nothing has been written as yet regarding their history. These considerations have, to a large extent, determined the method followed. The underlying purpose has been to show the causes that have produced the present system of Catholic schools, and an effort has been made to connect the movement, on the one hand, with the growth of the Church, and, on the other, with the religious, educational, social, and industrial movements in the country at large. During the colonial period particularly, when the Catholic school system was slowly forming in rough outline, these factors have been dealt with as extensively as was thought necessary, in order to enable the reader to see clearly the creative influences that were at work.

If the space devoted to the academic side of the Catholic school development seem unduly small, the fault does not lie with the plan of the author, so much as in the scarcity of materials. Exceedingly little has come down to us about the academic side of the early schools. There are several reasons for this. People did not write much about education in colonial times or even think about it much. And there was often a special reason for keeping silent about Catholic schools, in the fact of existing persecution and prejudice. But even for the post-Revolutionary period, the materials for a thorough study of the academic development of the schools are very scant and hard to be got at. Except in a few instances, nothing has yet been done to collect, from local sources, materials relating to the history of the schools during the last century. An abundance of data exists in local records, covering the history of the longer established schools during at least the past half-century. It would not be a difficult thing to gather this up and cast it into the form of local or diocesan school sketches. Several attempts of this kind have recently made their appearance, and it is evident that the importance of preserving the records of our schools is beginning to receive attention. It is hoped that the present effort to trace, in outline, the history of the school system as a whole, will stimulate many to take an interest in the history of local schools, and to collect and publish their records. Only after local and diocesan historians have done their work, can a history be written of the Catholic educational movement which will do justice to the subject in all its aspects.

Even in the case of the pre-Revolutionary period, it may be hoped that research will shed much further light upon Catholic schools. Several important facts in the history of the early Jesuit schools, gleaned by the author from the old Maryland Will Books, that go to disprove certain statements of educational historians which, in effect at least, have reflected more or less upon Catholic zeal for education, furnish an example of how much still remains to be done before the full history of the early Catholic schools will be accurately known. What has become of the records of the old Jesuit school at Bohemia, and of the records of the still older school and college at Newtown, as well as of the parish registers of that and the other Jesuit parishes in Maryland? A few precious manuscript records relating to these institutions survive at Georgetown, but the parish registers and the great bulk of the records are unknown. They may have been destroyed. Several disastrous fires occurred in Jesuit houses in America and England in which such records, if existing, would likely be stored.[1] Or, these records may still exist, forgotten and unknown, among the archives of Jesuit establishments in England or on the Continent. So too with the letters of the old Jesuit missionaries in Maryland and Pennsylvania, who were also the first Catholic school-teachers. Some have been religiously gathered up and treasured in the "Woodstock Letters," but the great mass of them have still to be found and published, if indeed they are to be found at all. The "American Catholic Historical Researches" is doing a service of the highest kind to Catholic history by searching out and publishing original letters and documents of this kind. The Catholic Historical Society, of Philadelphia, through its "Records," is doing a similar work, as is also the New York Catholic Historical Society, in its "Historical Records and Studies." The first two of these three last-mentioned publications have furnished a large share of the materials that went to

[1] Cf. Records of the English Province, vol. iii, p. 323.

make up the chapter on the schools in Pennsylvania.

There still remains, similarly, a large field for research in the history of the early Franciscan schools. There is reason to fear that many of the records pertaining to the early schools in New Mexico perished during the Indian uprising there in 1668. But much valuable material still exists, without doubt, relating to the Franciscan schools there, as well as in Florida, Texas, and California. In the archives of the Mexican National Library there are many volumes of still unpublished manuscripts dealing with the history of Spanish rule in the Southwestern States.[1] The extraordinary success attained by the Franciscans in converting and civilizing the natives, together with the reliance they placed upon education in effecting this result, would render every additional bit of information, from first-hand sources, bearing upon their work, an interesting and valuable contribution to the complete and comprehensive history of Catholic education in the United States,—a work which, as yet, belongs necessarily to the future.

[1] Texas Historical Association Quarterly, 1904.

CHAPTER I

EARLY MISSION SCHOOLS OF THE FRANCISCANS

NEW MEXICO

THE EARLIEST SCHOOLS

IN ATTEMPTING to trace the history of the Catholic parochial school system of the United States, we are led back step by step to the earliest organized work of the Church on the North American continent. In the Western World, as earlier, among the barbarian peoples of Europe, the work of the Church was one of Christianization and civilization, and it was clearly seen from the very first that the shortest and surest path to the attainment of this double end lay through the instruction of youth. Catholic schools sprang spontaneously from the development of Catholic life. The school-teacher followed close after the missionary and the explorer, and in many instances the first school-teachers were the pioneer missionaries themselves.

The earliest schools within the present limits of the United States were founded by the Franciscans in Florida and New Mexico. In the year 1629, four years before the establishment of the oldest school in the thirteen eastern colonies,[1] there were many elementary schools for the natives, scattered

[1] The oldest school in the thirteen English colonies was the school of the Reformed Dutch Church, established in 1633. The next was the Boston Latin School, opened in 1635 or 1636. Report of the Bureau of Education, 1903, vol. i, p. 555.

through the pueblos of New Mexico,[1] and from the number, character, and distribution of these schools, it is evident that the date for the foundation of the first school there must be set back considerably before the year 1629.

Doubtless the work of founding these schools was begun in 1598, the year in which Don Juan de Onate conquered and took effective possession of the country for the King of Spain.[2] Onate's force, which set out from Mexico early in that year, included seven Franciscan friars. As the expedition advanced northward into New Mexico and took possession of the country, the Franciscan Fathers were installed in the chief towns of the tribes, and the work of evangelization and education began. Churches were erected, as well as convents or dwelling-houses for the friars, and alongside of each convent, if not attached to it, was usually built a school.[3]

THE EDUCATIONAL MOVEMENT

Nor was this prominence given to education in the work of the missionaries due to circumstances or to accident. It had all been provided for almost a full century before, in the legislation framed for the liberty and protection of the natives of the New World by the great Ximenes, at the prompting of the saintly bishop Las Casas. That legislation dates from the year 1516.[4] By its terms, each village of the natives in New Spain was to have its

[1] Memorial of Benavides to the King of Spain, dated 1630, and printed at Madrid that year.
[2] Bancroft, Arizona and New Mexico, p. 124.
[3] Helps, The Spanish Conquest in America, vol. iii, p. 209.
[4] Ibid., vol. i, p. 353.

schools, as well as its church and hospital.[1] The sacristan of the village church was also to be the schoolmaster, and was charged with the duty of teaching the children to read, taking particular care to gradually accustom the Indians to the Spanish language. The parish priest was to see that each individual was taught according to his faculties, besides being instructed in the Faith. As early as 1531, the Bishop of Mexico was able to report that each convent of the Franciscan Order in his diocese had a school attached to it, and that the college which Peter of Ghent, a Franciscan lay Brother, had established in the City of Mexico, was attended by more than 600 Aztec youths.[2] The bishop also reported the foundation of many schools for girls.[3] For the native children schools were organized all through Mexico, and the work of erecting school buildings and organizing and teaching classes went on hand in hand with that of erecting churches, administering the sacraments, and preaching. The school, in fact, was considered essential to the complete organization of the parish. The aim was to give the entire native school population the benefit of at least a rudimentary education.[4]

Such was the system which led to the erection of schools alongside of the churches in New Mexico, as fast as the peaceful conquest of the country was

[1] Ibid.; von Hefele, Life of Card. Ximenes, p. 509 seq.
[2] Clinch, California and its Missions, vol. i, pp. 57, 63.
[3] Helps, The Spanish Conquest, vol. iii, p. 210.
[4] See in this connection the early Spanish educational legislation for the Philippine Islands, in Blair and Robertson's The Philippine Islands, vol. xliv, p. 184 seq.; also, Amer. Eccl. Rev., vol. xxxv, p. 595.

effected by Onate. The instruction given in these schools, in accordance with the plan of Ximenes, was of a twofold character. Up to nine years of age, the children were taught reading, writing, catechism, singing, and playing on musical instruments. Much stress was laid upon music, especially singing. It was an accomplishment that was made much of by the heathen medicine-men, and was held high in popular esteem. The native children took to it naturally, and the missionary Fathers themselves marveled and praised the Lord "to see in so short a time so many organ choirs."[1] Spanish was also taught.

A striking feature of this system of education was its practical character. From nine years of age on, the work of the pupil in school was almost wholly industrial. The common arts and trades of the civilized world formed the curriculum— tailoring, shoemaking, carpentering, carving, blacksmithing, brickmaking, stonecutting.[2] The girls were taught to sew and to spin. In their case also the instruction was admirably adapted to native character and talent, as well as to the needs of practical life. The Indians had a natural skill in many lines of industrial work, and the missionaries made the most of this in their system of instruction. So proficient did the pupils become in these trades, that, with the help of the women—upon whom, by a curious reversal of ordinary custom, the work of brickmaking and house-building fell, the men disdaining to take part in it—they were soon able to erect buildings for churches and schools which were

[1]Benavides, Memorial, p. 27.
[2]Ibid.

larger and finer than anything which the natives
had ever before attempted to build. "Over fifty
churches of very curious carved roof and the walls
very well painted" had been erected in this way by
1629.[1]

The missionaries themselves were the first
teachers. Some of them were men of eminent
learning, and nearly all had had the advantage of
years of experience in the missions of the Western
World.[2] They taught the elementary branches,
while training up the more promising pupils to become teachers. In course of time, probably, the
teaching came to be largely done by these natives,
but at the beginning the Fathers had to bear the
whole burden themselves. They taught the skilled
native artisans how to develop their trades along
European lines; they introduced domestic animals;
they taught the use of the horse, the cow, and the
sheep; they followed the plow, and sowed the
seed with their own hands, supplanting the primitive practices with the more scientific and fruitful
methods of agriculture brought from the Old
World.[3]

NUMBER OF SCHOOLS

The schools were scattered among the various
tribes inhabiting the region which extends for hundreds of miles along the upper Rio Grande. To

[1]Benavides, Memorial, p. 13.

[2]Among these may be mentioned Father Joseph Truxillo,
who had labored in New Mexico for many years preceding the
outbreak of the rebellion of 1680. He had acquired great renown in Mexico by his learning and eloquence. See Vitancurt, Teatro Mexicano, Menalogio, p. 87; Shea, History, vol. i,
p. 208.

[3]Benavides, Memorial, p. 27.

the westward, the missionaries penetrated far into what is now Arizona, and here too, among the powerful Mogui nation, churches and schools were established.[1] The Memorial or Report of Benavides shows that in 1630 there were about 50 Franciscans in New Mexico, serving over 60,000 Christian natives, in 90 pueblos, grouped in 25 missions, each pueblo having its own church.[2] Many of these pueblos had schools. Benavides does not give the exact number. He enumerates some dozen places where there were schools, but intimates that the inhabitants of all the pueblos had opportunity for instruction. Thus, speaking of the Tecas nation, he says: "All the pueblos have their churches, and they are very well instructed in all branches."[3] We can not be far from right, therefore, in concluding that the system of schools set up in New Mexico by the Franciscan missionaries comprehended in its scope the entire school population of the tribes or natives converted to the Faith. The fact is of interest when we reflect that it was not until some years later that the first school was set up in the English-speaking colonies of America, and, further, that at the time no comprehensive system of public schools existed in any European country.[4]

It is a matter of great regret that our knowledge of these schools and their practical working is so scant. Most of the knowledge we have of them is contained in the Memorial of Benavides. Nor have we any precise information about their influence. They must have been a potent factor in

[1]Bancroft, History of Arizona and New Mexico, p. 162.
[2]Benavides, Memorial.
[3]Ibid., Memorial, p. 8.
[4]Clinch, California and its Missions, vol. i, p. 57.

winning the good-will of the natives and effecting their conversion, and an evidence of their influence is to be seen in the conversion of entire tribes within a few years and their adoption of European standards of civilization. Not all the tribes were converted, but it is worthy of note that where the missionaries gained a foothold at all the conversion of a great part of the tribe almost invariably followed.

DESTRUCTION OF THE MISSIONS

Whether the schools were kept up until the very outbreak of the great rebellion in 1680, we have no means of knowing. Very likely they were. But the schools themselves, together with whatever records may have existed in New Mexico of their history and work, were completely destroyed in that uprising, and the only sources of information we have regarding them are contained in the accounts of the missions that reached the outer world before that date. Most of the friars were massacred. Schoolhouses, convents, and churches were burned or razed to the ground. In 1690 there was not a church, or priest, or Spaniard within the whole of New Mexico. Hatred of Spanish cruelty and tyranny seems to have been at the bottom of the revolt. Whether or not the friars themselves were partly responsible through imprudent zeal, they shared none the less in the general enmity toward everything Spanish which had gradually grown up in the minds of the natives during the years preceding the uprising. Unfortunately for New Mexico, and, no doubt, for the development of the entire southwestern section of our country, the friars do not appear to have ever fully regained their influence or their initiative in the missions of New Mexico. The rebellion was finally crushed. The friars came back; churches and convents were rebuilt; the natives were brought back gradually to the Faith, but a feeling of hatred, distrust, and fear lingered in the native mind. The long wars depopulated the country. There was no trade or industry, and the country was poverty-stricken. There were no material means to rebuild the schools, which had disappeared with the rebellion of 1680 as completely as if they had never existed. With the full restoration of the Spanish power, churches and schools were gradually re-established. In the year 1806, the schools of Santa Fe were attended by 480 children.[1]   But it was not until after the cession of New Mexico to the United States that, under the inspiration of an American bishop, and the breath of a new national spirit, evidence was given of the reawakening of a healthy Catholic life, by the foundation of a well-organized system of Catholic schools. Meanwhile, the Franciscans found new fields for the exercise of their zeal for Christian education in Texas and California.

TEXAS

The first Spanish expedition to Texas took place in 1689. It was followed by others, until gradually the whole country fell under the Spanish sway, and presidios or military garrisons were established among all the leading native tribes. Franciscan friars accompanied each of these expeditions, and when a presidio was planted, the work of civilizing

[1]Dexter, Hist. of Ed. in the U. S., p. 143.

and converting the natives was begun by the friars. Often, however, the missionaries preceded the soldiers. The Indians in most cases were friendly, welcoming the good priests with open arms, and being eager to learn from them the arts and manners of civilization, as well as to become Christians.

The Franciscans followed much the same methods they had made use of in New Mexico. Around the church and mission house, groups of buildings were erected, forming a little Catholic settlement, composed of the converted natives and their children. The real work of conversion and civilization was made to center about the children. Their moral training was carefully looked after, segregation of the sexes being practised to some extent, as was done later on in California. The girls were instructed in household arts, while the boys spent the greater part of their time at work in the shops or in the fields learning agriculture and stock-raising. There was a general instruction for all once a day at least, which was chiefly catechetical in character. Little attention was given to the study of the ordinary school subjects. The ideal was that of an industrial training, pure and simple.[1]

As in New Mexico and afterward in California, the educational work of the Franciscans in Texas was wonderfully successful, considering the difficulties in the way. The Indians in Texas were exceedingly hard to convert. "It is necessary first to transform them into men," said one of the missionaries, "afterward to labor to make them Christians."[2]

---

[1] Brown, Hist. of Texas, pp. 20-26; Yoakum, Hist. of Texas, pp. 53-64; Shea, op. cit., pp. 479-509; Garrison, Texas, p. 56.
[2] Yoakum, op. cit., p. 56.

Nevertheless, the missionaries succeeded. The Indians were converted, tribe after tribe, until nearly all except the Comanches and Apaches were Christianized. The mission region extended from the Rio Grande on the southwest to the Sabine River on the east, and from the Gulf of Mexico on the south to the mountainous region in North Texas. San Antonio was the chief center of the friars' work, five flourishing mission villages having been established in its vicinity.[1] What is more remarkable still, the Indians were led far along the way to material civilization and prosperity. They gave up, in large numbers, their wandering life. They substituted the plow for the bow and arrow, the quiet and peaceful life of the Christian presidio for the wild Arab life of their savage state. They became artisans, farmers, blacksmiths, bricklayers, carpenters, weavers. Many of their descendants are Christians to this day, even though ignorant and impoverished, owing to the operation of causes which have resulted in the entire disappearance of the Indians from other sections of our country.

The number of white settlers in Texas, as in New Mexico, was small, and this is probably the reason we do not hear of schools for Spanish children until a late date. San Antonio was the chief Spanish settlement, and a few years before 1789 a school was established there for the children of the colonists, which, although it had many ups and downs, continued to exist for a period of about thirty years.[2]

[1] Garrison, Texas, p. 60.
[2] A full account of this interesting institution, its curriculum, and curious disciplinary rules, is given by I. J. Cox, in the Texas Historical Association Quarterly for July, 1902.

FLORIDA

In Florida, the educational work of the Franciscans on a systematic scale dates from about the year 1594, when a band of twelve friars arrived from Spain to reinforce the four who were already laboring there.[1] The Franciscans, by their kind ways and methods of instruction, soon made many converts among the Indians. As in New Mexico, each mission house became a school of instruction for the natives, especially the children, in the arts of civilized life, as well as in the doctrines of Christianity. Missions were established gradually up and down the coast and far into the interior. But the work of the Franciscans did not meet with the same success in Florida as in the provinces to the west. This was due partly to the more savage and treacherous character of the Indians of Florida, and partly to the wars with the French and English, which resulted in the destruction of many of the mission houses and the dispersal of the missionaries.[2] For a time, however, much progress was made.

One of the first things the Franciscans did was to establish a classical school and preparatory seminary at St. Augustine, for the children of the Spanish settlers. This school existed as early as 1606, for in that year we find Bishop Cabezas de Altamisano of Santiago de Cuba, during the course of an episcopal visitation to Florida, conferring Confirmation upon several candidates for Holy Orders in St. Augustine.[3] In 1602, there were already 1,200 Christian Indians in Florida, and in 1612

[1]Shea, History, vol. i, p. 152.
[2]Fairbanks, Hist. of Florida, p. 177.
[3]Shea, History, vol. i, p. 160.

and the following year 31 new missionaries arrived from Spain, and the work of conversion and civilization was pushed rapidly on. The learned Father Francis Pareja, who was laboring among the Timuquan Indians at this time, published several catechisms, a grammar, and a number of other works in the native language, for the use of the missionaries and the instruction of the Indians.[1] By the year 1634, there were 35 Franciscans in Florida, with 44 missions, and 30,000 converts. Twelve years later, the number of missionaries had increased to 50.[2] That the Indians were instructed in reading and writing is evidenced by documents embodying petitions to the King of Spain and signed with their names by the chiefs of the various tribes.[3]

The prospects for Florida at this time seemed very bright, but they were soon overclouded. The tyranny of the civil authorities provoked the revolt of the powerful Apalache tribe, among whom a flourishing mission had been established, and the example of the Apalaches was followed by other tribes. The hostility of the English in the neighboring settlements, as they grew up, was another disturbing influence upon the Florida Indians, and a fruitful cause of dissatisfaction with the Spanish rule. The discipline of the missionaries also at times appears to have been somewhat harsh.[4] Owing to these and other causes, the missions, from about the middle of the seventeenth century, declined. Their record from that time on was one of stagnation or

[1] Shea, History, vol. i, p. 157.
[2] Ibid., pp. 163, 164.
[3] Ibid., p. 179.
[4] Ibid., p. 173.

decay, and presents little that is of educational interest until the year 1736, when Bishop Tejada, in attempting to bring about a revival of religion in Florida, reopened a classical school at St. Augustine,[1] the school being intended chiefly for the training of clerics. But it does not appear to have continued for more than a few years. In 1740, Governor Oglethorpe, of Georgia, led an expedition against Florida, and, in the long war which followed, the school probably disappeared, as no further reference to it is found after that date. In 1785, the Franciscans again opened a school at St. Augustine, the funds for its support being supplied by the King of Spain.

CALIFORNIA

The history of the school system established by the Franciscans in Upper California belongs, chronologically, chiefly to the post-Revolutionary period. The friars began their mission work there only in 1769, and the civilization and education of the native tribes went on under their direction until the year 1834. The mission schools of California, however, have a close historical connection with the school system established by the Jesuits in Lower California nearly a century before, and also with the school system set up in Mexico by the Franciscans, or under their influence, more than two centuries before. The regulations framed by the Franciscan Cardinal Ximenes for the education of the Indians furnished a practical educational ideal for the members of his Order doing missionary work

[1]Ibid., p. 470.

among the natives of the New World, as well as for all the other religious Orders. These regulations were, as we have seen, the guiding principle in the educational work of the Franciscans in New Mexico, Texas, and Florida. They were no less so for their work in California; only, as we shall see, they profited by the bitter lessons of their experience in New Mexico and modified the system somewhat in its external arrangement. At any rate, the mission schools of California belong to the great educational movement inaugurated by Ximenes and Las Casas. They have no connection with the educational work that was being done simultaneously in the English-speaking colonies. It seems best, therefore, to consider them in connection with the movement of which they formed a part.

EARLY JESUIT SCHOOLS

The Jesuits were the founders of the missions in Lower California, and the chief means they relied on for the success of their work seems to have been the building up of schools. As early as 1705, a school was set up at the mission of St. Xavier. This was followed by others, as fast as new missions were opened, each mission having two schools—one for boys, and another for girls. The subjects of instruction were Christian doctrine, reading, writing, music, and simple trades.[1] The school period lasted from the age of six to twelve. The Jesuits themselves, in the beginning, taught such trades as

[1] Clinch, California and its Missions, vol. i, p. 156; Gleeson, Hist. of the Cath. Church in Cal., vol. i, p. 258 seq.

farming, carpentry, smithing, and brickmaking, as well as the common branches of study. In the case of the girls, spinning and sewing took the place of the trades,[1] and, to crown the educational system, a boarding-school—a sort of normal school—was established in a central place, and to this the brightest boys were brought from each mission, and given a training in Spanish, as well as a higher training in the common branches. This school was counted on to furnish teachers for the other schools, as well as catechists and effective lay missionaries to aid the Jesuits in the extension of the mission work.[2]

Such were the remarkable educational achievements of the missionaries in Lower California when, in 1767, Charles III issued his fiat for the expulsion and deportation of the Jesuits from every part of the Spanish dominions. The Jesuits in Lower California were replaced by Franciscans. Sixteen Fathers, under the famous Junipero Serra, returned on the vessel which had carried the Jesuits away. They took up the missions and continued the work of the schools, but it was now found to be very up-hill work. The authorities threw obstacles in the way, and the natives were wasting away as the result of tyrannical oppression and disease.

THE FRANCISCANS

Father Serra, who was far-seeing and enterprising, as well as a saint, cast his eyes northward, and saw in the expedition which was being fitted out for the occupation of Upper California the oppor-

[1]Clinch, p. 105.
[2]Ibid., p. 156.

tunity for which he longed. An agreement with
the authorities was arrived at whereby the Franciscans were to take charge of the missions in the new
territory, and were to be given a free hand in their
work among the natives. The mission settlements
were to be entirely separate and at some distance
from both the presidios, or garrisons, and the
pueblos, or civil colonies. Father Serra had seen
the magnificent results of the Jesuits' work in
Lower California, where the plan had been to form
new settlements consisting of the converts alone,
and thus separate them completely from the bane-
ful influence of the gentiles, and especially the medicine-men. It was the same plan as the Jesuits had
carried out on a larger scale, and with even more
splendid results, in the famous "Reductions" of
Paraguay. He perceived, doubtless, that it was
the failure to separate the gentiles from the Christians which had led to the ruin of the missions in
New Mexico a century before.

It was natural that he should count largely on
education for the success of his plans. A Majorcan
by birth, the son of poor laboring people, he had
made a brilliant academic course, and, after teaching theology for three years with great applause,
received the degree of doctor.[1] He seemed destined to add another to the long list of names that
adorned the annals of Franciscan scholarship in Europe, and such, apparently, was what his superiors'
plans for him contemplated. But he longed for a
more apostolic career, and seized an opportunity

[1]Life of Ven. Padre Junipero Serra, written by his companion, Rev. Francis Pallou, p. 24; Hittell, Hist. of California,
vol. i, p. 301.

which presented itself of coming to America, where his learning, joined to the eminent holiness of his life, soon placed him at the head of the Franciscan missions in the far northwest.

CHARACTER OF THE SCHOOLS

Bancroft's summary statement, that there were no schools in California before Borica became Governor in 1793,[1] is true, so far as regards schools after the European fashion. But it is not true in the sense that nothing was done for the education of the natives. From the very first, the work of the friars was largely educational, and the whole routine of daily life devised for the converts who took up their residence at the missions formed a continuous educational process, in the large sense. Father Serra founded the first of the missions, at San Diego, in 1769. Others were founded by him year by year. San Gabriel was begun in 1771, and Father Font, a Franciscan who paid a visit to this mission in the year 1776, has left us in his diary a description of what he saw:

"The discipline of every day is this: in the morning at sunrise, Mass is said regularly, and in this, or without it if it is not said, all the Indians join together, and the padre recites them all the Christian doctrine, which is finished by singing the Alabado, which is sung in all the missions in one way and in the same tone, and the padres sing it even though they may not have good voices, inasmuch as uniformity is best. Then they go to breakfast

[1]Bancroft, Hist. of California, vol. i, p. 642.

on the mush (*atole*) which is made for all, and
before partaking of it they cross themselves and
sing the Benedito; then they go to work at whatever can be done, the padres inclining them and
applying them to the work by setting an example
themselves; at noon they eat their soup (*pozolo*)
which is made for all alike; then they work another
stint; and at sunset they return to recite doctrine
and end by singing the Alabado. . . .

"If any Indian wishes to go to the woods to see
his relatives, or to gather acorns, he is given permission for a specified number of days, and regularly they do not fail to return, and sometimes they
come with a gentile relative who stays to catechism,
either through the example of the others, or
attracted by the soup, which suits them better than
their herbs and eatables of the woods, and thus
these Indians are wont to be gathered in by the
mouth."[1]

The missions were, in fact, immense boarding-
schools. All the exercises of the day were in common. The great end in view was the formation of
Christian character. This was aimed at, in the
daily routine, by three means: religious practice and
instruction, industrial occupation, and strict discipline. The padre stood to the converts *in loco
parentis,* and the natives were treated as legal
minors under a guardianship.[2] The converts, on
the whole, accepted the conditions of life at the missions cheerfully. They loved the padres, and on
some occasions showed their love and veneration

[1] Garce's Diary, translated by Elliott Coues, vol. i, p. 262;
Gleeson, op. cit., vol. ii, p. 29 seq.
[2] Blackmar, Spanish Colonization in the Southwest, Johns
Hopkins University Studies.

for them by outward demonstrations which struck non-sympathetic observers with astonishment.[1]

As the formation of Christian character was the chief aim of the round of daily exercises prescribed for the convert, it was to be expected that special care would be bestowed upon the young. Father Serra early devised a system of training for girls, which became common throughout the missions, and a permanent feature of mission life. Font, in his description of the missions, refers to it thus:

"In the missions it is arranged that the grown-up girls sleep apart in some place of retirement, and in the mission of San Louis (Obispo) I saw that a married soldier acted as major-domo of the mission, so that the padre had some assistance, and his wife took care of the girls, under whose charge they were, and whom they called the matron, and she by day kept them with her, teaching them to sew, and other things, and at night locked them up in a room, where she kept them safe from every insult, and for this were they called the nuns; the which seemed to me a very good thing."[2]

It was the strict convent discipline, common in the bringing up of girls in Spain, which the friars introduced in the work of training the native girls. A soldier's wife took the place of the Spanish cloistered nun, and the domestic arts, sewing, spinning, and cooking, were substituted for the convent curriculum of studies. When De Mofras visited California, more than sixty years later, the native girls were still being trained in this way.[3]

[1] Vancouver's account of his visits to the missions, Hittell, Hist. of Cal., vol. i, p. 471.
[2] Garce's Diary, vol. i, p. 263.
[3] Blackmar, Spanish Colonization in the Southwest, p. 41.

FATHER LAZUEN

When Father Serra died in 1784, he was succeeded by Father Fermin Francis Lazuen. He was a man of refinement and scholarly attainments, even more markedly so than Father Junipero, and his administrative ability was equal to his learning.[1] For eighteen years he remained Prefect of California, founded many new missions, and labored to extend and perfect the work of the missionaries along the lines laid down by his predecessor.

Up to this time, there seems to have been no formal school work, outside of teaching the catechism. But little effort had been made to teach the natives Spanish. The boys spent most of the day in the fields.[2] Whatever teaching of the common branches there was, was done incidentally, or in the case of individuals. Father Lazuen, however, introduced schools, wherein reading, writing, and Spanish were taught, and singing by note, although only the most intelligent pupils were taught to read and write.[3] In the absence of books, these arts were not considered to have much practical value, but all were taught to sing, and were given plenty of practice in the daily religious exercises. Instruction in instrumental music was also given. Each boy was taught the rudiments of a trade, and much of the school-day went into practical lessons of this kind. Carpentry, blacksmithing, stonecutting, brickmaking, weaving, agriculture, and gardening, were the principal trades. Special stress was laid

[1]Hittell, Hist. of Cal., vol. i, p. 489.
[2]One of their chief tasks was to keep the birds away from the ripening fruits and crops.
[3]Shea, Hist. of the Cath. Church in the U. S., vol. iv, p. 345.

upon the value of steady occupation for the young, and habits of industry were inculcated as an essential to real Christian life.[1] Schoolhouses or schoolrooms were a regular feature of the mission buildings from this time on, but the training of the children continued always to be in the main industrial.

The slight importance attached to reading and writing and to the learning of Spanish, a knowledge of which was essential to the natives for much intellectual progress, is a point wherein the educational system established by the Franciscans in California is certainly open to criticism. Governor Borica, in 1795, issued a circular to the heads of the missions, directing them to form a school in every establishment, and teach the Indians to speak, read, and write Spanish, to the absolute exclusion of the native language. To this little attention seems to have been paid. Borica showed himself a strong friend of education, and besides encouraging it in the missions attempted to establish schools for the Spanish children in all the garrisons and pueblos. At this time the native Spanish population of California did not amount to more than 1,500.[2] It was very hard to find teachers, but Borica finally succeeded in starting several schools in the pueblos, a retired sergeant being the first schoolmaster, and the public granary at San José the first schoolhouse. The curriculum of these first public schools in California was very simple. Christian doctrine, reading, and writing, with perhaps the elements of arithmetic, were the only subjects taught.[3] Some

[1] Clinch, California and its Missions, vol. ii, p. 208.
[2] Bancroft, Hist. of Cal., vol. i, p. 603.
[3] Ibid., p. 643.

interesting facts respecting the illiteracy of the Spanish soldiers were brought to light by Borica's educational zeal. In 1791, only two out of 28 soldiers at San Francisco could write. In 1794, not a man in the garrison there was able to write, and the commandant asked that one who could write be sent from Santa Barbara. In 1800, many soldiers acting as corporals could not be promoted because they could not read.[1]

TECHNICAL TRAINING

Before passing judgment upon the neglect of thorough instruction in the common branches under the mission system, we must consider that the aim of the missionaries was not primarily intellectual, but spiritual, and that the system of instruction adopted for boys and girls, respectively, was held by the friars to be the best adapted to the immediate moral, material, and intellectual wants of a people who were in a state of transition from savagery to civilization. The natives were extremely lazy, and, generally speaking, stupid. Some among them were skilled in certain kinds of dyeing and carving, and they were all passionately fond of music. The missionaries, in framing their educational system, tried to adapt it to the characteristics and needs of the natives, just as they had done in New Mexico. All the children were taught to sing, and those who had inclination for it were taught the use of the musical instruments common in Europe. They were taught the manufacture and dyeing of cloths

[1]Ibid.

and fabrics of various kinds, from materials raised on the mission farms. With the help of skilled artisans, brought from Mexico for the purpose, they were schooled in the arts of masonry and carpentry, and the old mission churches still standing testify, although in ruins, to the high degree of technical skill they acquired, as well as to the architectural genius of the padres.

After all, was it not more important, at least for the first generation of converts, to learn to till the soil and to support themselves by the labor of their hands, than to learn to read and write? As between knowledge and industry, the friars might very sensibly have inclined to the belief that, in view of the inherited indolence of the natives, the first and most essential thing to teach them was work, and that it would be time enough to set up schools after the European fashion when their pupils had mastered the more elementary and necessary arts which would provide for them food, clothing, shelter, and other common conveniences of civilized life. When schools were actually established, the plan was to give instruction chiefly to the children who were brightest, with a view to making them teachers and superintendents of the others in the various trades and occupations. Eventually, there were schools established at most of the missions, and probably more or less common school education came to be given to every child. As late as 1829, however, several of the missions are reported as having no schools, and the complaint of some of the padres at that time, in reply to the circular letter of the Governor enjoining the establishment of schools, that the boys had little time for learning on account of their work,[1] shows us the relative importance the missionaries attached to book knowledge as compared with industrial skill.

RESULTS

If we would judge fairly of the wisdom and value of the educational methods of the friars, we must view their methods in the light of the results achieved. The test of the value of a method is in its working out. Certainly, the results achieved by the friars in the civilization of the natives of California were without parallel in the English-speaking colonies, and were not surpassed even in Mexico or Paraguay. "History," says a careful and learned modern critic, "records no better work ever accomplished in modern times for an inferior race."[2] At the end of sixty years, there were twenty-one prosperous missions, on a line extending from south to north about seven hundred miles. More than thirty thousand Indian converts were lodged in the mission buildings. They had been brought from the state of savagery, taught to wear clothes and accustomed to a regular life of toil, taught to read and write, instructed in music, accustomed to the service of the Church, partaking of its sacraments, and indoctrinated in the Christian religion.[3] De Mofras has left us a brilliant picture of the material prosperity of the missions at the time they reached their greatest development. The line of missions linked together the most fer-

[1] Bancroft. Hist. of Cal., vol. ii, p. 680.
[2] Blackmar, Spanish Colonization in the Southwest. p. 47.
[3] Blackmar, ibid.; Dwinelle, Colonial History of San Francisco, p. 84.

tile valleys of the coast. In the year 1834 they
produced 100,000 bushels of grain. They possessed 424,000 horned cattle, and 100,000 cattle
were slaughtered every year, yielding a return of
ten dollars per head. The total annual product of
the missions amounted to more than $2,000,000,
and the valuation of the movable stock, aside from
the buildings, orchards, vineyards, etc., was not less
than $3,000,000. Besides this, the "Pious Fund"
yielded an annual income of $50,000.[1] The mis-
sions had, in fact, grown wealthy, and a second line
of missions, farther back from the coast, and extending parallel with the first, was being projected.

RUIN OF THE MISSIONS

But the material prosperity of the missions
proved, in a way, to be their undoing. The country was filling up with colonists, and they looked
with a covetous eye upon the fertile valleys from
which the simple natives, under the mission discipline and management, were extracting all this
wealth. Agitation for the secularization of the
missions had been long going on, and was growing
stronger every year. Mexico, meanwhile, had
thrown off the Spanish yoke, and the Government
of the new republic was violently hostile to the
friars. In 1834 the blow fell. The Governor of
California, acting at the instance of the Mexican
authorities, issued an edict for the "secularization"
of the missions. The friars were driven off, and
the property taken possession of by the Government. The poor Indians, of course, got little or

[1]Blackmar, p. 47.

nothing. The final result of the process of "secularization," as might have been expected, was the plunder and complete ruin of the missions, and the demoralization and dispersion of the Christianized Indians.[1]

The best tribute to the work of the Catholic missionaries, and to the effectiveness of the methods they employed for the civilization and education of the native races, is to be found in the contrast between the results produced under the system they established, and the systems that have been tried by other agencies. It is interesting to note that the United States Government, after experimenting for over a hundred years in the education of the Indians, is tending more and more toward the adoption of the methods used by the Franciscans in California over a century ago.[2] If we contrast the labors of the Franciscans for the Indians of California with the work of the Government and other agencies for them since, we shall not find it difficult to accept as just the following judgment of the work of the friars, by one who was competent to speak with authority upon the subject:

"If we ask where are now the thirty thousand Christianized Indians who once enjoyed the beneficence and created the wealth of the twenty-one Catholic missions of California, and then contemplate the most wretched of all want of system which has surrounded them under our own Government, we shall not withhold our admiration from those good and devoted men who, with such wis-

[1] Dwinelle, op. cit., p. 63.
[2] Blackmar, op. cit., p. 48. Cf. also Report of the Commissioner of Indian Affairs, 1905.

dom, sagacity, and self-sacrifice, reared these won-
derful institutions in the wilderness of California.
They at least would have preserved these Indian
races if they had been left to pursue unmolested
their work of pious beneficence."[1]

[1]Dwinelle, Col. Hist. of San Francisco, p. 87. It may not be
amiss to quote here what a distinguished English traveler,
Mr. Alleyne Ireland, in a recently published book, The Far
Eastern Tropics (1905), has to say about the methods of education employed in the case of the native peoples of the Orient.
Indirectly, his remarks form a striking tribute to the efficiency
of the educational methods employed by the Franciscans in
California and the Spanish missionaries generally in dealing
with the native races in the Western World.

Speaking of the educational system we have set up in the
Philippine Islands, he says: "Every effort is being made in the
Philippines to give the people whatever advantages may be
attached to a wide diffusion of educational facilities; but when
it is reflected how small a proportion of the Filipinos can
ever be utilized outside the field of manual labor until a great
increase in industry has provided work of a higher character,
it is at least open to doubt whether the present attempt to
increase the literacy of the people is not premature.

"I may add in this connection that in fifteen years of travel
in tropical countries in which education has been in operation
for more than a generation I have observed no indication that
the spread of instruction has had the effect of making the
natives appreciate the dignity of manual labor. In fact, for
every skilled workman turned out by the industrial schools
in the tropics, the schools of general instruction have cast upon
the country twenty men who from the very fact of their education refuse absolutely to have anything to do with any
employment which involves manual labor" (p. 242).

CHAPTER II

CATHOLIC COLONIAL SCHOOLS IN THE FRENCH POSSESSIONS

NEW ORLEANS

EARLY CONDITIONS

THE CITY of New Orleans, which was founded in the year 1718, was described by Charlevoix, who visited it on his journey down the Mississippi four years later, as follows:

"A hundred barracks, placed in no very good order; a large warehouse, built of timber; two or three houses, which would be no ornament to a village in France; one-half of a sorry warehouse formerly set apart for divine service, and was scarce appropriated for that purpose, when it was removed to a tent. . . . What pleasure, on the other hand, must it give to see this future capital of an immense and beautiful country increasing insensibly and to be able to say that this wild and desert place, at present almost entirely covered over with canes and trees, shall one day, and perhaps that day is not very far off, become the capital of a large and rich colony."[1]

The place in its moral aspect was even more uninviting. The inhabitants were largely drawn from the outcast and criminal classes in France.[2] The number of negro slaves was greater than the number of whites. Yet there were some colonists of

[1] Journal of a Voyage to North America, vol. ii, p. 276.
[2] Gayarré, Hist. of Louisiana, vol. i, p. 248.

the better class, and the colony possessed in Bienville, the Governor and founder of the city, a man who united administrative ability with the highest ideals of moral and intellectual life.

Bienville saw clearly from the first that the only hope of the colony lay in education. If the criminal classes were to be elevated socially and morally, if the better class of inhabitants was to be kept in the colony and added to, it would be necessary to provide for the teaching and Christian bringing up of the children. One of his first acts, after the founding of the city, was to arrange for the bringing over of Capuchin friars, to take charge of the parish and to teach. Two Capuchins came from France in 1722,[1] and one of them, Father Cecil, opened a parish school for boys.[2] The school was, no doubt, very small, for the town, which had just been made the capital of New France, contained no more than 300 souls.[3]

Bienville was exceedingly anxious to get the Jesuits to come to New Orleans to found a school for the education of the boys of the more well-to-do colonists. The Jesuits established a missionary station there, but saw no means whereby they could establish and support a college. Bienville petitioned the King for this purpose, setting forth that it was essential to the colony that there be established a college "for the study of the classics, of geometry, geography, biology, etc., and where the youth of the colony would be taught the knowledge of religion, which is the basis of morality."[4] But

[1]Relation du Voyage des Dames Religieuses Ursulines, p. 115.
[2]Records Amer. Cath. Hist. Soc., vol. i, p. 219 seq.
[3]Gayarré, Hist. of La.
[4]Ibid., vol. i, p. 522; Fay, Hist. of Ed. in La., p. 11.

the colony was regarded by the King as too unimportant for the financial outlay required.

A description of the character and occupation of the boys of New Orleans which has come down to us, makes it easy to understand the anxiety of Bienville to get the Jesuits. Writing about 1740, an officer of the garrison in New Orleans says:

"The youth here are employed in hunting, fishing and pleasuring; very few learn the necessary sciences, or, at best, it is what is least attended to. The children, even of the best sort, know how to fire a musket or shoot an arrow, catch fish, draw a bow, handle an oar, swim, run, dance, play at cards, and understand Paper Notes, before they know their letters or their God."[1]

THE FIRST URSULINES

But though he could not succeed in getting the Jesuits, he was able at an early date, thanks to the good offices of the Jesuits, to get a band of trained teachers belonging to the foremost teaching sisterhood in France, to come over to take charge of the education of girls. This event, so notable in the history of American education, took place in the year 1727. On February 22 of that year, ten Ursuline Sisters, drawn from various convents of the Order in France, set sail at l'Orient, in a ship called the *Gironde,* accompanied by several Jesuits. The following is the list of the Sisters composing this little band, who probably have the honor of being the first professional elementary school-

[1] Present State of the Country and Inhabitants of Louisiana, p. 29.

teachers to set foot upon the soil of the United States:

Mère Marie Tranchepain de St. Augustin, of Rouen.

Sœur Marguerite Judde de St. Jean l'Evangéliste, professed, of the Community of Rouen.

Sœur Marianne Boulanger de St. Angélique, of Rouen.

Sœur Madeleine de Mahieu de St. Francis Xavier, professed, of the Community of Havre.

Sœur Renée Guiquel de Ste. Marie, professed, of Vannes.

Sœur Marguerite de Salaou de Ste. Thérèse, of Plœrmel.

Sœur Cécile Cavalier de St. Joseph, professed, of the Community of Elbœuf.

Sœur Marianne Daiu de Ste. Marthe, professed, of the Community of Hennebon.

Sœur Madeleine Hachard de St. Stanislaus, novice.

Sœur Claude Maffy, a secular choir sister.

Sœur Anne, a secular *converse* sister.[1]

The Superioress of the Sisters was Mother Tranchepain, a woman of scholarly attainments, and a convert to the Faith. All the Sisters had offered themselves voluntarily for the work of teaching in the far-off colony of New Orleans, though this involved so many hardships and a lifelong exile from home. Among them was a young novice, Sister Stanislaus, known in the world as Madeleine Hachard, who has left us, in a series of letters to her tenderly-loved parents, a fascinating narrative of the voyage and of their early life in

[1] Fay, Hist. of Ed. in La., p. 124.

New Orleans.[1] Madeleine Hachard was a Norman by birth, and was eager to imitate, even in a humble way, the heroic exploits of her great compatriot, La Salle. Her narrative breathes a love of adventure encountered in the service of the Cross, together with that quiet, cheerful humor which is characteristic of convent life. The account of the voyage reads in these days like a romance. And in truth, the voyage was romantic enough. The ship encountered terrible tempests, and several times seemed on the point of going down. Once she struck upon a rock. Corsairs got on her track again and again, and on one of these occasions, when capture seemed to be inevitable, the Sisters were stowed away in the captain's cabin. To add to their sufferings, the captain treated them at times with brutal harshness.[2] Five months were thus consumed, and everybody both at home and in the colony had given them up for lost. Finally, reaching the mouth of the Mississippi, the *Gironde* stuck fast in the mud, and the Sisters were forced to make their way up the river as best they could in small boats and dugouts, going ashore at night and sleeping in the forest. After two weeks of this rough canoe life, they reached New Orleans on August 7, 1727. "The city is very beautiful," naïvely writes Sister Stanislaus, "but it has not all the beauty the songs attribute to it. I find a difference between it and Paris; the songs may persuade those who have

[1]Relation du Voyage des Dames Religieuses Ursulines. Sister Stanislaus continued to teach in New Orleans until her death there, August 9, 1760.
[2]Relation, Circular Letter on the death of Mother Tranchepain, p. 58.

never seen the capital of France, but I have seen it, and they fail to persuade me."

The Sisters were joyfully welcomed, and installed in the best house in the city, which had been used by the Governor. Here these brave and noble women established a convent and Sisters' school, the first within the present limits of the United States. A hospital was also started, and later an orphan asylum. There were plenty of pupils—rich and poor alike sent their daughters, and on Sundays and in the evenings even negro and Indian women, along with their children, came to be instructed in the catechism. The Sisters did not teach boys. Part of the house was set apart for a boarding-school and academy for the education of the children of the better classes. All the inhabitants who could not afford to send their children to the academy were invited to send them to the day-school, in which the teaching was free of charge. They began with 24 boarders and 40 day-scholars.[1]

URSULINE IDEALS

Before proceeding to give an account of the matter and methods of the teaching in this venerable Catholic parochial school, it will be useful to consider the ideal of teaching proposed by the Ursuline Order, which still occupies an important place among the teaching Orders in the United States. This will help the reader to understand the teaching ideal of the Catholic sisterhoods in general engaged in school work, for they are all alike in this respect. It will enable him also to

[1]Relation des Dames Religieuses, p. 115.

understand the heroism of these first parish-school teachers, abandoning home and country, and meeting a thousand perils on the sea, in order to set up Christian schools in the wilderness of America, and thereby help to win its youth to Christ.

"The Ursuline Order has been instituted, not only for the salvation and perfection of its members, but also in order that these may help and serve their neighbor by the instruction of young girls, whom they must labor to bring up in the fear and love of God, leading them in the way of salvation, teaching them every social and Christian virtue, and preparing them to be a source of edification to others by the practice of these virtues.

"This vocation is eminent, and it ought to be esteemed by those whom God has called thereto; for in following it they are doing with advantage the office of the Guardian Angels, an angel being charged to guard a single soul, and that by ways secret and invisible; whereas an Ursuline can direct several souls by ways exterior, sensible, and proportionate to their capacity. And this need not astonish us, as God has, since the Incarnation of His Divine Son, raised men above angels, to aid and co-operate in the works of grace.

"The principal end of the Ursulines' vocation being to give a good and solid education to young persons, according to their condition, all the teaching religious ought to prepare themselves in the sciences and arts, so as to be always capable of meeting the exigencies of the times, and to be thoroughly master of all they may be called on to teach.

"The Sisters will rejoice in the Lord and take a special pleasure in teaching poor girls, honoring therein the mission of our Divine Saviour, sent to evangelize the poor.

"And, as there is a vast difference between engaging in some great employment and applying one's self to it through a spirit of vocation and grace when one is called by God; so it is very important for Ursulines to know and understand that they have been called by God to instruct young girls, and that they will receive grace to acquit themselves well of the duties of this vocation. Hence they ought to apply themselves cheerfully to these duties for the sole glory and love of God."[1]

THE URSULINE SYSTEM

In the Rules for the Ursuline Religious printed at Paris in 1705, a well-thumbed copy of which, brought by the Sisters to New Orleans in 1727, is still preserved in the Ursuline Convent there, we have an outline of the course of studies followed in this primitive parish school, as well as a great deal of valuable information regarding the methods of teaching employed by the Ursulines in France at the beginning of the eighteenth century.

The following is the program of studies prescribed in this ancient manual, and immediately after it, for the sake of comparison, is given the program prescribed in the revised rules, edition of 1860. It will be observed that the subjects in the two are substantially the same, as also their order of arrangement, the chief difference being that the sessions in the second are longer and the exercise, named manual labor, is put first on the list for the afternoon. In the first program, manual labor is given as an alternative exercise to reading, the

[1]Constitutions of the Ursuline Order, New Orleans.

custom being to permit the more advanced pupils to occupy at least a part of the reading-hour in manual work.

Program of Studies, 1705

Morning (1½ hours).
> Prayers.
> Reading (manual work).
> Arithmetic.
> Writing.
> Recess.

Afternoon (2½ hours).
> Prayers.
> Reading (manual work).
> Religious instruction.
> Prayer, examen.
> Recess.[1]

Program of Studies, 1860

Morning.

8.30	Prayers, recitation of lessons, correction or preparation of duties.
9.30	Reading.
10.00	Lesson in arithmetic.
10.45	Lesson in writing.
11.30	Recess.

Afternoon.

1.30	Lesson in manual work, during which there is recitation of beads and spiritual reading.

[1] Rules of the Ursuline Religious, Part Second, Day School, Paris, 1705.

3.15   Lesson in grammar, exercises in orthography, or other exercises.
4.15   Religious instruction.
4.45   Prayer, examen.
5.00   Recess.[1]

The school-day was very short in the early period—only four hours. But so was the vacation period, which covered only three weeks. However, there were many feast-days, and Saturday afternoon was free.

Reading, writing, and arithmetic, together with catechism and industrial training, made up the simple but substantial program. Of the first three, reading was regarded as of the most importance. It was taught both morning and afternoon, and all other secular instruction centered about it. The more advanced pupils read first, and then, while the others were being heard, they practised writing and "casting accounts." In teaching reading, the teacher read the lesson first aloud, slowly and distinctly, the pupils following in a low tone. The pupils were then called upon, one after the other, to repeat parts of what had been read, the teacher correcting the mistakes. Spelling was taught in connection with the reading lesson.

Comparatively little attention was given to arithmetic. For writing, there was a long table, provided with quill pens and inkstands, together with written models which the pupils set themselves to copy.

But the exercise which was regarded always as of first and most fundamental importance was re-

[1]Revised Rules of the Ursuline Religious, appendix, 1860.

ligious instruction. This included prayers, daily examination of conscience, preparation for the sacraments at stated times, and the daily study of the catechism. It was for this chiefly that the school existed, and at her first entrance to school the pupil was to be taught that the principal purpose for which she was received was "to learn to know, love, and serve God, in order by this means to become one day blessed."[1]   It was sought to fix in the mind of the pupil the view that this life is destined to be but a preparation for a higher and more blessed life to come, and that the chief business of education, consequently, was to enable one so to live and work in this world as to attain most securely and most perfectly to the possession of life in the world to come. This idea lies at the root of all Catholic educational work, and constitutes to-day a mark of fundamental difference between the Catholic school system and the system of public schools.

Sister Madeleine de Mahieu was the first to have charge of the day-school. She was a talented teacher, who, as soon as the news of the founding of New Orleans reached France, ten years before, had offered herself for the work. The teaching of the poor children who flocked to the school was her delight. Nothing made her more happy than to see their number increase, and the more ignorant they were the more she attached herself to them.[2] Most of them were densely ignorant. By the rules of the Order, pupils were supposed to be at least six years of age, and to know the alphabet before

[1] Rules, 1705 edition.
[2] Relation du Voyage des Dames Religieuses Ursulines, p. 43.

being admitted to school;[1] but this requirement could not be exacted in New Orleans. There were some pupils fifteen years old who had never been to confession or to Mass, and some had never even heard tell of God. "When we tell them the most common things," wrote Sister Stanislaus, "they take them for oracles which fall from our lips."[2] The pupils were docile and eager to learn. They loved the Sisters who had come so far to teach them, and their love for them was shared by all the people of the town. Good Sister Madeleine, sad to say, lived only a year after the opening of school. She fell a victim of the swamp fever and to the lack of suitable medical attention. Three other Sisters also died within a few years, among whom was the Superioress, Mother Tranchepain. All of them suffered much from sickness during the first years of their residence in New Orleans.

Some features of the Ursuline system of teaching were surprisingly modern, and throw a new light upon the educational ideas and methods of the period. One of these features was the employment of pupil-teachers, called in the Rules *"dizainières."* They were selected from among the brightest and best-behaved girls, and their office was to assist the teachers in class-work and in the maintenance of discipline. They were to be changed every three or four months. Each *dizainière* had her group of ten or so to look after. She admonished them of their faults, of which she was not, however, to inform the teacher, except it be-

[1]Rules, Paris, 1705.
[2]Relation du Voyage des Premières Ursulines, p. 99.

came necessary for their correction. Among other duties, she distributed the text-books to her charges at the beginning of class, and locked the books up again carefully just before school was dismissed. Text-books were free, although they were precious things in those days, and hard to obtain. She taught the prayers to beginners, and often helped during the recitations, standing near the teacher, and interrogating the members of her band. The system was in many respects like the system of pupil-teaching which Lancaster almost a century later introduced into the United States.[1]

Another interesting feature of the Ursuline method of teaching was specialization. The "teacher of writing" devoted her time chiefly to that particular branch, and went from class-room to class-room to supervise the work of the pupils in learning to write. There were special teachers also for arithmetic and industrial training.[2] It is probable, however, that some time elapsed before the principle of specialization was put into practice in New Orleans, on account of the scarcity of teachers.

It will be noticed that a great deal of time was devoted to industrial work. This was a feature of the Ursuline school everywhere. The pupils began by learning to knit and to stitch, and were taught gradually how to mend and make their own garments, as well as various articles of utility in the household. From work of this kind, which it was considered necessary in those days for every good housewife to know, they passed on in the course of

[1]Gordy, Rise and Growth of the Normal School Idea, p. 23.
[2]Rules of the Ursulines, edition of 1705.

time to ornamental work, such as embroidery in muslin and silk, crocheting, the making of artificial flowers, etc. While the pupils were engaged in this work, the Sister in charge, or one of the pupils, often read some interesting and instructive sketch or story. Three times a year there was a public exhibition of the work of the pupils, with distribution of prizes to those who excelled. Industrial training of this kind must have had a great social value in a primitive community such as New Orleans was in those days. Taken in connection with the refining religious influence created by the noble lives of the good nuns, it enables one to realize how, as we are told, emigrant girls taken from the streets or correctional houses of the great cities of France became in New Orleans good wives and devoted mothers, and how their descendants, a generation or two after, came to form the most sturdy element in the moral make-up of the city.[1]

ATTITUDE OF THE STATE

From the beginning, the Ursulines were treated with the greatest kindness by the mother country. The expenses of the voyage were paid for them, and they were given a fixed salary until the institution became self-supporting. In 1740, they figure in the budget of the colony for 12,000 livres, for the support of twelve Sisters and the orphans.[2] The Government encouraged education, and aimed to provide full educational opportunities for both

[1] Gayarré, vol. i, p. 390.
[2] The Ursulines in Louisiana, p. 18; Publications of the Louisiana Hist. Soc., vol. ii, part 4, appendix.

sexes, and for all classes of the population. The school for boys in charge of the Capuchins seems to have been continued right along, and in course of time other schools also were opened.

The Spanish Government, when it assumed control of Louisiana in 1769, continued the same policy of encouraging education. Governor Miro, in 1788, reported six schools in the city—a Spanish school, four French private schools with 400 pupils, and the school and academy of the Ursulines. The Spanish school was intended for a high-grade classical college. The Government sent out several fine professors, chosen from the universities of Spain, but the institution does not appear to have ever advanced beyond the rank of an elementary school. Nobody came to study Latin, and the number of pupils never exceeded thirty.[1] The reason of this lay, very likely, not so much in lack of interest in higher studies, as in dislike of the Spanish. New Orleans is reported as having a population at this time of about 12,-000, including the colored race, but this estimate seems too high.

The Spanish authorities were greatly chagrined at seeing the ill support of the Government school, while the French private schools and the schools of the Ursulines were in such a flourishing condition. Bishop Penalvert, of Havana, visited New Orleans in 1795, and found the Spanish school still continuing. In view of the French Revolution, he was naturally solicitous for the faith of the children who were being educated in the private schools. Referring to them, he says: "As I was ignorant of

[1] Fay, Hist. of Ed. in La., p. 15.

the faith professed by the teachers and of their morality, I have prescribed for them such regulations as are in conformity with the provisions of our legislation."[1] The bishop praised the schools of the Ursulines, in which, he said, "a good many girls" were educated. The Sisters also had been made to feel the effects of the persistent efforts made to replace French by Spanish as the language of the colony. The bishop complains that the nuns are too French, that they refuse to admit Spanish postulants, unless they adopted the French language and customs, and that they shed many tears at being obliged to use Spanish books in their spiritual exercises, as the authorities made them do.[2] Spanish text-books were no doubt prescribed for the schools.

From the reports of the Governor and bishop, it is evident that very considerable opportunities for education, both elementary and higher, existed in New Orleans during the second half of the eighteenth century. It may indeed be questioned if any such opportunities for the education of girls existed in the English-speaking colonies at that time as were afforded by the free school and the academy of the Ursulines in New Orleans.

LETTER OF JEFFERSON

Notwithstanding the petty persecution to which they were subjected by the Spanish authorities, in common with the other French schools, the Ursulines in New Orleans prospered and by degrees

[1]Fay, op. cit., p. 17.
[2]Ibid.

became contented with the new conditions. The Government encouraged their work, and a number of Spanish postulants were received. So great, in fact, was the change effected in their attitude, that it was a terrible blow to them when, in 1803, Spain restored Louisiana to France. The horrors of the French Revolution were fresh in the minds of the nuns. Many of them felt that the doom of the convent was sealed, and resolved to take refuge, before it was too late, in one of the neighboring Spanish colonies. In spite of all efforts to keep them, the prioress, with fifteen other Sisters, embarked for Havana, where they soon were enabled to establish a convent of their order. The nine Sisters who remained behind in New Orleans bravely endeavored to continue the work of the schools. Efforts were made to get Sisters to come to their assistance from Canada and France, and they were successful. But in the meantime, Napoleon had sold Louisiana to the United States, after keeping possession of it for only twenty days. The Sisters knew little of the character and spirit of the new Government, and the French Revolution had filled their minds with a profound distrust of republics. They feared confiscation or exile. The air was full of alarming rumors. Friends assured them that the best they could expect was leave to remain in their convent undisturbed until death, when the convent, together with their lands in the city and suburbs, would be seized by the Government. Under these circumstances, the Mother Superior, in 1804, wrote to President Jefferson, appealing to him for protection, and received from him in reply the following letter:

"The President of the United States to Sœur
Thérèse de St. Xavier Farjou, Supérieure, and
the Nuns, etc.

"I have received, Holy Sisters, the letters you
have written to me, wherein you express anxiety
for the property vested in your institution by the
former Government of Louisiana. The principles
of the Government and Constitution of the United
States are a sure guarantee to you that it will be
preserved to you sacred and inviolate, and that
your institution will be permitted to govern itself
according to its own voluntary rules, without inter-
ference from the civil authority. Whatever diversity of shade may appear in the religious opinions
of our fellow-citizens, the charitable objects of your
institution can not be indifferent to any; and its
furtherance of the wholesome purposes of society
by training up its young members in the way they
should go, can not fail to insure it the patronage
of the Government it is under. Be assured it will
meet with all the protection my office can give it.
"I salute you, Holy Sisters, with friendship and
respect.[1]

"THOMAS JEFFERSON."

The first American Governor, Claiborne, treated
the Sisters with equal respect. Nuns came from
France and Canada to replace those who had de-
parted, and soon the convent schools were again
in a flourishing condition.

At the battle of New Orleans, the class-rooms of
this venerable institution were turned into infirm-
aries for the sick and wounded soldiers, and the

[1] The Ursulines in Louisiana, p. 32; Education in New Orleans in Spanish Colonial Days, Amer. Cath. Quart. Rev., vol.
xii, p. 267.

Sisters devoted themselves to nursing them. Andrew Jackson, in the midst of the ovation accorded him by the city after his great victory, graciously acknowledged the patriotic charity of the Sisters by paying a visit to the convent, and thanking them for what they had done for him and his soldiers by their prayers and kindly ministrations. In after years, when he returned to New Orleans as President of the United States, he did not fail to revisit this historic sanctuary of religion and learning and give expression anew to the esteem in which he held the good Sisters and their work.[1]

French Settlements in the North

Outside of New Orleans, there were several schools in existence during the eighteenth century in various parts of the French possessions. As a rule, wherever there was a French settlement with a resident priest, a school was established for the education of the children of the settlement in the common branches, the parish priest being most often the first teacher. The education given, however, was only of the most elementary kind, and the existence of these schools was not always con-

[1]The Ursulines in Louisiana, p. 37. The Ursulines in New Orleans have continued to carry on the work of their academy and free school down to the present day. In 1824 they built a magnificent new convent farther out from the city, and here they have developed one of the largest and finest educational institutions for girls in the South. The free school is now known as St. Angela's Free School, and in 1905 it numbered thirty pupils. The old convent and school on Chartres Street, which they had occupied for ninety years, became, in 1824, the residence of the bishop, part of it being used temporarily for a boys' school.

tinuous. The priest was often absent for long periods, and years elapsed at times without there being anything like a regular school. In a general way it may be said that educational conditions in the province of Louisiana during the eighteenth century, outside the city of New Orleans, approximated the educational conditions which had existed in the English colonies a century before.

In the country round about New Orleans there were no schools properly so called, beyond those already mentioned. The country was but sparsely settled, and it was very difficult to get teachers of any sort. Planters who could afford it picked up any one happening to come along who was able to teach, and gave him lodging, board, and a trifling wage, to instruct their children at home.[1] The Ursuline Sisters did not attempt any new establishments until toward the middle of the nineteenth century, and these were made in Texas.

ST. LOUIS

St. Louis had a resident priest soon after its foundation in 1764, and also Ste. Genevieve, near by. In both places, also, schools were soon established in which children were taught reading, writing, and arithmetic. At St. Louis, the first permanent school was opened in 1774 by Jean Baptiste Trudeau, who in that year arrived from New Orleans. Trudeau continued his school for almost fifty years. He was well educated, and the best families of the place sent their sons to him. Another school was opened in 1797 by the widow,

[1] Fay, op. cit., p. 22.

Madame Rigauche, but it probably lasted only a couple of years. The first English school was opened in 1804. At the time of the cession of Louisiana to the United States, St. Louis counted no more than 180 houses, and from 1,500 to 2,000 inhabitants. Sons of the more wealthy families were often sent to Canada to be educated. Some were sent even to the universities of Europe.[1]

KASKASKIA AND MACKINAW

At Kaskaskia (Ill.) and Mackinaw Straits (Mich.), schools were also established at an early date by the Jesuits. Charlevoix, who visited Kaskaskia in 1721, found four Jesuits there, in charge of a thriving French settlement and two Indian villages.[2] The French settlement had probably a school of its own. At both Kaskaskia and Mackinaw, there were schools for the Indians, in which the boys were taught to read, write, sing, and work at some trade; and the girls, besides learning to read and write, were taught to sew, knit, and embroider.[3] The importance attached to industrial training by the Jesuits, in their efforts to educate and civilize the Indians, is worthy of notice. Some historians have asserted the existence, during this period, of a college in the modern sense at Kaskaskia, but this assertion is without good ground. The records do indeed state that there was a "col-

[1] Scharf, The History of St. Louis, p. 823; Report of the Celebration of the Anniversary of the Founding of St. Louis, Feb. 15, 1847, p. 12 seq.; Carr, Missouri, Amer. Commonwealth Series, p. 47; Address on the Centenary of the Cathedral Church of St. Louis, Aug. 27, 1876.
[2] Charlevoix, Journal, Oct., 1721, vol. vi, p. 139.
[3] Wisconsin Hist. Collections, vol. v, p. 327.

lege" of the Jesuits there, but the term "college" was evidently used in its medieval sense, and meant simply a residence.

DETROIT

There is evidence that Detroit had a school dating almost from the foundation of the city. Writing from there in 1703, about the time of the first settlement of the place, Cadillac, the founder, said:

"Permit me to insist upon the great necessity there is for the establishment of a Seminary at this place for the instruction of the children of the savages with others of the French, instructing them in piety, and, at the same time, teaching them our language."[1]

The school was undoubtedly established. In the course of time, there were probably two schools in Detroit, one for the whites and another for the Indians, for in 1755 we find a mention of the "Director of the Christian Schools." The schoolhouse was built "just outside the fort on the West."[2] The Franciscans and Jesuits successively had charge of the parish there during many years, and both Orders were noted for their zeal for education. The priests themselves sometimes had to do the teaching in the school. A visitor to Detroit in 1729 described the pastor as a man who was fond of study, and says that he had taught some of the inhabitants.[3]

[1]Farmer, History of Detroit and Michigan, p. 720.
[2]Ibid.
[3]Ibid., p. 530.

VINCENNES

Vincennes had a school in 1786, and probably for many years before. In a letter to the Bishop of Quebec the famous Father Peter Gibault, then pastor at Vincennes, writes that he taught the children there not only the Christian doctrine, but also "to read and write."[1]

MAINE

Among the Indians of Maine, a school or seminary was established about 1640, by French Capuchins who were laboring in that region. Of special interest in connection with this institution is the fact that Cardinal Richelieu took an active interest in its foundation and maintenance, and transferred to the Capuchin Fathers certain property rights, in order to secure its permanent endowment.[2]

[1]Shea, Hist. Cath. Church in the U. S., vol. ii, p. 471.
[2]Ibid., vol. i, p. 237.

CHAPTER III

EARLY JESUIT SCHOOLS IN MARYLAND

THE BEGINNINGS of Catholic educational work in the English colonies date back to the arrival of the Maryland colony. It was a day full of significance for the future of education in America that brought to our shores the Jesuits, the most successful teachers of youth, perhaps, that Europe had yet known. Tracing things to their commencement and their causes, we must attribute to the Jesuits, more than to any other single influence, the establishment of the Catholic school system such as it exists to-day. It was the Jesuits who opened the first schools, gave them their present form, and made them a function of organized parish work. Long before the advent of the hierarchy in the person of the venerated Bishop Carroll, Catholic schools existed, flourished, and had been molded into a kind of system, under the Jesuit pastors and missionaries.

EDUCATIONAL PLANS

The educational activity of the Jesuits may be said to have begun with their first arrival in Maryland. On March 25, 1634, the colony sent out by Lord Baltimore landed on St. Clement's Island, in the lower Potomac, and soon after a permanent settlement was founded at St. Mary's. Two Jesuit Fathers and a lay Brother accompanied the

expedition.   At their head was Father Andrew
White, one of the foremost English Jesuits of the
time, a scholarly man, who had held the offices of
Prefect of Studies, and Professor of Sacred Scrip-
ture, Dogmatic Theology, and Hebrew, in the English colleges at Valladolid and Seville.[1]   Father
White immediately set about acquiring the language of the Indians, and had soon prepared a native grammar and vocabulary, as well as a catechism, the latter being still extant.   The conversion
of the most important Indian chieftain in Maryland, with many of his subjects, was the result of
these zealous labors.   Shortly afterward, we are
told, the newly converted king brought his daughter, who was seven years old at the time, to St.
Mary's "to be educated among the English."[2]

It is certain that the matter of educational provision for the children of the colonists occupied
the attention of the Jesuits from the very beginning.   As early as 1640, when only four settlements had been formed, the question of establishing a college was discussed by members of the
Order in Maryland and their higher superiors.[3]   It
is not the fault of the Jesuits if Maryland is not
able to contest with Massachusetts the honor of
having founded the first American college.   Writing to the Superior of the Maryland Mission on
September 15, 1640, the Superior-General of the
Jesuits said:

"The hope of establishing a college which you
hold forth, I embrace with pleasure; and shall not

[1]Records of the English Province, vol. iii, p. 334.
[2]Letter of 1640, Records, vol. iii, pp. 379, 382.
[3]Records Amer. Cath. Hist. Society, vol. xi, p. 185.

delay my sanction to the plan, when it shall have reached maturity."[1]

But the Jesuits found their plans continually thwarted. Lord Baltimore, through an unfortunate chain of circumstances, was led to assume an attitude of hostility to them, and laws were framed and measures taken which could not fail to effectually cripple their activity along educational as well as other lines. As a climax to these difficulties, the rebellion of Claiborne and Ingle broke out in the beginning of the year 1644, resulting in the banishment of the Jesuits from the colony and the loss or destruction of much of their property. When they returned, after an absence of three years, and set about repairing the work of destruction accomplished by the rebels, they seem to have taken up again the project of the college. But times had changed. The Parliamentarians had gained the ascendency in England, and soon made themselves masters in Maryland. They were bitterly hostile to the Catholics, and with the overthrow of the Proprietary Government in Maryland in 1652, the Jesuits found it impossible to do anything openly. It was not until after the Restoration in England and the manifestation of the friendly disposition of Charles II toward the Church, as we shall see, that they ventured to engage openly in the work of education, and to carry out their long-cherished plan of founding an institution of higher education for the benefit of Maryland Catholics.

In the meantime, they were quietly preparing the

[1]United States Cath. Magazine, vol. vii, p. 580.

way for this event, by encouraging elementary education, and by establishing at least one school for the teaching of the elementary branches. It appears to have been about 1640 that this school was started. In that year, Ralph Crouch, "the first schoolmaster to make his way across the Potomac,"[1] came from Europe, and began an educational service that lasted for twenty years. He was a layman at this time, but he had been a Jesuit novice. For some reason not recorded, he left the novitiate in 1639 and came to Maryland. The official chronicles of the Order in England represent him as a man of some education, full of zeal and charity and ready for every good and pious work.[2] He was called the "right hand and solace" of the Fathers of the Society in Maryland, and he was continually associated with them in his educational and charitable work. Having joined the Order again in 1659, he was sent to Europe to complete his noviceship, but never returned. He died a Jesuit priest in 1679.

SITE OF FIRST SCHOOL

At the time of Ralph Crouch's arrival in Maryland, the center of Jesuit activity was at Newtown, having been shifted from St. Mary's, probably because of the hostility of the authorities there, and also because of the number of Catholics in the vicin-

---

[1]Dexter, History of Education in the U. S. This author represents Ralph Crouch as having come from Virginia, and says nothing about his connection with the Jesuits. It is not improbable that Crouch was sent to Maryland by the Jesuits, and sent for the express purpose of founding Catholic schools.
[2]Records of the English Province, vol. v, p. 953.

ity of Newtown. The Jesuits had a manor-house at this place,[1] which very likely served as a church on Sundays and as a schoolhouse during the week, a not infrequent combination during colonial days. The house lay not far from Britton's Bay, and from its windows could be had a view of the distant Potomac, with some charming vistas of the bays, creeks, and forests that abound in the vicinity.[2] Such was, apparently, the site of the first formally established Catholic school in the English-speaking colonies. It was here probably Ralph Crouch came after his arrival in Maryland in 1640, and began the work of teaching the children of the neighboring Catholic planters during the week and giving catechetical instructions on Sundays, while assisting the Fathers in visiting and caring for the sick, and in the numerous other duties in connection with their work which ordinarily fell to the lot of the temporal coadjutors of the Society.[3]

CATHOLICS AND EDUCATION

Some of the Catholics in the vicinity were wealthy, according to the standards of those times, and it was natural that the Jesuits should look to these for the means which were necessary to endow the school and insure its existence permanently. The Catholic colonists were generous, and attached to the Church by ties which had been rendered stronger and more tender by persecution and suffering. The strength and depth of their attach-

[1] Woodstock Letters, vol. xiii, p. 269.
[2] Ibid., p. 73.
[3] Records, vol. v, p. 953.

ment to the Church, as well as their practical generosity, is evidenced by the fact that no less than
42 Catholics, between the years 1650 and 1685,
made the Church or the clergy a beneficiary in
their wills.[1] They were zealous for education, too.
It is a grave mistake to assert that the sentiment in
Maryland was "opposed to free schools for the
people."[2] On the contrary, Catholics and Protestants alike were eager to provide the best facilities
possible in the way of education. The more
wealthy colonists frequently employed private
teachers for their children; a strong desire, however, was manifested for the establishment of
schools. This is proved by the fact that several
generous bequests were actually made during this
period for the establishment of "free schools."
One of these bequests will be given here in full; in
addition to which, mention may be made of the will
of John Price, February 16, 1660, in which part
of the estate was set aside for the establishment of
a "free school;" also, of that of Thomas Pacey,
May 2, 1667, in which provision was made for the
founding of "free schools." Price was a Protestant, and a very prominent personage in early
Maryland history, having been a member of the
Governor's Council and having held important
military commands; and the fact that he was a
soldier and an illiterate man makes his interest in
the establishment of schools all the more remarkable.[3] Surgeon Henry Hooper also, who died

[1]Maryland Calendar of Wills, vol. i; Annapolis Will-books,
lib. i, ii, iv, v, ix.
[2]Dexter, Hist. of Education, p. 65.
[3]Davis, Day Star. p. 183; the wills of Price and Pacey are
to be found in the Will-books at Annapolis, lib. i.

about the year 1650, left a legacy to Ralph Crouch for such "pious uses as he thinks fit," the intention being probably to found a school. The insecure position of Catholics in Maryland at the time made the more general designation, "for pious purposes," the more prudent form to employ in an educational bequest.[1] Several other wills made during this period testify to the generally felt need of schools.[2] Nor did the authorities in the province lack interest in education. In 1673, Charles Calvert, the Governor, wrote that he was endeavoring to found a private school at St. Mary's. Two years before this date, a bill for "the founding and erecting of a school or college within this province for the education of youth in learning and virtue," was accepted by the Catholic upper house of the Assembly, but was killed by amendments added to it by the lower house, which was Protestant. The amendments had reference to the religious differences which existed between the two bodies, and were distasteful to the Catholics.[3]

COTTON'S ENDOWMENT

Among the "loving friends" of Ralph Crouch, and one of his most generous supporters in his educational and charitable work, was a rich and influential Catholic planter near Newtown named Edward Cotton. He was a member of the Assem-

[1] Neill, The Founders of Maryland, p. 127.
[2] See the will of Augustus Herman, 1684, in Steiner, Hist. of Ed. in Maryland; also that of Walter Hall, made in 1678, and referred to in the Maryland Calendar of Wills.
[3] Steiner, op. cit., p. 15.

bly in 1648, and represented 9 votes.[1] He was un-
married, it would seem, and when he died, in
1653, he made Ralph Crouch one of his two executors, and left the bulk of his estate, consisting of
450 acres of land and many cattle, for the endowment of the Catholic school. His will contains the
first bequest made in behalf of education in Maryland, and the first made in behalf of Catholic education, so far as is known, on this side of the
Atlantic. It is given here almost in full for this
reason, only the minor items being omitted.

"*The Last Will and Testament of Edward Cotton*
made the 4th of April 1653 he having perfect sense
and memory as followeth. First, I give and bequeath
my soul to God my Maker and Redeemer to the
fellowship of all the holy Angells and Saints and
my body to the earth from whence it came to be
decently buried with all Christian Rites and Ceremonies according to my quality. . . . Thirdly, I
doe appoint my Loving friends Thomas Mathews
and Ralph Crouch my Executors Equally to have
Power to take and Dispose of all my whole Estate
whatsoever in manner and form as followeth, not
to be accountable unto any person or persons whatsoever. *First,* to pay all my Debts whatsoever in
the first Place. *Secondly,* to sett my man David
Thomas free at the time of my Death, provided
that he do discharge my Executors from a bill of
Fifteen hundred weight of Tobacco which I am
bound for unto Walter Beane. *Thirdly,* to give
unto Mr. Starkey [the parish priest at Newtown]
my old Chestnutt Colloured Mare and my horse
now 3 years old, this Spring. . . . *Ninthly,* I doe
give all my female Cattle and their Increase for

[1]Davis, Day Star, p. 144.

Ever to be disposed of by my aforesaid Executors as they shall think fitt unto charitable uses which may be most to God's honor, the Stock to be preserved and the Profitt to be made use of to the use of a schooll, if they shall think convenient, and for the Male Cattle that are or that hereafter shall encrease I doe give to the aforesaid use reserving to my aforesaid Executors the privilege to Kill for their own use some of the Male Cattle, the better to Enable them to do Charitable offices presuming that they will make no Waste contrary to this my Will and all the rest of my estate to be disposed of as aforesaid to good uses as they shall think fitt. . . . *Eleventhly*, I doe give them power to appoint at their death some other faithful person in their stead whom they shall think fitt with the same power as they or he hath. *Twelfthly*, my desire is if they shall think Convenient that the Schooll be kept at Newtowne, and that the Cattle may be in the Care of John Warren upon such agreement as my Executors shall make Provided that this my desire do not hinder them from doing a greater good to the honour of God otherwise which I doe leave absolute in their power and to their Discretion. . . .

"In Witness whereof I have hereunto sett my hand.

"EDWARD COTTON."[1]

The gift of a herd of cattle, with "their increase forever," as an endowment for a school, strange as it may seem nowadays, was natural enough in the early years of the Maryland colony. A codicil

[1] Will-books in the office of the Register of Wills, Annapolis, lib. I, p. 46. There is another will of Edward Cotton recorded in the same book, on p. 203, but it is almost word for word the same as the above, and is evidently a misplaced copy of it.

to the will provided that the 450 acres of land, together with one of the negro servants, should be leased to John Warren for eight years, the executors to receive yearly in return "one thousand pounds Weight of good sound Merchantable leaf Tobacco and Cask." Cattle and tobacco were, in fact, the most ordinary standards of value at the time, and by the endowment settled upon the school in these two things, there was provided for it a capital which was at once the safest and the most in demand.[1]   A pound of tobacco at the time was worth about threepence in English money.[2]

CHARACTER OF THE SCHOOL

What was the character of the school which was thus so generously endowed? Here we have little that is authentic to guide us. There are only some scattered references, from which inferences must be made, and which have to be supplemented by conjecture. It can hardly be doubted that an elementary school existed at Newtown at this time and for ten years or so before, although its existence

[1] In 1649 cattle were used in Maryland for the payment of soldiers. Maryland Hist. Soc., vol. ix, p. 275. Tobacco served as a standard of value until near the Revolution. A lady who died in 1660, in Calvert County, provided that the private tutor who was charged with the education of her children should be paid two hogsheads of tobacco (4,000 pounds) yearly, besides his "lodging, Dyett & Walking." This was very fair pay for a private teacher.

[2] Davis, Day Star, p. 49. Steiner seems not to have known of the existence of this will of Edward Cotton, for in his learned and invaluable work, "The History of Education in Maryland," the will of Augustus Herman, a Protestant, who left his estate contingently for the founding of a school, is quoted as containing "the first bequest for educational purposes made by a citizen of Maryland." Herman died in 1684.

may not have been continuous at that place.[1] The "three R's" represented the ideal of education most in favor with the old Maryland colonists, or, as one of them put it, "Wryteing and reading and Learning to Cast accompt."[2] The education of girls was not neglected, but the standard was not the same as in the case of boys. A Catholic who died in 1664 provided that his children

"Should have such education in Learning as to write and read and cast accompt. I mean my three Sonnes, my two daughters to learn to read and sew with their needle and all of them to be Kept from Idleness."[3]

The "three R's" doubtless constituted the main curriculum of studies in the Newtown school, but there can be no doubt that Latin was taught, and perhaps Greek also. Ralph Crouch, whom the English "Records" refer to as having "opened schools for teaching humanities,"[4] must have known both these languages, and good Father Starkey or another Jesuit Father was probably there to assist him in teaching the larger boys in the more advanced classes. The school must have been, in fact, a preparatory college as well as an elementary

[1] Woodstock Letters, vol. xiii, p. 73 seq.
[2] Maryland Will-books, lib. i, p. 136.
[3] Ibid., p. 183. A curious instance, illustrative of the fervor of the devotion of the old Maryland Catholics to the Church, is afforded by the will of Jane Fenwick, which provided that "William Payne the negro boy servant in case he survive my three children shall be then free, he paying yearly to the Roman Catholic Church for Ever one hhd. of tobacco, and in case the said William continue not always a member of the said Church that then he shall be forever a slave to the aforesaid Catholic Church." Lib. i, p. 114.
[4] Vol. xii, p. 593.

school. This is rendered the more likely from the constantly adhered to plan of the Jesuits to establish a college in Maryland, and from the fact that a college for the teaching of the classics or "humanities" was sometime afterward actually begun at Newtown.[1]

The endowment made by Edward Cotton offered a good opportunity, in fact, for the starting of this long projected institution. In 1668, the neighboring manor of Mr. Britton, a wealthy Catholic, was purchased, and about the same time, probably, another story was added to it.[2] A chapel had been erected by the congregation at Newtown some years before.[3] At this time, under the administration of Father Henry Warren, the Superior, there were four Jesuit priests in Maryland and two lay Brothers.[4] Besides assisting the priests, the lay Brothers taught in the elementary school, one of them at a time having charge of it.[5] One of these lay Brothers, named Gregory Turbeville, came to Maryland shortly after Ralph Crouch's departure, and remained until his death in 1684—a service of 22 years.[6] The Superior often resided at Newtown, and it is likely that there were two Fathers constantly there. As the Jesuit priests in Maryland were, as a rule, remarkably learned men, there was thus a chance for them to lay the foundation for college work by the gradual introduction of such classes as would form the curriculum of a clas-

[1] Woodstock Letters, vol. xiii, p. 269 seq.
[2] Ibid., p. 73.
[3] Shea, History, vol. i, p. 76.
[4] Records of the English Province, Collect., Hist. Intr.
[5] Woodstock Letters, vol. xiii, p. 269.
[6] Records, Collectania.

sical preparatory school. In the will of Luke Gardner, a Catholic, made in 1673, there is a recognition of the existence of such a preparatory school in the provision made for the education of his sons until they reached the age of eighteen:

"My will is that my three sons, John, Luke and Thomas Gardner be kept at School and have such education as this country and their estates will afford them until they successively attain unto the age of eighteen years."[1]

THE FIRST COLLEGE

We are prepared, therefore, to learn that not long afterward a college, or "school for humanities," was officially announced as having been opened in the year 1677, and that two of the Jesuit Fathers had been assigned as its "directors." In the annual letter to the higher superiors in Europe of the date of 1681, this event is referred to as the one of greatest interest and importance in the recent history of the colony:

"Four years ago, a school for humanities was opened by our Society in the center of the country, directed by two of the Fathers; and the native youth, applying themselves assiduously to study, made good progress. Maryland and the recently established school sent two boys to St. Omer who yielded in abilities to few Europeans, when competing for the honor of being first in their class. So that not gold, nor silver, nor the other products of the earth alone, but men also are gathered from

[1]Will-books, lib. i, p. 634.

thence to bring those regions, which foreigners have unjustly called ferocious, to a higher state of virtue and cultivation. Two of the Society were sent out to Maryland this year to assist the laborers in that most ample vineyard of our Lord."[1]

St. Omer's was a college established by the Jesuits in Belgium, for the education of the Catholic youth of English-speaking countries. It had a complete college curriculum, as well as preparatory studies. One of the two pupils of the college alluded to as having gone to St. Omer's to finish their studies was Robert Brooke, who was born in Maryland in 1663. He subsequently entered the Society of Jesus, being the first priest of the Order ordained from Maryland. He labored for many years in the Maryland Mission.[2] The other youth was Thomas Gardner (Gardiner), a son of the Luke Gardner mentioned above. He also became a Jesuit scholastic, but left the Society before he was ordained. The sending of students to St. Omer's from the Newtown school would indicate that the latter institution had not developed a full collegiate curriculum at this time. The higher classics were probably not taught as yet. As a matter of fact, we have no positive evidence that a complete college curriculum was ever attained at Newtown, but the indirect evidence at hand would lead us to the

[1]Records, vol. iii, p. 394. Dexter, Hist. of Ed. in the U. S., p. 65, following Steiner, erroneously supposes that the college thus established was an Indian school. The term "native youth" used in the above letter is evidently used to designate those born or brought up in Maryland, as distinguished from the "Europeans" mentioned in connection with St. Omer's. It is unlikely that there were any Indian youth at the college at Newtown.
[2]Shea, op. cit., vol. i, p. 84.

conclusion that it was. This evidence centers chiefly about three points: the eager desire of the Jesuit authorities to establish a complete collegiate institution in Maryland; the need existing for such an institution there; and the actual strengthening of the faculty of the Newtown school about this time. At any rate, whether the institution ever developed a *complete* college curriculum or not, it must be admitted that a college was established at Newtown, and that this college was the second institution of the kind, in point of time, established within the present limits of the United States, being preceded only by Harvard.

The two members of the Society alluded to in the above letter as having been sent to Maryland in 1681, were a lay Brother and Mr. Thomas Hathersall, the latter being a scholastic or one not yet ordained to the priesthood. He was the only Jesuit scholastic ever in this country in the colonial period, and he continued unordained until the time of his death, which occurred in Maryland in 1698.[1] Coming to Maryland at the age of forty-two, he was sent to the college at Newtown, where we have references to him as teaching the classics—"letters and humanities"—during a period of fifteen years, between 1683 and 1698.[2] In the year 1682 another Jesuit, a priest, came over to Maryland, probably to teach in the college. At this time there were nine Jesuits in Maryland—five priests, three lay Brothers, and the scholastic above men-

[1] MS. Records of Bohemia and Newtown, in Georgetown University.
[2] MS. Records, Georgetown University; Treacy, Old Catholic Maryland and its Early Jesuit Missionaries, p. 95.

tioned.[1]   The college was evidently prospering.   It had good teachers, and even Protestants sent their sons there.[2]

JESUIT SCHOOL IN NEW YORK

At this time also the Jesuits ventured to open a school in New York City, under the patronage of the Catholic Governor, Colonel Thomas Dongan. The institution was begun originally as an Episcopalian school, about 1684, but it did not prosper, and after a time was closed.   It stood on the site of Old Trinity Church, at Broadway and Wall Street.   One of the Jesuits who arrived in New York in 1683 or 1684, probably Father Henry Harrison, reopened the school at the Governor's instance.   The classics were taught, and doubtless the elementary branches also.   The Governor urged King James to endow it with a tract of land known as "the King's Farm,"[3] but it does not appear that this petition was granted.   There were not many Catholics in the city, but some of them were men of influence who held high offices in the colony, and these eagerly seized the opportunity of affording their sons an education under Catholic auspices.   In spite of the statement of Leisler, that "the college vanished" for lack of support, there is good reason for believing that the institution was

[1]Records of the Eng. Prov., Collect., Hist. Intr.
[2]Shea, Hist., vol. i, p. 345.
[3]Broadhead, Hist. of the State of N. Y., vol. ii, pp. 407, 487; Documents relating to the Colonial History of the State of New York, vol. iv, p. 490; Bayley, History of the Catholic Church in New York, p. 31.

successful and had ample support, as long as Dongan was Governor.[1]

THE ERA OF PERSECUTION

It was just at this time, however, when the prospects of the Church in New York seemed so bright,
and the long cherished and so often thwarted hope
for the establishment of a Catholic school and college in Maryland was so happily realized, that the
era of most bitter persecution was about to be
ushered in. The revolution which broke out in
England in 1688 and resulted in the overthrow of
James II gave birth to corresponding revolu-
tions in Maryland and New York, directed chiefly
against the Catholics. In New York, the government of Dongan was overthrown, and the Jesuits
were driven out. In Maryland, the statutes guar-
anteeing religious freedom were repealed, and the
Church of England was made the established form
of religious worship for the colony.[2] The Jesuit
Fathers soon encountered the gravest difficulties in
ministering to their flocks. It was to be expected
that the college and school at Newtown, as the
chief nursery of Catholic life in the colony, would
be the first to suffer. Whatever the nature of the
practical measures taken to bring about the result
may have been, it is certain that the educational
establishment there, after some years, was closed.
The Jesuits engaged in teaching were scattered, and
the institution was never afterward reopened, at
least at Newtown. The precise date of the final

[1]Documentary History of N. Y., vol. ii, p. 22.
[2]Thomas, Chronicles of Maryland, p. 70.

suspension of educational work is not known, but it was probably not until the closing years of the century. Thomas Hathersall continued to live at Newtown until 1698, and no doubt some teaching continued to be done until about that time. By 1699, the number of Jesuits in Maryland was reduced to three priests and two lay Brothers. The last specific reference we have to the Newtown school is found in the will of Thomas Rasin, made April 18, 1687, saying that "My desire is that if Mr. Pennington desires to have the educating of my youngest son that my Executors do put him to him." "Mr. Pennington" was the Rev. Francis Pennington, the Jesuit Superior in Maryland, who died at Newtown in 1699.[1] In 1704, a law was passed which provided that,

"If any persons professing to be of the Church of Rome should keep school, or take upon themselves the education, Government, or boarding of youth, at any place in the province, upon conviction such offenders should be transported to England to undergo the penalties provided there by Statutes 11 and 13, William III, 'for the further preventing the growth of Popery.' "[2]

One of the principal features of this long period of persecution, which lasted down to the outbreak of the American Revolution, was a continual effort to prevent Catholics from giving a Catholic education to their children. It was sought to render impossible the establishment of Catholic schools,

[1]Woodstock Letters, vol. xiii, p. 271; Annapolis Will-books, lib. iv, fol. 302.
[2]Shea, op. cit., vol. i, p. 358.

the teacher being liable to perpetual imprisonment.[1] That Catholics would seek to evade the laws and escape the legal penalties by employing teachers of their own faith to give instruction to their children at home, or to the children of a neighborhood together in some convenient house, was anticipated, and even this was interdicted. A Catholic father was liable to a fine of 40 shillings per day if he employed any but a Protestant teacher or tutor to instruct his child.[2] If he sought to procure a Catholic education for his son by sending him across the sea to St. Omer's, or some other of the Jesuit colleges in Europe founded for this very purpose, he became liable to a fine of £100.[3] Poor Catholics were thus effectually deprived of all opportunity to give their children a Catholic education, except in so far as they were able to instruct them themselves. Wealthy Catholics fared somewhat better, as it was easier for them to secure a private tutor, and it was less difficult for them to conceal the fact. They could afford, too, to send their sons to Europe to study, and, in spite of the stringency of the laws and the vigilance of the authorities, they often found means to do so without being discovered. One great help to this end was afforded by the use of an *alias,* the student assuming a new name by which he was known during the time of his journey to Europe and his stay there. This was a favorite practice of the Jesuits during times of persecution.

These harshly proscriptive measures appear all

[1]Shea, vol. i, p. 358; Devitt, "A Dark Chapter in the Hist. of Md.," U. S. Cath. Hist. Mag., vol. i, p. 144.
[2]U. S. Cath. Hist. Mag., vol. vii, p. 532.
[3]Ibid.; Shea, loc. cit.

the more odious in view of the fact that the men who were so bent upon making every species of Catholic educational work impossible did so little themselves to further the cause of public education during this period. Up to 1694, practically nothing had been done. In that year, an act was passed by the legislature for the establishment of free schools, and two years later it was amended and sent to the King for his approval.[1] The act provided for the erection of a free school in each county of the colony; but nothing came of it, except the establishment of King William's School at Annapolis, which subsequently developed into St. John's College, and even this school owed its foundation in large part to private generosity. King William's School continued to be the only public school in Maryland until the year 1723. Money was scarce, and it was found to be exceedingly difficult to raise money for schools.[2] Taxes were imposed upon all sorts of things for the purpose, but without much avail. In 1717, the Irish Servant Bill was re-enacted, a duty of 40 shillings being put upon each Irish Catholic servant imported into the province, "to prevent the growth of Popery."[3] The duty upon negroes was also raised, and the money collected from these sources was to be devoted to the schools.[4] Catholics were to be rigorously excluded from any share in the management of the schools; the trustees were all to be Protestants; the teachers, members of the Church of Eng-

[1]Brown, The Making of Our Middle Schools, p. 56; Clews, Educational Legislation and Administration, p. 411 seq.
[2]Clews, op. cit., p. 423; Steiner, Hist. Ed. in Md., pp. 23, 24.
[3]Clews, p. 425; Shea, vol. i, p. 373.
[4]Report Amer. Hist. Assoc., vol. i, p. 250.

land; and the Anglican rector of the parish was to be the chairman of the school board.[1] Under the Act of 1723, schools were gradually introduced into a number of the counties, but the terms of the legislation, coupled with the spirit of bigotry that prevailed, left little hope to the Catholic parent of being able to bring up his children in his own faith, if he attempted to make use of the only educational facilities which the laws allowed him. The alternative was plain; it was, apostasy or ignorance.

BEGINNINGS AT BOHEMIA

Under these circumstances, when the number of Catholics in the colony had dwindled to one-twelfth or less of the population,[2] and the faith of the rising generations of Catholics seemed so gravely imperiled, the Jesuits again attempted to come to the rescue by establishing a Catholic school. The history of this institution is interesting, but the information that has come down to us regarding it is brief and fragmentary. Its origin is wrapped in obscurity; it was begun by stealth; its existence was precarious; and it appears to have been closed several times, owing to fresh outbursts of persecution. But it did, nevertheless, a great work: it helped to keep alive some sparks of the old Maryland faith, and provided a generation of educated Catholics—small in number but strong in faith and knowledge—who were fitted to champion the cause of the Church's freedom by word and deed, in the

[1]Clews, p. 429 and passim; U. S. Cath. Hist. Mag., vol. i, no. 2, passim.
[2]Life and Select Letters of Rev. Thomas Bray, p. 160.

era of universal liberty ushered in by the Revolution. It was the last educational effort of the Jesuits in colonial Maryland, but the tattered pages of its register which still survive bear some of the most illustrious names in American Catholic history.

The spot selected by the Jesuits for the new school was Herman's Manor of Bohemia, on the eastern shore of Maryland. The place was in Cecil County, which borders on Pennsylvania and Delaware, and forms the extreme northeast corner of Maryland.[1] It is easy to understand why this comparatively remote section of the colony was chosen. Pennsylvania was the home of religious freedom in colonial times, and the new establishment, while being less liable to observation on the part of the Maryland authorities, would form a convenient base for missionary work among the neighboring Quakers. To Bohemia accordingly, in the year 1704, the Rev. Thomas Mansell, S.J., came, and soon afterward he took out a patent for 458 acres of land. The country was a wilderness, the Catholics in the vicinity few.[2] In 1738, the Rev. Thomas Poulton took charge, remaining there until 1745. He had one assistant, and under him the school was organized about the year 1744. The branches taught were both elementary and preparatory, that is, they included the "three R's," which formed the almost invariable curriculum for beginners in those days, and such subjects as Latin, algebra, history, and perhaps Greek, which were

[1] Shea, Hist. of the Cath. Church in the U. S., vol. ii, pp. 27, 28.
[2] Woodstock Letters, vol. xiv, p. 347 seq.

calculated to prepare the pupil for college.[1] The charge was 40 pounds per annum for the preparatory students, and 30 pounds for the elementary.[2] This included board and other expenses, as most of the pupils came from a distance, and it was necessary for them to live at the college. The building must have been of goodly size, for at one time it held as many as forty pupils. There is no evidence that anything higher than a preparatory school ever existed at Bohemia. For further studies, the students were sent to St. Omer's, in Flanders.[3]

FAMOUS STUDENTS

This school was evidently a great boon to the Catholics of Maryland, for it was patronized immediately by some of the leading Catholic families. A fragment of the record book for 1745-6 contains the names of Peter Lopez, Edward Neale, and Daniel Carroll, who entered their sons there that year. The latter was father of John Carroll, the future Archbishop of Baltimore. John was the youngest of three brothers, and it was probably one of his elder brothers who entered the school at that time. John Carroll, according to his biographies, entered when he was twelve years of age, and this date coincides with the year 1747.[4] An entry of April 22, 1748, records that he came there a second time, having returned home, apparently,

[1] MS. Records of Bohemia, Georgetown University.
[2] Ibid.; Shea, vol. i, p. 404.
[3] Shea, ibid.
[4] Shea, vol. ii, p. 27; Boyle, Biog. Sketches of Disting. Marylanders, p. 104.

before his first year was finished.[1] In 1748, or early in 1749, he left Bohemia to go to St. Omer's, where he completed the classical course, remaining there six years. Among the other early pupils of the school were Benedict, Edward, Charles and Leonard Neale, the latter destined to become the second Archbishop of Baltimore; James Heath, Robert Brent, and Archibald Richard.[2] Charles Carroll of Carrollton, future signer of the Declaration of Independence, was also a pupil at Bohemia about this time, entering in 1747, when ten years of age; the following year he accompanied his cousin John to St. Omer's, going thence, after six years, to the Jesuit college at Rheims, and afterward to the college of Louis le Grand, at Paris.[3]

The Bohemia school seems to have been continued during the greater part of the summer.

[1]MS. Records of Bohemia.
[2]MSS. Records; Shea, vol. i, p. 404.
[3]Rowland, Life and Correspondence of Chas. Carroll of Carrollton, vol. i, p. 18; Shea, vol. ii, p. 28; U. S. Cath. Hist. Mag., vol. i, p. 72; Boyle, Biog. of Disting. Marylanders, p. 81.

Of Charles Carroll as a student, we have a description by a teacher, who wrote of him as "one who, during the whole time he was under my care, never deserved, on any account, a single harsh word, and whose sweet temper rendered him equally agreeable both to equals and superiors, without ever making him degenerate into the mean character of a favorite, which he always justly despised. His application to his Book and Devotions was constant and unchangeable." He himself, in his old age, was often heard to speak of his Jesuit teachers in terms of the deepest affection, gratitude, and reverence. "To them he attributed all that he knew, to their solicitude he referred all that he valued in his acquirements; and particularly that deep and hallowed conviction of religious truth which was the ornament of his youth, and the solace of his old age. When any one uttered a sentiment of astonishment, how in his advanced years he could rise so early and kneel so long—'these good practices,' he would answer with his high tone of cheerfulness, 'I learned under the Jesuits at the College of St. Omer's.' "—Rowland, pp. 62, 63.

There is a record extant of students entering during the months of April, June, and August. A note in the register records the fact that on July 8, 1748, "Jackey Carroll went to Marlborough," such being the name the future archbishop was known by among his fellow-scholars.[1] As the institution was a boarding-school, some of the pupils doubtless remained there all the time until they had finished. The uncertainty attaching to the existence of the school, owing to the laws and the attitude of the civil authorities, may have afforded a special reason for keeping up class-work during the entire summer.

OTHER MARYLAND SCHOOLS

There is evidence that the Maryland authorities were not lacking in vigilant determination to prevent the introduction of Catholic schools into the colony. Encouraged by the success of the Jesuits at Bohemia, several schools were opened by Catholics in other parts of Maryland. In 1752, a school was established by Daniel Connelly and Patrick Cavanaugh near My Lady's Manor. In the year 1757, when Baltimore was a little struggling town, with probably not more than a hundred Catholic inhabitants, Mary Anne Marsh opened a Catholic school there; whereupon the Rev. Thos. Chase, of St. Paul's Parish, complained to the Assembly, alleging that the Protestant schoolmaster "had lost many of his scholars, which were immediately put to the popish seminary." The magistrates were accordingly ordered "to call all persons before them who were keeping public and private schools,

[1]MS. Records.

and to administer to them the oaths to the Government required by law, which oaths if any refused to take, and afterwards kept school, they were to prosecute them according to law."[1] The "oaths" were, of course, those involving abjuration of the Catholic faith. A Catholic schoolmaster named Elston was, in 1752, conducting a school within a few miles of Annapolis. He had previously taught school at the Jesuit missions of Portobacco in Arundel County, and Deer Creek in Baltimore County, as we learn from the following extract from a "Report by the Committee of Grievances and Courts of Justice, June 17th, 1752," of the Assembly of Maryland:

"Your Committee conceive it their indispensable Duty to Report to your honorable house the many Dangerous Innovations against Law made by the Popish Interest within this province and ye great growth of popery and extensive acquisitions of popish priests or Jesuits within ye same.

"1. That contrary to the statutes a papist keeps a School for the education of youth within six or seven miles of Annapolis, ye seat of Government as appears by ye following Declaration of Benja Wright who says: Y^t a certain James Elston, a papist, keeps a School near his House which is about seven miles from Annapolis. y^t he has heard Elston say y^t he w^d educate such of ye peoples Children in ye Romish Religion as approved of it & such as did not he w^d educate in ye protestant way. that he Elston told him he was a papist and went to Mass. That he Wright had been at ye Schoolhouse & heard Elston teach y^e

[1] U. S. Cath. Hist. Mag., vol. viii, no. 10; Scharf, Hist. of Balt. City and County, p. 526.

Children in yᵉ Common prayer book their prayers according to yᵉ Church of England. That there is a Child of one Mr. Ireland a papist yᵗ goes to yᵉ school & Believe there may be fifteen or sixteen children taught by yᵉ sᵈ Elston at his School. that he knows that yᵉ sᵈ Elston taught at portobacco in Arrundel Co & heard him say that he had kept school at Deer Creek in Baltimore Coty before that time."

Nor did the school at Bohemia, amid the remote fastnesses of Cecil County, escape the prying eyes of the persecutors. In 1760, the Rev. Mr. Reading, an Episcopal minister at Apoquiniminck, Del., reported that there was "a very considerable Popish Seminary in the neighboring province of Maryland, under the direction of the Jesuits."[1] The Anglican rector of St. Stephen's Parish, near the school, was aware of its existence, and made vigorous efforts to secure the enforcement of the laws against those who were conducting it.[2] Nevertheless, amid increasing difficulties, involving fines and other legal penalties, the Jesuits at Bohemia kept bravely on. One of the features of their work there, as it had been at Newtown, was a circulating library, Catholic books of instruction and of controversial character being loaned out to Catholic families for many miles around.[3]

The recrudescence of the persecution which was brought on by the French and Indian War gave rise to the enactment of still more oppressive laws against Catholics, and, with the sharpened vigilance of the authorities, their position in the colony be-

[1]Amer. Cath. Hist. Researches, vol. xi, p. 60.
[2]Shea, vol. i, p. 405.
[3]Ibid., p. 405.

came well-nigh intolerable. It was during this period that a law was passed laying a double tax upon the property of Catholics. So unrelenting had the war upon them become, that a general desire prevailed on the part of Catholics to migrate from the colony.[1] The Jesuits were the principal object against which this anti-Catholic agitation was directed. The proposition of seizing and confiscating all their property in Maryland was discussed in the papers, and a bill looking to this object was actually passed by the lower house of the Assembly.[2] But the bill failed to become a law, and the school at Bohemia continued for some years longer, though with a diminished faculty and a small number of pupils. About the year 1765, one of the two Fathers still remaining there was withdrawn, and the school was closed.[3]

CONNECTION WITH GEORGETOWN

After the American Revolution, or, it may be, during it, the school was opened again on a small scale. The Society of Jesus had, in the meantime, been suppressed, but the members continued to labor in the old missions as secular priests. In the year 1789, Georgetown College was founded. The institution was projected and organized by the former members of the Society, the prime mover in the matter being the former pupil of the Jesuits at Bohemia, who had become a Jesuit priest after finishing his studies in Europe and was now Pre-

[1] Shea, vol. i, p. 416; U. S. Cath. Hist. Mag., vol. iii, p. 147.
[2] Ibid., p. 417.
[3] Woodstock Letters, vol. xvi, p. 229.

fect-Apostolic of the Church in the United States, the Rev. John Carroll. The first students were received at Georgetown in 1791,[1] and not long afterward, it would seem, classes were discontinued at Bohemia.[2] It is important to note the coincidence, for, taken in connection with the fact that the new institution at Georgetown was founded by the Jesuits, it goes to show that Georgetown College has a close historical connection with the Bohemia school and, if we go farther back, with the old college and school at Newtown—the second college established within the United States. The foundations of Georgetown College were, in fact, laid long before the days of John Carroll. The new institution was, in reality, only the old Jesuit school that had existed more or less continuously, in one place or another, for a hundred and fifty years before. The change of site, the larger building, the broader plans, the open appeal to the Catholic public, the rapid development of the college —these and other things of the same kind gave to the institution an aspect of complete newness. They showed that an era of educational freedom had been ushered in by the Revolution; but they showed also what would have been the possibilities of Catholic educational development in colonial days, had the Jesuit Fathers been at liberty to carry out the broad educational plans which they had cherished from the very beginning.

In endeavoring to arrive at a just estimate of the influence and value of the old Jesuit schools of Maryland, the words used by an eminent historian

[1]Georgetown College Catalogue, Introduction.
[2]Records Amer. Catholic Hist. Soc., vol. i, p. 119.

in speaking in general of the work of the Jesuits in the colony may appropriately be recalled:

"No stone marks the grave of these devoted men. Of most of them even the names have passed into oblivion, and of the rest we have little more than a few faded yellow lines of antique writing scattered among moldering and forgotten archives. The tribes among whom they labored have long since passed away. But their work has not perished with them; and if the peaceful, equitable, and generous spirit which characterized the early days of the colony, secured its growth and permanence, and has left its stamp on Maryland institutions, is something to remember with pride, let it not be forgotten how large a part of this is due to the truly Christian example and teaching of the early missionary Fathers."[1]

[1]Scharf, History of Maryland, vol. i, p. 192. The house of William Britton, at Newtown, which was purchased by the Jesuits, enlarged, and probably used as a school and college building, is still standing, and is in an excellent state of preservation. The school building at Bohemia, however, has entirely disappeared. The spot on which it stood is still pointed out, and the bricks that composed it were used in putting up the present dwelling-house of the Jesuits there. See Shea, op. cit.

CHAPTER IV

CATHOLIC COLONIAL SCHOOLS IN PENNSYLVANIA

ATTITUDE OF THE QUAKERS

WHEN THE Jesuits established themselves at Bohemia, it was, as has been observed, partly with the purpose of making that place a base for missionary work in the newly founded colony of the Quakers to the north. The broad-minded tolerance of Penn in religious matters attracted people of all creeds to his colony. A strong stream of emigration set in early from Germany, which Penn himself visited for the purpose of securing emigrants.[1] Many of these came from the Rhine provinces, and among them were a considerable number of Catholics. Most of the German emigrants were farmers, and naturally continued the same occupation after their arrival in this country, taking up lands to the west and northwest of Philadelphia. Emigrants came in large numbers from Ireland also, though somewhat later. The proportion of Irish became noticeably large about the year 1717, and ten years later the Irish outnumbered greatly all other nationalities in the list of emigrants for the year.[2] Most of these were from the north of Ireland, and were Protestants, but there were some Catholics among them. The tendency of the

[1]Bolles, Hist. of Penn., vol. ii, p. 146.
[2]Amer. Cath. Hist. Researches, vol. xvi, p. 68 seq., and vol. xviii, p. 99.

Irish was to settle in Philadelphia or the other towns.

Teaching school was a favorite occupation of the better educated Irish emigrants after their arrival, at least until something more advantageous offered. Many of the emigrants were "redemptioners," or indentured servants, being bound to service for a term of years in payment for their passage to America or for other obligation, and some of these engaged in school-teaching. There are frequent references to Irish schoolmasters in Pennsylvania during the first half of the eighteenth century, and mention is made of several who were Catholics. A letter of the Rev. Mr. Backhouse, an Episcopalian clergyman, of Chester, Pa., written in 1741, to the Society for the Propagation of the Gospel, in London, has a special interest in this connection, in that it discloses the attitude of the Quakers toward Catholics in general, and incidentally, to some extent, toward Catholic schools. It appears that the Episcopalians of Chester had brought a school-teacher of their faith from Maryland, 'with the object of having him open a school. As they were not numerous enough themselves to support him, they endeavored to induce the Quakers to patronize the school. What the Quakers did, we are told by Mr. Backhouse in words that still glow with the fervor of his astonished indignation:

"They did what none but Quakers dare do, in a country under the government of a Protestant king; that is, they engaged by their great encouragement a rigid, virulent Papist to set up school in the said town of Chester, in order to oppose and impoverish the said Protestant teacher. Under such proceedings we meekly and seriously debated the matter with him. . . . Yet, notwithstanding they did, and still persist to encourage the same. Nay, they carried their implacable malice so far as to occasion by threats and promises most of the children who were under the said Protestant teacher's tuition to be taken from him without being able to give any reason for such their proceedings."[1]

Writing again to the Society the following year, he is obliged to complain that the Quakers "still maintain their Papist master purely in opposition to ours." The Quakers were, in fact, friendly to Catholics, as they were in general to all denominations, and Catholics in Pennsylvania appear to have enjoyed the full religious liberty guaranteed by the charter of William Penn, notwithstanding the existing proscriptive laws against them in England.[2]

FIRST JESUITS

A favorable opportunity thus offered in Pennsylvania for the work of the Jesuits. From about the beginning of the eighteenth century, the scattered Catholics there were visited from time to time by missionaries from Maryland. In 1730, Father Greaton, S.J., came from Maryland, and established himself in Philadelphia. Out of a total population of about 10,000 in the city, he organized the first little Catholic congregation, consisting of 37 persons, and four years later was able to erect a modest church.[3] The influx of Catholic emi-

[1] Amer. Cath. Hist. Researches, vol. xi, p. 62.
[2] Ibid., vol. ix, p. 24.
[3] Ibid.

grants soon called for additional laborers in this ripening harvest-field, and in 1741 Father Greaton was joined by the Rev. Henry Neale, S.J. The same year, the German Province of the Society of Jesus sent out two priests to minister to the German Catholics in the colony. These were Father Wapeler, who founded the missions of Conewago and Lancaster, and Father Schneider, who took up his residence at Goshenhoppen, in Berks County. Other German Jesuits came later on, one of these being the celebrated Father Farmer.[1]

There is no documentary proof to show the time of the establishment of the first Catholic schools in Pennsylvania, but there is strong traditional evidence for the belief that they date back to the time of the very first organization of the Church in the various centers of Catholic life. Local traditions indicate that in nearly every instance the organization of a Catholic parish was attended, if not preceded, by the organization of a parish school, the priest himself, in some cases, being the first school-teacher.[2] Mr. Martin I. J. Griffin, a competent historical authority, has summed up the result of a thorough investigation of the subject in the statement that "wherever throughout Pennsylvania prior to 1800 there was a chapel, there was undoubtedly, where there was a number of children, and where Catholics were in fair numbers, some system of instruction, even though the method was crude and but elementary in its extent."[3] This con-

---

[1]U. S. Cath. Mag., vol. iv. no. 4, p. 249 seq.

[2]Wickersham, Hist. of Education in Penn., p. 115 seq.; Riley, Conewago.

[3]Letter to the Superintendent of Catholic Schools, Philadelphia, 1905.

clusion is further supported by the fact that the other religious denominations in the colony, especially those which were German, almost invariably signalized the beginning of church work in a locality by the establishment of schools.[1] It is reasonably certain that the Jesuits, with their known zeal for education, were not behind the ministers of other denominations in practical effort to furnish the children of their respective flocks with the opportunity for at least a rudimentary schooling.

FIRST SCHOOLS

There seems to be a recognition of the existence of a school in Philadelphia for some time and of the need of providing larger and better accommodations for the pupils, in the will of James White, a merchant, made in 1767, and bequeathing 30 pounds "toward a schoolhouse."[2] This is the earliest known bequest made in behalf of Catholic education in the colony. Again, in 1782, there is evidence that a school had long been in existence there, in the fact that a subscription was taken up for the purpose of paying for the "old schoolhouse and lot" just purchased from the Quakers, and of erecting a new school building. Previous to this date, the school was probably taught in the paro-

---

[1] Wickersham, op. cit., passim.

[2] Rec. Amer. Cath. Hist. Soc., vol. vi, p. 459. The James White here mentioned was the ancestor of a Catholic family that has figured largely in the history of the Church in this country. Edward Douglas White, who was appointed an Associate-Justice of the U. S. Supreme Court in 1894, is a great-grandson of this first lay benefactor of Catholic education in Pennsylvania. Ibid., p. 467.

chial residence.[1] Among the German Catholics scattered through the counties farther west, a school was probably started near Conewago by Father Wapeler, a few years after his arrival there,[2] and probably, also, in the course of time, at several of the missions attended from Conewago, chief among which were Sportsman's Hall, Carlisle, Milton, York, Taneytown, Frederick, Littlestown, Brandt's Chapel, now Paradise, and Hanover. About 1787 the school near Conewago was so far developed as to be able to engage the services of the very capable schoolmaster at Goshenhoppen, for we find him moving there at that time.[3] Goshenhoppen, too, where Father Schneider resided, became the center of a circle of missions, a number of which also had schools. From the will of John McCarthy, we have evidence of the existence of a school at one of these missions, Haycock, in 1766; and again, in 1784, the marriage of Ferdinand Wagner, "our schoolmaster at Haycock," is recorded in the Goshenhoppen register.[4] There was thus a Catholic school at Haycock long before there was a Catholic church there. According to local tradition, Mass was said in McCarthy's house, and school was kept in another building on the premises until the erection of a permanent school building with the church later on. Reading was another

[1]Amer. Cath. Hist. Res., vol. x, p. 60; Woodstock Letters, vol. xiii, p. 33; Letter of Mr. Martin I. J. Griffin.
[2]Wickersham, op. cit., p. 115.
[3]Riley, Collections and Recollections, History of the Gubernator Family, vol. vii, p. 530 seq.; Letter of Mr. John T. Riley to the author.
[4]Goshenhoppen Registers, in Records of the Amer. Cath. Hist. Soc., vol. viii, p. 388.
[5]Letter of Mr. Martin I. J. Griffin.

mission station which in all probability had a Catholic school soon after the organization of the Catholic congregation there in 1755.[1]

GOSHENHOPPEN

A peculiar interest attaches to the school at Goshenhoppen.[2] The Jesuit missionaries in America, it has already been observed, were men of marked abilities and learning, as a class; men, oftentimes, who had occupied places of distinction in the seminaries or universities of the Order in the Old World. The German Jesuits who labored in the rough mission fields of Pennsylvania during those early days were men of this kind. Of Father Wapeler, Bishop Carroll wrote that "he was a man of much learning and unbounded zeal." He referred to Father Schneider as a "person of great dexterity in business, consummate prudence and undoubted magnanimity," and said that "he spread the faith of Christ far and near."[3] An old Jesuit catalogue refers to the founder of the Goshenhoppen mission as, *"Theo. Schneider, qui docuit Philos. et controv. Leodi. et fuit rector magnif. Universi. Heidelbergensis."*[4] Father Schneider was born in Germany in the year 1700. He entered the Jesuit Order while still young, and his superior talents caused him to be sent, after ordination, to the famous Jesuit seminary at Liège, in Belgium, where he taught both philosophy and theology. Subsequently, he was sent to Heidelberg, to teach in the

[1]Ibid.
[2]Now known as Bally, in Berks County.
[3]U. S. Cath. Mag., vol. iv, p. 250.
[4]Ibid.

university or the college established by the Jesuits
in connection with the university in 1703. Heidelberg was a Catholic university then, the Faculty
of Philosophy, from the year 1716, being under
the control of the Jesuits.[1] In this way, Father
Schneider came to be chosen and installed as rector
in December, 1738, his term of office lasting until
December of the following year.[2] It was a high
distinction to have come to one comparatively so
young—a fine tribute to his talents as well as to his
popularity, and it opened up the prospect of a brilliant career. But a nobler and holier fire than that
of intellectual ambition burned in the soul of Father
Schneider. Like St. Francis Xavier, he turned
aside from the shining heights of academic fame,
to devote himself, as a poor and humble missionary in a distant land, to the ministry of souls.
There was a call for German priests from the far-
off frontiers of Pennsylvania, and Father Schneider
was one of the two who were sent from Germany
to inaugurate the apostolic work.

It is interesting to contemplate the brilliant
young priest, fresh from the honors and the experience gained while fulfilling the office of *Rector
Magnificus* of Heidelberg University, gathering
the poor German children of Goshenhoppen and
vicinity about him in his little room, to teach them,

[1] Paulsen, Geschichte des Gelehrten Unterrichts, p. 278.
[2] For the date of Father Schneider's rectorship of Heidelberg University, I am indebted to Professor Wille, of that institution, who, at my request, made a search of the archives
for the purpose. The archives reveal nothing more about
Father Schneider than the fact of his having held the office
of rector and the dates. For the manner of electing the rector,
and the duties and honors attaching to the position, see
Raumer, Geschichte der Pedagogik, Vierter Theil, S. 18 seq.

along with the simple catechism, the rudiments of a brief pioneer education. There can be no doubt that he himself took up the work of teaching, soon after his arrival in 1741. Reading, writing, and spelling were about all that was taught at that early period in the schools that were being started everywhere in the colony.[1] Little if any attention was given to what is now called arithmetic. The term of schooling was brief, the pupils were few and of all ages. There was no church in Goshenhoppen as yet, Mass being said in one of the farmers' houses. Father Schneider took up his residence in a two-story frame house, the largest, probably, in the vicinity, and here, according to local traditions, he began his school.[2] The school was eagerly attended by the children of the whole neighborhood, Protestant as well as Catholic, it being the only one in the place. Father Schneider, in fact, soon made himself greatly beloved by the members of all denominations, and there is a tradition that when, in 1745, he commenced the work of building a church, the Protestants of the region were not less generous than the Catholics in helping to furnish the necessary material means.[3] It is pleasant to record that the educational zeal of the first schoolmaster at Goshenhoppen was not forgotten by the descendants of the early settlers. More than a century afterward, the public school authorities of the district showed their appreciation of what he had done, by an arrangement which

[1] Wickersham, op. cit., passim.
[2] Ibid., p. 115; Amer. Cath. Hist. Res., vol. xvii, p. 98; Letter of Father Bally, pastor of Goshenhoppen, in Woodstock Letters, vol. v, pp. 202, 313.
[3] U. S. Cath. Mag., vol. iv, p. 250 seq.

provided for the education of the children of the Goshenhoppen parish school at the public expense.[1]

Under Father Schneider, the work of organizing the parish at Goshenhoppen, as well as the neighboring Catholic missions, went steadily on. A church was built, a tract of about 500 acres of land purchased, and the land sold off from time to time in small portions, with the result of bringing about a considerable settlement of Catholic families near the church. For twenty-three years he lived at Goshenhoppen, ministering to the Catholics there and in the region for fifty miles around. He was skilled in medicine, and was frequently called upon to minister to the sick in the capacity of a physician. As "Doctor Schneider" he was often enabled to gain access to persons and places which he could not otherwise have visited. We have an evidence of his love of books, as well as of his incessant activity, in a beautifully bound manuscript copy of the entire Roman Missal, transcribed by his own hand—a piece of work that doubtless helped to fill out many a long wintry day, a work that witnesses, too, to his life of extreme self-sacrifice and poverty.[2] Before he died, in 1764, he had the satisfaction of seeing the Church firmly established in Pennsylvania; and in the building of churches, schools, and mission chapels, together with the increasing influx of Catholic emigrants, he must have discerned the prospect of a much greater and more rapid growth in the future.

[1]Woodstock Letters, vol. v, pp. 202, 313.
[2]U. S. Cath. Mag.. vol. iv, p. 249 seq.

For many years, however, the growth of the Church in and around Goshenhoppen was slow, and Father Schneider's school remained small. The French and Indian War came on, and the country became the scene of the most savage depredations on the part of the Indians. After Braddock's defeat, in 1755, Berks County was laid waste with fire and sword, hundreds of houses were burned, and many of the settlers slain and scalped, or dragged away into captivity to undergo a fate worse than death.[1] In 1757, the total number of adult Catholics in the county was only 117.[2] Yet Father Schneider seems to have kept up his school all this time, and to have gradually increased the number of pupils attending, for in 1763, about the time of the close of the war, we find that the school was large enough to engage the services of a paid school-teacher. The baptismal register of Goshenhoppen for that year records the private baptism of a child, when eleven weeks old, by "Henry Fredder, the schoolmaster at Conisahoppen."[3] A schoolhouse, too, apparently had been built. From this time on, there are frequent references to the schoolmasters in the parish records.

[1] Egle, Hist. of Pennsylvania, p. 384.
[2] Amer. Cath. Hist. Res., vol. vii, p. 88.
[3] Records Amer. Cath. Hist. Soc., vol. ii, p. 328. The spelling of the name of the place must have been a perpetual puzzle to the children of Father Schneider's school, since even the pastor, as is evident from the above entry, did not seem to be able to fix upon any definite form. "Goshenhoppen" was the more commonly used form, but no less than seventeen different ways of spelling the name occur in the parish records between 1735 and 1787. Besides the two already given, we have Gosshehopen, Cossehoppa, Quesohopen, Cushenhoppen, Cowshoppen, with others quite as curious. Ibid., vol. viii, p. 341.

GOSHENHOPPEN SCHOOLMASTERS

The schoolmaster was evidently looked upon as a person of distinction in the little world of Goshenhoppen, contrary to the custom which prevailed in the colonies generally. He stood next to the parish priest, and was his right-hand man, a sort of lay assistant, in matters relating to the temporal, and even the spiritual welfare of the Catholic flock. Three schoolmasters are mentioned in the parish registers between 1763 and 1796, Henry Fredder, Breitenbach, and John Lawrence Gubernator. Breitenbach does not seem to have stayed for more than a short time, as we have only a single mention of him, as standing sponsor for a child, with "his wife Susan," in 1768. He was preceded by Henry Fredder, who is mentioned occasionally between 1763 and 1768. There is an interval then of sixteen years, during which we have no means of knowing who the school-teacher was, for if his name is given in the registers, as it probably is, the title of his office is not subjoined. John Lawrence Gubernator, the most distinguished of the Goshenhoppen schoolmasters, and the ancestor of the numerous Pennsylvania families who have borne that name, appears first on the parish registers in 1784. He was born in Oppenheim, Germany, in 1735, served as an officer in the army of the Allies in the Seven Years' War, and came to America during the Revolutionary War. He landed in Philadelphia, and made his way to Goshenhoppen, where he was engaged by Father Ritter, then pastor, to take charge of the school. He seems to have been a finely educated man, and a devoted teacher, and rendered great services to the cause of Catholic education in Pennsylvania during a period of twenty-five years. He served as organist as well as schoolmaster. Not long after coming to Goshenhoppen, he was married to a widow named Johanna Darham. It was made a gala day in the old Catholic settlement, and the chronicle of the happy event in the parish records, brief as it is, affords us a pleasant glimpse of the position of social prominence accorded to this successor of Father Schneider in the Goshenhoppen school.[1] He subsequently taught school near Conewago, returned to Goshenhoppen, and, after several years, finally settled down as a teacher in the newly started preparatory seminary of the Sulpicians at Pigeon Hills, Pa. His son also became a schoolteacher and had charge for a time of the school near Conewago.[2]

There is reason for believing that a school was founded at Lancaster also at a very early date, although local tradition is silent on the point. Father Farmer was there from 1752 to 1758, and he was not the man to permit the parish to be behindhand in the matter of education, even if Father Wapeler had not been able to see his way to the establishment of a school at an earlier date. When the Rev. John B. Caussee took charge of the parish in 1785, he probably found a Catholic school in existence. We find him petitioning the State authorities for the establishment of a "charity school" at Lancaster. Instead of a "charity

[1] Goshenhoppen Parish Registers, in Rec. Amer. Cath. Hist. Soc., vol. viii, p. 388.
[2] Riley, Collections and Recollections, History of the Gubernator Family, vol. ii, p. 530.

school," however, he started an institution of a higher grade, in conjunction with the other denominations of the place, which was chartered by the legislature under the name of Franklin College.[1]

FATHERS FARMER AND MOLYNEUX

Father Farmer, whose real name was Steinmeyer, was a famous figure in the history of the Church in Pennsylvania. Born in Germany in 1720, he passed through a university course, devoting special attention to physics. When twenty-three years of age he joined the Jesuit Order, and was sent to America in 1752. After being six years at Lancaster, he was called to Philadelphia, especially to minister to the Germans there, and continued to make that city the center of his extensive missionary labors until his death in 1786. He founded mission stations in New Jersey, and organized a Catholic congregation in the city of New York. His genial temperament and lively charity endeared him greatly to the inhabitants of Philadelphia, regardless of religious beliefs. He was a member of the famous Philosophical Society of Philadelphia, and was made a member of the Board of Trustees of the University of Philadelphia, when that institution was chartered in 1779.[2] Another learned Jesuit who labored in Philadelphia during the Revolutionary War was the Rev. Robert Molyneux, the companion of Father Farmer during many years at St. Mary's Church.[3]

[1]S. M. Sener, in U. S. Cath. Hist. Mag., vol. i, p. 215.
[2]U. S. Cath. Mag., vol. iv, p. 249; Amer. Cath. Hist. Res., vol. ii, new series, p. 72.
[3]The new church built by Father Harding in 1763 was called St. Mary's.

He was an Englishman by birth, and a man of extensive knowledge, his society being eagerly sought for in the most polite circles of society in Philadelphia. He was a favorite guest at the house of the Marquis de la Luzerne, Minister Plenipotentiary from France, and became instructor in English to him.[1]

Under the direction of these able and universally respected priests, the Church made rapid progress in Philadelphia, and broad and firm foundations were laid for a system of Catholic schools. It is impossible to tell how much we are indebted to these two men for the change which came over the Continental Congress and the country generally during the Revolutionary War in respect to the Catholic Church. There were, of course, deeper causes at work, but surely something must be credited to the personal influence of Fathers Molyneux and Farmer, who, in character, seemed each to combine the finest traditions of Jesuit scholarship and Jesuit piety, and who, in their daily lives, were thrown into frequent contact with many of the men who were engaged in framing the new government and informing it with its spirit. Many were the notable gatherings that St. Mary's Church witnessed during the Revolutionary War. It was the place of worship for the diplomatic representatives of the Catholic powers. Washington was twice at Vespers there, and more than once it is recorded that the members of Congress attended the services in a body.[2]

[1] U. S. Cath. Mag., vol. iv, p. 249 seq.
[2] Amer. Cath. Hist. Res., vol. xiii, p. 174; new series, vol. i, p. 161.

The education of the Catholic children of Philadelphia claimed the special attention of Fathers Molyneux and Farmer. Father Molyneux was the first in this country, so far as is known, to get out text-books for the use of Catholic schools. He had a catechism printed, and other elementary books, among which was "a spelling primer for children with the Catholic Catechism annexed," printed in 1785.[1] The latter were probably reprints of commonly used text-books for spelling and reading, with modifications and additions to make them adaptable for use in Catholic schools. He was the first to make extensive use of the press to disseminate religious truth, importing Catholic books from England, and causing to be reprinted in Philadelphia such works as Challoner's "Catholic Christian Instructed," and "The History of the Bible."[2]

THE EDUCATIONAL PURPOSE

It was from the beginning the steady purpose of those in charge of the church in Philadelphia to provide a training under Catholic auspices for *all* the Catholic children of the city. A clear evidence of this purpose is afforded in the case of the children of the exiled Acadians, a colony of whom took refuge in Philadelphia. In 1771, a petition was forwarded to the General Assembly of Pennsylvania, praying for the granting of relief to some of the Acadians who were sadly in need of it, and among others to Ann Bryald, a Catholic lady who had been engaged to teach their children. The

[1] Sketches of Father Molyneux, in U. S. Cath. Mag., vol. iv, p. 249 seq.; Amer. Cath. Hist. Res., vol. v, p. 31.
[2] U. S. Cath. Mag., loc. cit.

petition refers to her as "Ann Bryald, a woman
who acts as Schoolmistress to the Children, and
on that account in need of assistance, as she can not
work for a livelihood, her whole time being taken
up in the Care of them."[1]   The event shows how
careful the good pastors were that no portion of
their growing flock should be left without the opportunity of a sound religious and secular education.   The difficulty of securing a Catholic teacher
who understood French would account for the
anxiety to retain the services of Ann Bryald.   The
parish was poor, too.   The total annual revenue
from all sources at this time amounted to only
about 90 pounds;[2] and the support of the regular
parish school must have been felt as a burden
already sufficiently heavy.   Another illustration of
this broad educational purpose was afforded on
the occasion of the yellow fever scourge.   In the
year 1798, and during several preceding years, the
city was ravaged by the disease, and hundreds of
Catholics fell victims to it.   To care for the help-
less orphans left behind, an association was formed
which succeeded in establishing a Catholic orphans'
home and school, and this institution developed
subsequently into St. Joseph's Orphan Asylum, the
first Catholic orphan asylum within the limits of
the United States.[3]

PROGRESS OF THE SCHOOLS

Toward the close of the Revolutionary War,
with the influx of Catholic emigrants, there was a

[1]Amer. Cath. Hist. Res., vol. xviii, p. 141.
[2]U. S. Cath. Mag., vol. iv, loc. cit.
[3]Shea, Life and Times of Archbishop Carroll, p. 414.

great increase in the Catholic population of Philadelphia. Two more priests arrived, and the number of adult Catholics in the city, in the year 1784,
was reckoned by Father Molyneux to be about
2,000.[1] The number of children in the school
was correspondingly increased, and the need was
felt of larger and better quarters. The old schoolhouse and lot of the Quakers was purchased for
400 pounds in 1781. A new schoolhouse was built
for 440 pounds, and subscriptions were started to
meet the cost of these extensive improvements,
which involved a total debt of approximately 1,000
pounds. The general interest of Catholics in the
matter of education was shown by the ready and
generous response to the appeal of Father Molyneux, a sum of over 320 pounds being raised by individual subscriptions within a year. Among the
largest contributors were, besides Father Molyneux
himself, Captain Baxter's wife, Captain John
Walsh, Captain James Byrne, James Oeller, the
Catholic ambassadors, and Thomas Fitzsimons, a
signer of the Constitution, who was a member of
the parish and a staunch advocate of Catholic
schools.[2]

The new schoolhouse was finished in 1782, and
probably opened for the first time in August of that
year. It was two stories high, and was no doubt
regarded by the Catholics of Philadelphia as a
thing perfect in its kind. The walls were plastered,
and the interior woodwork painted. One of the
items of expense was "308 panes of window glass,"
each 8×10 inches. Firewood was to be supplied

---

[1] U. S. Cath. Mag., loc. cit.
[2] Rec. Amer. Cath. Hist. Soc., vol. iv, passim.

regularly and abundantly for the new building. Light, heat, and sanitation were evidently carefully looked after according to the standards of the time. The school was divided into two sections. The upper schoolroom was reserved for the younger children, the lower for "such as shall be fit for Writing & Cyphering."[1] Two teachers were consequently employed. The affairs of the church and school at this time were administered by a board of managers, at the head of which were the pastors. Later on, when the church was incorporated, the board of managers became the board of trustees.

The school was called a "free school," but the term then did not mean precisely what it does now. It was hoped, however, to make it in time an endowed school, and thus relieve parents of the necessity of paying tuition for their children. As a step in this direction, and with the view of providing for the education of the poorer children of the congregation, the managers resolved, in 1783, that each of the teachers should furnish instruction gratis to six poor scholars annually.[2] From the rest they were to receive payment. In 1794 the tuition charge was 17s. 6d. for the pupils in the upper room, and 20s. for those in the lower. But there must have been difficulty in collecting the money, for this plan was soon abandoned, and the teachers were paid a fixed salary out of the parish treasury, the money being raised by means of "charity sermons," church collections, and occasional gifts. The salary of the head schoolmaster, in 1788, was 75

[1]Minutes of the board meeting, Sept. 1, 1783, in Rec. Amer. Cath. Hist. Soc., vol. iv, p. 268.
[2]Minutes of the board meeting, ibid.

pounds per annum. The cost of text-books, considering the scarcity of books at the time, was not great. Spelling-books sold for 10d. apiece, catechisms for 5d., and "fables," or readers, for 3s. 9d. Children were received as young as six years of age.

The managers were determined to bring the work of the school up to the highest possible standard of excellence. One of the means adopted for this purpose was the offering of cash premiums to the pupils having the best records. It was resolved that, "as an encouragement to the Children's improvement at school, premiums be given them four times in the year, viz., the first Mondays in February, May, August & November, to the value of Twenty shillings each time."[1] Very little vacation, if any, it would appear, was allowed during the summer months.

The greatest difficulty experienced by the managers in their efforts to improve the school came from the lack of good teachers. Between 1787 and 1800, the head-teacher was changed eight times. The plan of having a woman teacher for the girls was tried, and found to give satisfaction. A constant effort was made to secure better teachers. It must be remembered that teaching was not regarded as a profession in those days, and most of those who took up the work continued in it only until they were able to get something better. To meet this difficulty, the salaries of the teachers were raised again and again. In 1795, the salary of the head-master was $400, but out of this he had to pay "a female assistant to the care of the girls,"

[1] Minutes of the board meeting, ibid.

which assistant was "subject to his jurisdiction and
to the approbation of the Trustees." There seem
to have been three teachers employed at this time,
as, besides the head-teacher and his assistant in
charge of the girls, we find that there was another
teacher who was known as the "Master of the
Poor School."[1] The "Poor School" consisted of
those pupils who were unable to pay their tuition,
and also, probably, the small boys. The salary of
the "Master of the Poor School" was 210 pounds
(Pennsylvanian standard), or about $337. The
known teachers of St. Mary's School up to 1800
were Hugh Sweeney, Edward Barrington, Patrick Brady, Mrs. Short, Mr. and Mrs. McLaughlin, T. Reagan, Mr. Brady, Mr. Graham, Mr.
Chapman, James Reagan, Terence Byrne, and
P. J. Doyle.

SUPPORT OF THE SCHOOLS

The school was thus growing, the class-rooms
were crowded, and an enlargement of the building
had to be made. New problems were springing
up as the result, involving the separation and classi-
fication of the pupils and the differentiation of the
teaching. The solution of these problems meant
increased expense. Collections were taken up in the
church at intervals for the benefit of the school,
and the interest of the people in education and in
the efforts that were being made toward its improvement may be gaged, in some measure, by the
extent of the response to these appeals. The collection was generally preceded by a "charity ser-

[1] Ibid.

mon," or an address by one of the more able preachers, upon the object to which the proceeds were to be applied. In 1788, the collection for the school which was taken up on May 4 brought 50 pounds, while in November of the same year the collection amounted to 39 pounds. Besides this, there were individual gifts, which were often of a considerable sum.[1]

The general interest in education, and the generosity of the people in contributing to its support, is shown even more notably by the donations and bequests made from time to time, having for their object the permanent endowment of the school. Between 1788 and 1810 there were twelve bequests or donations made to the school with this end in view. Some of these gifts were in the form of houses or lands, others in cash or bonds. The largest was that of James Costelloe, whose will was made in Philadelphia in 1793. He bequeathed 20 acres of land on Boon Island, Kingsessing, "the rents, issues and profits to be divided into equal parts, one moiety or half to be forever appropriated toward the maintenance and support of the Free School of St. Mary's."[2] This property was subsequently sold for $2,000. Among the benefactors of St. Mary's School was Commodore John Barry, the "Father of the American Navy." In 1803, he left an annuity of 20 pounds, the principal of which, on the death of his negro man, was "to be given to the Trustees of the Roman Catholic Society worshipping at the Church of St. Mary, in the city of Philadelphia, for the use and benefit of

[1]Minutes of the board meeting.
[2]Amer. Cath. Hist. Res., vol. viii, p. 19.

the poor school of said church." The principal, when turned over to the corporation, amounted to $900.[1]

An interesting feature of the school, which serves to show the efforts made to reach all classes of the Catholic population, was the giving of instruction in the evening to such as, for one cause or another, were unable to come during the day. It may also have been due partly to lack of room in daytime. There is no evidence to show when this "night-school" was started, or how long it continued, but it was in existence in 1805, as on the evening of May 21, in that year, the meeting of the trustees— they met in the schoolhouse—could not be held on account of the session of the "night-school."[2] A "singing-school" was also established, to prepare singers for the choir, but it probably had no connection with the regular school.

THE MOTHER-SCHOOL

If the account of St. Mary's School has been somewhat long and detailed, it is due to a desire to set forth, as fully as the documentary evidence will permit, the plan of the school, and above all, the motives which lay back of its organization and development, for it may be said to have been the mother-school of all the parochial schools in the English-speaking States. Philadelphia was the largest city, and St. Mary's was the largest and richest Catholic parish, in the United States. It was the center of Catholic power and influence, and

[1]Ibid.
[2]Griffin, History of Bishop Egan, p. 15.

other parishes, as they grew up, especially in the cities, naturally looked to it for guidance in the solution of the many problems that confronted the newly organized Catholic congregation under New-World conditions—foremost and most far-reaching of which was the problem of religious education. The problem had been solved in Philadelphia, solved apparently to the satisfaction of both clergy and laity, as the result of a process of development responding to newly developed needs. The solution resulted in fixing an educational ideal which has struck its roots deeper and more firmly into the Catholic American mind with every year that has since elapsed.

The influence of this ideal was shown shortly in the organization of other parishes in Philadelphia. The Germans broke off from St. Mary's Parish in 1788, and soon afterward built a church of their own—Holy Trinity. Provision was immediately made for a parish school. As they were not able to build a schoolhouse as yet, the basement of the church was set apart for that purpose, and fitted up as a schoolroom. The church was described as being "100 feet long and 60 feet broad, and underneath was a comfortable schoolroom."[1] A few years later, with the rapid growth of the parish, the need of a separate schoolhouse was felt, and the congregation had recourse to a lottery—a commonly employed means of raising money for charitable purposes at the time. The sum of $10,000 was wanted, and the legislature of Pennsylvania was petitioned for the legal power to create a lottery in that amount. The Act was passed in 1803,

[1]Hist. Sketches of the Cath. Church in Phila., p. 43.

and the lottery was a great success. The tickets were sold for $6 apiece, and there were 6,274 prizes, amounting to $8,700.[1]

A third parish in Philadelphia was organized in 1796 by members of the Augustinian Order, and became known as St. Augustine's. For some years the members of the new parish continued to send their children to St. Mary's School, but in 1811 a school was begun at St. Augustine's which combined instruction in preparatory and collegiate, as well as elementary branches. It opened with 39 pupils. The example set by St. Mary's was imitated by other parishes also as they grew up, a school being usually begun as soon as the congregation was organized and a place of worship secured.[2]

The factional troubles which broke out in St. Mary's Parish in 1812 and continued for many years, to the great detriment of the Church in Philadelphia, had a very injurious effect upon the school in point both of efficiency and of attendance. Nevertheless, the old school continued to exist and to render valuable service to the cause of Catholic education. St. Mary's School was not attached to St. Mary's Church, but was back of Walnut Street, next to the "Old Chapel" of St. Joseph's. The school building which had been erected in 1782 was torn down in 1838, when the present St. Joseph's Church was built, St. Joseph's having become a separate congregation after 1821. After 1838, school was kept in the basement of St. Joseph's Church, until 1852, when

[1]Ibid., p. 44.
[2]Ibid.

a three-story school building, which is still standing, was built on the northern part of St. Joseph's lot, with the entrance from Walnut Street. The present schoolhouse annexed to St. Mary's Church was built in 1843.[1]

[1]Letter of Mr. Martin I. J. Griffin to the author.

CHAPTER V

CHARACTERISTICS OF CATHOLIC COLONIAL SCHOOLS

NUMBER OF SCHOOLS

IT HAS been shown that it is to the Spanish Franciscans the credit is due for the first schools set up by Europeans within the limits of the United States. Benavides' account of their New Mexican schools was *published* several years before either the Boston Latin School or the Dutch School in New Amsterdam was established, and the *earliest* Franciscan schools in New Mexico were probably begun a quarter of a century before. The first Franciscan schools in Florida were begun at an even earlier date. We have a reference to the existence of a classical school at St. Augustine in 1606, which was 29 years before the foundation of the Boston Latin School, and 27 years before that of the Dutch School in New Amsterdam.

The founders and first missionaries of the other Catholic colonies were not less zealous for education than the Franciscans in New Mexico and Florida. We have seen that, in every instance, a system of education was provided for in the plans of the founders, and that in each case, in spite of difficulties, the plan was wrought out in practice to some extent, with more or less success and permanency. The educational efforts of the Spanish friars in New Mexico, Texas, Florida, and California; the French schools in New Orleans, Detroit, and throughout the Mississippi Valley; the schools of the Jesuit missionaries in Maryland and Pennsylvania, taken all together form, in view of the circumstances of the time, a record of educational ideals and achievements of which Catholics may well be proud. Probably more than 70 schools were established by Catholics on the soil of the United States during the colonial period.

SOCIAL AND POLITICAL CONDITIONS

In studying the schools which existed in colonial times, one is constantly reminded of the vast differences between social, political, and religious conditions then and now. It is impossible to understand the character of the early schools, or the difficulties which were involved in their establishment and maintenance, without taking this into account. This is more especially true of Catholic schools. The condition of Catholics differed in many ways from that of the other elements of the population. Catholics in the English colonies were ground down by oppressive laws, which affected their relations with each other, as well as with their fellow-colonists of other religious beliefs. They were a class apart, outside of the general social and political environment, and beyond the reach of some of the strongest influences which were making for the enlightenment and general educational advancement of the colonies. In the west and south, Catholics, while free from persecution, lived in a social environment which contained elements that were entirely absent in the eastern colonies. The political conditions in the west were quite different too.

In Maryland and Pennsylvania, up to near the Revolution, there was but a thin population, spread over an immense expanse of territory. There were no towns at all in Maryland worthy of the name. St. Mary's, for 60 years the capital and the most populous place, was never more than a small village, and Annapolis, the new capital, contained about the year 1700 no more than 40 dwelling-houses.[1] It was the same in Pennsylvania, outside of Philadelphia.[2] Such places as Goshenhoppen and Conewago were mere straggling country villages with a few houses grouped about the church, the rest of the population that made up the parish being scattered through the district round about for several miles. In the country districts proper, the population was still more sparse, many miles often intervening between nearest houses. People had to travel for hours, and sometimes even for days, to reach the nearest church, and there were vast stretches of forest land which contained no inhabitants at all.

In Maryland, there was considerable diversity likewise in the social standing of the inhabitants. A colonial nobility existed in fact, if not in name, patterned after the English nobility. A great many of the inhabitants of the colony were either indentured servants or tenants living upon the great landed estates or manors. In all the English colonies the wealthier classes naturally looked to England as the ideal place for the education of their

[1] Steiner, Hist. of Ed. in Md., p. 16.
[2] Wickersham, Hist. of Ed. in Penn., passim.

sons, both on account of the reputation enjoyed by its schools and colleges, and the social advantages a residence in the mother country offered.

All these things operated together to prevent the establishment of schools and to diminish their attendance and efficiency. Catholic schools were affected by these conditions equally with the schools of other denominations. Father Schneider reported in 1757 that the number of Catholics in Berks County, Pa., was only 117 men and women.[1] At the close of the Revolution, the total Catholic population of Pennsylvania was about 7,000, that of Maryland 16,000. The Catholic population of the United States in 1789 has been estimated at 35,000, out of a total population of about 3,000,-000.[2] This estimate includes the Catholics living west of the Alleghenies, in the region that had been wrested from France during the French and Indian War.

Throughout the French and Spanish colonies of the west and southwest which came subsequently to form part of the United States, there were even greater difficulties in the way of the establishment and maintenance of schools. The country was larger and wilder, and contained only the merest fraction of the population of the eastern colonies. Thus, in the region that now comprises the Middle Western States, it is estimated that there were in 1789 only about 5,500 whites,[3] with but seven places that had churches and priests.[4] The effect

[1] Amer. Cath. Hist. Res., vol. vii, p. 88.
[2] Historical Records and Studies, U. S. Cath. Hist. Soc., vol. iii, part i.
[3] Ibid.
[4] Shea, History, vol. ii, p. 386.

of this condition in preventing the development of education is seen in the fact that the Ursuline Sisters, who settled in New Orleans in 1727, confined their work strictly to that city, and did not attempt to found new establishments outside of it for over a hundred years. The tendency of the French and Spanish colonists to cluster in settlements already formed, rather than to spread out over unsettled territory after the manner of the English, while it retarded the development of the country as a whole, was favorable to the establishment of churches and schools. It has been shown that in nearly all the settlements of the kind schools of some sort existed.

Another fact which had a strong bearing upon educational work in the French and Spanish colonies was the success of the missionaries in converting the Indians, and the greater or less commingling of the converted Indians with the whites. This condition did not exist in the eastern colonies. There were some schools for the Indians in the east. Many were converted there through the efforts of the Jesuits and zealous Protestant ministers like John Eliot; but there was no intermixture of the two races. How great an influence this condition had upon education in the French and Spanish provinces is shown by the fact that many of the schools in these sections were for the Indians alone, the converted Indians in many places far outnumbering the white settlers or soldiers who dwelt among them and intermarried with them. The educational system planned by Cadillac for the newly-founded city of Detroit comprehended a school for the Indians side by side with the school for the whites. The Creoles in Louisiana were admitted to the Ursuline convent as day-scholars and as boarders, on a footing of equality with the children of parents who had come from France. In the primitive schools of the west and southwest, Indian children often attended along with the white children, or, formed into separate classes, were taught in the same building before or after the regular school hours. The position of social equality, so freely accorded the native race by the French and Spanish, goes far to account for the great advancement in civilization made by the Indians in these sections, as compared with the Indians in the east, but it must have proved a serious obstacle to the educational efficiency of the schools for the children of the French and Spanish themselves.

Another condition that must be taken into account in this connection is the relation of the French and Spanish colonies to their respective home governments. There was far less of local and individual freedom than was enjoyed in the English colonies. Union of church and state in the French and Spanish colonies meant union also of state and school. The government was looked to for the support of the schools as well as the churches, and the government was usually generous to both. The arrangement had its advantages, especially in the beginning; but it produced grave inconveniences also. It went far to destroy individual initiative and denominational zeal, which were such powerful factors in the development of education in the English colonies. It bound church and school so closely to the military administration in the minds of the natives, that rebellion against the one was conceived to involve necessarily the destruction of the others as well, as in New Mexico and Florida. It left the schools and their maintenance at the absolute mercy of governmental policy. We have seen how this resulted in the complete destruction, by a stroke of the pen, of the flourishing schools in California, with all the bright hopes they inspired for the future of its Christianized and civilized Indians.

RELIGION AND THE SCHOOLS

Practically all the schools established in the English colonies, as well as those set up by the French and Spaniards prior to 1800, were religious schools, in the sense that denominational and dogmatic religious doctrines were supposed to be taught by them along with secular knowledge. To the minds of the colonists, Protestants as well as Catholics, religious instruction was the first duty the school owed to its pupils. The belief was firm and universal that religious instruction in the school was the best means to insure the virtuous bringing up of the young. Moreover, every religious body had its system of schools, and it was considered that the school owed it to the denomination which had established it to instruct its pupils thoroughly in the faith professed by its founders. The more general intermingling of the denominations, which was brought about gradually by the natural movement of the population, gave rise to the first undenominational schools. This tendency became especially manifest after the Revolutionary War. But the great majority of the schools continued to be strictly denominational down to near the middle of the nineteenth century.

This fact—the out-and-out "sectarian" character of all the existing schools—played an important part in the rise and development of the Catholic school movement. Coupled with the greater or less but never-ceasing grind of persecution to which Catholics were subjected, it forced them to establish and keep up a system of schools and colleges of their own. Catholic schools became a necessity for the preservation of Catholic children's faith. The necessity was so plain and urgent that Catholics thought no sacrifice too great which insured a Catholic education for their children. Even in the face of the Maryland penal code, a Catholic school was kept alive by the Jesuits. Long after the Revolution had put an end to religious persecution, the sectarian character of education in general continued to act as a spur to the establishment of Catholic schools. For a brief period after the Revolution, the head of the Catholic Church in the United States, the Very Rev. John Carroll, seemed to entertain some hope that Catholics might be able to unite with their non-Catholic fellow-citizens in building up schools and colleges on some basis which would be mutually satisfactory from a religious point of view. The establishment of a system of Catholic schools, adequate to the needs of the rapidly growing body of the faithful, considering their scattered condition and their poverty, must have seemed to him a gigantic task. Writing to the Propaganda, February 27, 1785, and giving an official report of the status and prospects of the Church in the United States, he said:

"There is a college in Philadelphia, and it is proposed to establish two in Maryland, in which Catholics can be admitted, as well as others, as presidents, professors, and pupils. We hope that some educated there will embrace the ecclesiastical state. We think accordingly of establishing a seminary, in which they can be trained to the life and learning suited to that state."[1]

An ecclesiastical seminary was apparently the only thing contemplated at the time. The next year he took a prominent part in the movement for the establishment of an academy or college in Baltimore, which was to be non-sectarian.[2] But his hopes in this respect were short-lived. It was found that even institutions supported by the State and professing to be non-sectarian were offensively Protestant in tone and management, and could not be frequented by Catholic students without peril to their faith. A change of views appears to be evidenced in the pastoral letter which he addressed to the Catholics of the country in 1792, making known to them the regulations adopted at the First Catholic Synod, which had been held a short time before. Education was the opening theme. The necessity was emphasized of "a pious and Catholic education of the young to insure their growing up in the faith." Alluding to the newly established college at Georgetown, the hope was

[1] Shea, History, vol. ii, Life and Times of Archbishop Carroll, p. 260.
[2] Ibid., p. 286.

expressed, that while the number educated there would be necessarily small, the graduates, on returning to their homes, would be able "to instruct and guide others in local schools."[1] He had thus arrived already at a belief in the necessity of a comprehensive system of Catholic schools and colleges, and taken the resolution to proceed with the work of their establishment. The adhesion of both clergy and laity to that belief and resolution has never wavered since. The Catholic school system was already an accomplished fact, at least in embryo. It was necessary only to develop it along the lines already laid down.

ACADEMIC CHARACTER

Something has already been said about the character and methods of the French and the Spanish schools. At the close of the Revolution there were about 15 Catholic schools in existence in Maryland and Pennsylvania and the territory to the west under the jurisdiction of the Very Rev. John Carroll. It is to be regretted that we do not know more about the character and methods of the Catholic schools in the English colonies, out of which chiefly the Catholic parochial school system developed. Very little knowledge of this kind has come down to us. Beyond some incidental al-

[1]Ibid., p. 399. The movement for the establishment of Georgetown College took definite shape toward the end of the year 1786. There was some opposition to the project at first, for certain reasons. Referring to this opposition, the Very Rev. John Carroll said: "God is my witness that in recommending a school at first, and in still persisting in that recommendation, I think I am rendering to Religion the greatest service that will ever be in my power."—Shea, loc. cit., p. 305.

lusions to the work of the schools in the letters of the missionaries in charge of them, we have nothing to guide us here except a knowledge of the methods employed by the Jesuits in teaching and the methods of colonial schools in general, joined to a knowledge of the circumstances under which Catholic schools were established and maintained. The persecution to which Catholics were subjected rendered it advisable to carry on the work of the schools as secretly as possible.

One of the schools in the English colonies was, as we have seen, an academy or preparatory college, all the others being parish schools in which only the common branches were taught. The schools west of the Alleghenies were, as a rule, French. St. Mary's, in Philadelphia, was an English school. Outside of that city, the schools in Pennsylvania were mostly German. The Catholics of Berks County were almost exclusively German, and the school at Goshenhoppen long continued to be taught in German. The schools at Lancaster, Hanover, and other places were also German.

HISTORICAL PROTOTYPES

What were the historical prototypes of the Catholic colonial schools? It has been shown that the various denominational school systems which sprang up in the colonies were copied more or less closely after the school systems which existed in the respective European countries from which the first settlers came,[1] and we should be led to expect

[1] Eggleston, The Transit of Civilization; Wickersham, Education in Penna.; Brown, The Making of Our Middle Schools.

the same result in the case of Catholic schools. But this is only partially the case. To speak only of the schools in the English colonies, there was less tendency on the part of Catholics to copy the Old-Country schools. This was partly due to the fact that the first Catholic settlers had often had no opportunity of becoming acquainted with the schools of the mother country, being obliged because of persecution to make their studies abroad. To the devout English Catholic, the English grammar schools of the time were the hotbeds of heresy, to which no Catholic child could with safe conscience be sent. It was also due to the fact that Catholics, on settling in some of the colonies, found all around them other denominational schools, which had been already modified and adapted from their European models to meet the new conditions under which the settlers had to live and work and rear their children. The Jesuit college, or "school of humanities," which was established in Newtown in 1677, was, of course, modeled upon the *Ratio Studiorum*. Its courses, so far as they went, were probably parallel to those at St. Omer's, where most of its teachers had been students and some of them professors.[1] The elementary school which Ralph Crouch set up at Newtown about 1640 was also very likely modeled upon the elementary school which formed part of the establishment of St. Omer's,[2] although he may also have been influenced by the early Virginia elementary schools, several of which existed in the Virginia settlements about the Potomac

[1] Records of the English Province, passim.
[2] Ibid.

River and the Chesapeake when he came from England the year before.[1] "To read, write, and cipher" was the simple but all-sufficient program of these Virginia schools, which had no relation to the parish or the State authorities, but were established spontaneously by the people.[2] Their number and popularity rapidly increased, and they were undoubtedly known to the Jesuits of Maryland, who often made long journeys into Virginia. When the Jesuits penetrated into Pennsylvania, and found the way open for educational work, they established similar elementary schools in their parishes, but under parish control.

It is impossible to say definitely, however, just how much connection there was between the Virginia elementary schools and the first Catholic parish schools in Pennsylvania. Other influences were undoubtedly at work. There were elementary Quaker schools in Philadelphia and scattered throughout the colony, at the time Father Greaton organized the first Catholic church and school in the colony.[3] Schools of other denominations were springing up too. It is probable that the first English Catholic parochial schools were a compound of all these influences—the elementary schools conducted by the Jesuits in Europe,[4] the Virginia popular private schools, and the existing denominational schools of Pennsylvania.

The German schools set up by Father Schneider

[1] Eggleston, The Transit of Civilization, p. 222.
[2] Ibid., p. 223.
[3] Wickersham, Hist. of Ed. in Penna., passim.
[4] Although their chief work was in the field of higher education, a number of elementary schools were conducted by the Jesuits in various parts of Europe. See Schwickerath, Jesuit Education, p. 106.

and other German Jesuits were undoubtedly modeled after the *Volks-schulen,* which were comparatively numerous in Germany in the beginning of the eighteenth century.[1] These schools usually taught reading, writing, religion, singing, and a bit of reckoning. But they received scant support in Germany from either the people or the State. The teacher was most often a craftsman, who plied his trade while teaching or conducting the school. An ordinance of one of the German States in 1722 prescribed the kinds of crafts whose masters were supposed to be eligible for teaching school, and another of 1736 allowed the school-teacher, in case he had no trade, a vacation of six weeks each year to go out and earn something for himself, whereas, if he were a craftsman, he would be able to support himself by his work, and would need no vacation.[2] The teaching of even the rudiments attempted was wretched, and in the cities matters were but little better. Such were the schools for the common people in Germany in the days of Father Schneider. The school system was, to use the cautious phrase of the historian, "in the lowest stage of development."[3]

The *Volks-schulen* must have been thoroughly familiar to Father Schneider and the other German Jesuits. Coming directly from Germany to a district which was largely peopled by Germans, they were not apt to be influenced by the efforts that were being made in several of the Eng-

[1]Biedermann, Deutschland im Achtzehnten Jahrhundert, II. Band, S. 486 seq.; Raumer, Geschichte der Pedagogik, III. Theil, S. 21 seq.
[2]Biedermann, loc. cit.
[3]Ibid., p. 485.

lish colonies to build up a system of schools for the common people in which the reading and writing of English should be substituted for the Latin of the English grammar schools. The schools established by the German Jesuits in Pennsylvania, in the beginning, bore a marked resemblance to the elementary schools in Germany, although they did not long continue to resemble them. At first the merest rudiments were taught, and the first teachers hired were probably men who supported themselves, at least partly, by other means, as in the case of the *Volks-schulen* in the mother country. In the course of time, however, teachers were secured who were better equipped, and who devoted their whole time to the work. The getting of such a teacher as John Lawrence Gubernator, at Goshenhoppen and Conewago, shows the extent of the development of these German Catholic schools within a period of forty years or so. The fact exemplifies the rapid and wide divergence of the American colonial school from its prototype across the water, and its development along lines traced out for it by the different social, economic, and religious conditions in the New World.[1]

BUILDINGS, TEXT-BOOKS, AND TEACHERS

In respect to material conveniences and general equipment, Catholic colonial schools were like those of other denominations,[2] except that, owing

[1] Eggleston, The Transit of Civilization, chap. v.
[2] For a description of colonial schoolhouses and their equipment, and also for the methods of teaching and the studies, see Wickersham, op. cit., chap. x.; Eggleston, The Transit of Civilization, chap. v.

to the social and economic effects of the laws against Catholics, they were more handicapped in the way of material resources. The Jesuit missionaries received little or no support from the congregations. Their support was derived from the lands they had taken up, and even these were held in the name of laymen, for fear of confiscation. There was little money, therefore, to be had for the schools. The first schools were held in the priest's house, or rather in his room, for he most often took up his residence with some Catholic family, and the priest himself did the teaching. As the number of Catholics increased, a little church was built, or a farmhouse converted in whole or in part into a place for divine worship; and on weekdays, the place came naturally to be used as a school. In some instances, one of the outbuildings connected with the farmhouse—the first log-dwelling, probably—was used for the school. Separate schoolhouses were not erected until many years after teaching was first begun. Small and rough looking as they were, they marked a new era in school development, an era of longer school hours, of greater continuity in school work, of a larger field of studies, and, above all, of school-teaching by men who gave their whole time to the task.

Little is known about the text-books that were used. The Jesuits, no doubt, employed at Newtown the manuscript text-books which were in use in their schools in Europe, and some of these may also have been brought to Philadelphia. Just what these were, however, it is impossible to say. Father Schneider may, similarly, have brought from Germany copies of the crude print or manuscript books used for teaching reading, writing, singing, figuring, and catechism in the Catholic elementary schools there; or he may have composed some himself. At any rate, he could not have made use of the German text-books published in his time by the other German denominations in the colony, as it was the custom in those days and for long afterward to employ primers, readers, spellers, writing models, and even arithmetics and other text-books as vehicles for the inculcation of religious and denominational teaching.[1] As time wore on, however, the religious instruction was gradually eliminated, until it often became possible, by means of a few changes, to make such books entirely inoffensive to Catholics, or even, by certain additions, as well as eliminations, to turn them into distinctively Catholic text-books. Some of the first Catholic school-books published in this country were but new editions of commonly used text-books, revised and recast, more or less, to give them a Catholic tone.

The studies followed in the primitive Catholic schools have been already sufficiently dwelt upon. It is not the purpose here to attempt a description of Catholic schools, except in so far as they differed from other schools of the time. So far as regards studies and methods of instruction, Catholic elementary schools do not seem to have differed in any important respect from other colonial schools; and the studies and methods of instruction of the schools in general in Pennsylvania and Maryland during the pre-Revolutionary period have been care-

[1] See Wickersham, op. cit., chap. x.

fully studied and fully described by several well-known educational historians.[1]

In respect to teachers, Catholic schools were not, to say the least, inferior to other schools. Good teachers were exceedingly scarce in colonial times. Teaching was but a poorly paying occupation, and indeed was scarcely regarded as an honorable one. Few took to it except out of necessity and for a time. The descriptions that have come down to us of the character of the teachers in some of the colonies seem almost incredible to-day, in view of the high esteem in which the teacher is now universally held, and the time and expense lavished upon the teacher's preparatory training. Many of the early teachers in Pennsylvania, as has been noted, were "redemptioners," or, in other words, indentured servants. In Maryland matters were much worse. The Rev. Jonathan Boucher, who was a neighbor and friend of Washington, and who had taught school in Maryland himself, writing as late as 1773, complains that

"At least two-thirds of the little education we receive are derived from instructors who are either indentured servants or transported felons. Not a ship arrives either with redemptioners or convicts in which schoolmasters are not as regularly advertised as weavers, tailors, or any other trade; with little other difference that I can hear of, except perhaps that the former do not usually fetch as good a price as the latter."[2]

[1] See the educational histories of Steiner, Wickersham, Brown, and Eggleston.
[2] Boucher, A View of the Causes and Consequences of the American Revolution, Sermon on Education, p. 184; see also Clews, op. cit., p. 425; Steiner, Ed. in Md., p. 38.

Of the twelve school-teachers in St. George County in 1754, six were free men, two were indentured servants, and four convict-servants.[1] So greatly was the efficiency of the schools impaired as a result of this condition, that we are assured that the usefulness of the county schools, established by the Maryland legislature, had in most cases practically ceased at the time of the Revolution.[2]

Catholics, it is true, were less able to afford the money necessary to hire good teachers, but this disadvantage was more than compensated for by the presence of a long series of brilliant Jesuit scholars in Maryland and Pennsylvania, as pastors of the churches and directors of the parish schools, and often teachers in them. The elementary school and the college at Newtown had teachers of perhaps unrivaled academic ability in colonial America. The revived school at Bohemia, almost lost to the public eye in the most remote corner of the eastern shore of Maryland, had, as teachers of reading, writing, spelling, and the elementary classics, men who were fitted to take charge of professors' chairs in the great Jesuit colleges of Europe.[3] The parochial school at Philadelphia was under the direction of such men as Fathers Molyneux and Farmer, who, no doubt, taught catechism and perhaps other classes in it. The school at Goshenhoppen, started by the learned former rector of Heidelberg University, and under his charge for twenty years, was during the twenty-three succeeding years in charge of Father

[1] Steiner, op. cit., p. 34.
[2] Ibid., p. 34.
[3] See the biographies of the Maryland Jesuits in the Records of the English province.

Ritter, S.J., a man of scarcely inferior ability.
The other parishes and missions were served by
priests whose learning and ability are witnessed
in many records of the colonial era, and whose zeal
for education was shown in founding or maintain-
ing schools in the face of almost insuperable obstacles, involving sometimes, as we have seen, the
teaching of all the classes by the priest himself.
The Jesuit Order, during the three centuries and a
half of its existence, has done much for the advancement of education in almost every country of the
world; but it may be doubted if its educational zeal
has ever been more finely displayed than it was
in English America during the colonial period.
The results elsewhere may have been larger and
more striking, and may have attracted greater attention from educational historians; but surely nowhere have they, in the long run, been more fruitful, for, as has been shown, it is principally to the
Jesuit schools in Maryland and Pennsylvania
that we owe the development of the Catholic
parochial school system in the United States.

A SYSTEM IN EMBRYO

One other point remains to be noticed. The
Catholic schools existing in the English colonies
at the time of the Revolution were already, to some
extent, thrown into the form of a system. They
were all under the control of the Jesuit Order.
In the case of religious instruction, if not of all
the subjects taught, their work was based upon an
ideal common to all institutions in charge of that
great teaching body. They were looked upon

also as but the base of an educational edifice which was to be made to include, in time, facilities for the complete education of Catholic youth under Catholic auspices. And they were regarded as an indispensable adjunct of parochial organization. New parishes, accordingly, as they grew up, gave rise to new parish schools. The grain of mustard-seed planted by the pioneer Jesuit educators had, by the time of the Revolution, struck its roots deep into the soil. We shall see how rapidly it grew and developed, and how far it threw out its branches, under the influence of the universal stir and movement to which the Revolution gave rise.

CHAPTER VI

EDUCATIONAL INFLUENCES OF THE AMERICAN REVOLUTION AND OF THE FRENCH ÉMIGRÉS

THE NEW CONDITIONS

THE CHANGES which the American Revolution produced in the condition and prospects of Catholics in this country were many and far-reaching, but it is intended here to trace the influence of only such of these changes as had a direct, causative effect upon Catholic educational activity.

For Catholics outside of Pennsylvania, the most immediately felt effect of the Revolution was the cessation of the bitter persecution to which they had so long been subjected. The laws which bore so heavily upon them were repealed, or at least, as time wore on, gradually relaxed, and a kindlier spirit was everywhere manifested toward them. Catholics woke up, on a sudden, to find themselves free to practise their religion, to build churches and schools, and to set the organization of the Church in America upon a permanent foundation.

Together with religious freedom, there came to the Church almost immediately, as a result of the Revolution, a great increase in members. Emigration brought a steadily growing stream of Catholics from Ireland and other countries of Europe. The great region west of the Alleghenies, which had been wrested from England during the struggle, was peopled largely by Catholics. In some parts of it, the population, both white and native, was entirely Catholic. The westward movement of the population in the Eastern States attracted many Catholics. In the new territories, Catholics shared the hardships and the dangers of pioneer life with their non-Catholic fellow-settlers, and, when the time came, they took part with them in the work of organizing these territories into States and framing their respective constitutions. Both in the east and in the west, the gate of opportunity was thus opened wide for the Church. The laborers were few, and entirely inadequate to the need, but the French Revolution cast opportunely upon our shores a body of exiled priests who were destined, in the providence of God, to do for the Church in America even more than the enemies of the Church in France had undone. Well educated, thoroughly disciplined, pious and zealous, the coming of these exiled members of the French clergy gave an immense impetus to the growth of the Church under the newly established order of the national existence. Their influence was especially marked in the field of education. Several of them became bishops. Some of them had been professors in the colleges and seminaries of France, and all of them shared the conviction of Bishop Carroll and his clergy that the success of the Church in the new Republic would be proportionate to the successful establishment of Catholic colleges, seminaries, and schools. So thoroughly persuaded were they of this, that many of them, as we shall see, like the old Jesuit missionaries, in the absence of other teachers turned schoolmasters themselves, ministering to their flocks on Sundays, and teaching school during the rest of the week. Between the years 1790 and 1798, sixteen French priests, mostly Sulpicians, arrived in America. Previous to their coming, there were only about two dozen priests in the whole country.

THE EASTERN STATES

GEORGETOWN AND ST. MARY'S SEMINARY

The influence upon Catholic educational activity of the new conditions ushered in by the Revolution was manifested almost immediately. The Very Rev. Prefect-Apostolic, John Carroll, brought the subject of the foundation of an academy or college before the meeting of his clergy at Whitemarsh, in 1786, with the result that a movement was inaugurated which led to the opening of a college at Georgetown in the year 1791.[1] About the same time, the exiled Sulpicians, at the instance of Father Carroll, founded St. Mary's Seminary, Baltimore, for the training of ecclesiastical students.[2] These were the parent institutions of the Catholic college and seminary systems respectively in the United States, and they have continued to exist down to our own day. From the very beginning of their existence, these two institutions exercised a potent influence upon Catholic educational activity the country over, not only as regards colleges and seminaries, but also elementary and secondary schools.

[1]Shea, op. cit., vol. ii, p. 301.
[2]Ibid., p. 380.

ELEMENTARY SCHOOLS

While Catholic higher education was thus being provided for, efforts were also being made to establish parochial or elementary schools. The Germans in Philadelphia, as has been noted, organized a parish and school soon after they separated from St. Mary's Church, in 1788. In 1799, a school was opened in Georgetown by Miss Alice Lalor, who had come from Philadelphia for the purpose, on the invitation of Father Leonard Neale, President of Georgetown College.[1] About the same time, an academy or school for lay pupils was started by the Sulpician Fathers on the grounds of the Seminary in Baltimore. It was attended by both Catholics and Protestants, and some years later was chartered by the legislature as St. Mary's College.[2] At McSherrystown, Pa., a school appears to have been opened in 1800.[3] At Conewago, the Rev. F. X. Brosius, a learned German priest who had come to America in 1792,[4] was teaching a school about the same time. How long it lasted we do not know; but a school, taught now by the priest, and again by a lay teacher, was maintained more or less continuously from this time on at Conewago, until the erection of two schoolhouses there in 1830.[5] In 1806, Father Brosius opened a school or "seminary" at Mt. Airy, near Philadelphia. In this school, it is said, black-

---

[1] The Ave Maria, "An American Community," vol. lxi, p. 584.
[2] Shea, Hist. of the Cath. Church in the U. S., vol. ii, p. 607.
[3] Wickersham, Hist. of Ed. in Penna., p. 115.
[4] Shea, ibid., p. 443.
[5] John T. Riley, McSherrystown, Pa., letter to the author; see Conewago, p. 80.

board and chalk was made use of for the first time in this country. Father Brosius continued at the head of Mt. Airy Seminary until 1813.[1]

MT. ST. MARY'S

In 1790, a school was begun at Pigeon Hills, Pa., four miles from the old Catholic settlement of Conewago, by a pious French Catholic named Heront, who later became a Sulpician priest. This school led eventually to the foundation of an institution by the Sulpicians at Pigeon Hills known at first as the "Seminary Farm," and intended to serve as a preparatory school to St. Mary's Seminary, Baltimore.[2] It was founded by the Sulpician Fathers Nagot and Dilhet, in 1807, but was soon transferred to Emmittsburg, Md., where, passing under the control of the diocesan authorities, it developed into Mt. St. Mary's College and Seminary, the second oldest Catholic college in the United States, and the venerated Alma Mater of hundreds of illustrious Catholic names—bishops, priests, and laymen, who have contributed largely to the development of the Church and of Catholic education in our land.

NEW YORK CITY

In the year 1800, or early the following year, at the instance of Bishop Carroll, a "free school" was established at St. Peter's Church, on Barclay

[1]Hist. of Mathematics, a Monogram published by the U. S. Govt., referred to in Rec. Amer. Cath. Hist. Soc., vol. xii, p. 19; Amer. Cath. Hist. Res. for 1888, p. 155.
[2]Riley, letter to the author; Shea, op. cit., p. 611.

Street, New York City, the Rev. William
O'Brien, O.P., being pastor.[1] This was the only
Catholic parish in the city at the time, the church
having been built only in 1786. St. Peter's School
soon grew to be the largest of the several schools
in the city, counting 100 pupils in 1805.[2] It contained almost all the Catholic children in New York
who attended school, since the registers of the
schools under the control of the Free School Society
showed, some years later, the names of only nine
Catholics out of a total attendance of 798 pupils in
the two schools of the society.[3] Besides the Catholics, the Episcopalians, the Dutch, and the Presbyterians had each a school in New York. How
strongly rooted in men's minds the idea of the
necessity of religious instruction in the school was
at that period, is shown by the fact that even the
Free School Society, which was established in 1805
for the purpose of providing "for the education of
such poor children as do not belong to, or are not
provided for by any religious society," and which
gradually led to the formation of the present public school system of New York, imposed religious
instruction in its schools. The society required the
whole of each Tuesday afternoon to be devoted to
this purpose. On Sunday mornings also, the pupils were to assemble at the schools and then proceed, under the care of a monitor, to the respective
churches designated by their parents or guardians.[4]

[1]Rev. J. H. McGean, in Hist. Records and Studies, vol. iii,
part ii.
[2]Amer. Cath. Hist. Res., vol. vii, p. 142; Boese, Hist. of
Pub. Ed. in City of N. Y., p. 24.
[3]N. Y. City Education Pamphlets, Document No. 41.
[4]Ibid.

A petition signed by 3,000 persons was presented to the legislature by a Catholic member in 1806, asking that a portion of the moneys devoted by the State to educational purposes might be allotted to St. Peter's School. The petition was granted, and in the State Senate there was only one opposing vote.[1]

SCHOOL-BOOKS

An evidence of Catholic educational activity at this time is afforded by the publication of school-books for the use of Catholic pupils. The growing demand in this way was recognized by several Catholic publishers, among whom was the celebrated Matthew Carey, of Philadelphia, who brought out a number of Catholic text-books. Among these were "The Catholic Christian Instructed," used as a reader, Reeve's "History of the Old and New Testament," besides catechisms and "spellers," or primers. New editions of text-books which were in common use in other denominational schools were also published, with such emendations as would render them unobjectionable to Catholics.[2]

WESTERN PENNSYLVANIA

ST. VINCENT'S ABBEY

The movement of the population westward during and after the Revolution carried many Cath-

[1]Boese, Hist. of Pub. Ed. in City of N. Y., p. 24; Considine, Brief Chron. Acct. of the Cath. Ed. Ins. in N. Y., p. 8.
[2]Correspondence of Matthew Carey in Rec. Amer. Cath. Hist. Soc., vols. ix, x, xi, passim.

olics from Eastern Pennsylvania and Maryland across the Alleghenies, to settle in Western Pennsylvania and Kentucky. In some cases, groups of Catholic families set out together, and took up lands near each other in the west. Little Catholic colonies or settlements were thus formed which became the nuclei of the subsequent growth of the Church in the new regions. About 1787, a number of Catholic families from Goshenhoppen crossed the Alleghenies and settled in Westmoreland County, at a place called Sportsman's Hall. Their pastor, Rev. Theodore Browers, bought a farm of several hundred acres of land, and at his death, a few years later, he left all his property to the Church. The estate subsequently fell to the Benedictines, and upon it was built St. Vincent's Abbey and College, the mother-house of the numerous convents, colleges, and schools of this religious Order in the United States. There was a Catholic school at Sportsman's Hall very early, if not from the very founding of the settlement; for the Benedictines found, on their arrival there in 1846, among other buildings, "a little schoolhouse."[1] The fact has a special interest in that it affords a thread of connection between Father Schneider and his educational work, in the old Catholic colony of Goshenhoppen, and St. Vincent's, the mother-house of the Benedictine Order, which has had so large a share in Catholic educational development in the United States during the past fifty years.

[1] Wickersham, op. cit., p. 116; Lambing, A Hist. of the Cath. Church in the Dioceses of Pittsburg and Allegheny, p. 375.

FATHER GALLITZIN

Another Catholic colony from the east settled in Cambria County in 1790. The famous Russian priest, Prince Demetrius Gallitzin, went there in 1799, and at once set to work to build a little log church. The next year a school was opened near Loretto. The schoolhouse was, like many other Pennsylvania schoolhouses of the time, "a small log building, daubed with mud, and heated by means of a large stone fireplace."[1] Children traveled a distance of four or five miles to attend the school. A man by the name of O'Connor was the first teacher. Father Gallitzin, although voluntarily engaged in the roughest kind of pioneer missionary work, was a ripe scholar, and a firm believer in education. In the course of time, he established schools at several other missions which he founded. As there was the greatest difficulty in procuring good Catholic teachers, he planned to establish a community of teaching Sisters. Some steps were actually taken with this end in view, but the project failed through the scarcity of candidates for the community.[2]

KENTUCKY AND INDIANA

While Catholic schools were thus springing up in various parts of the Eastern States, the West became the theater of Catholic educational movements which were not only interesting and important in themselves, but which, owing to their react-

[1] Wickersham, op. cit., p. 117.
[2] See Brownson, S. A., Life of D. A. Gallitzin, p. 189 seq.

ing influence upon the movement in the East, greatly contributed to the establishment of a uniform Catholic educational ideal the whole country over. In respect to Catholic educational development, Kentucky soon became to the Middle West what Maryland and Pennsylvania had been to the East.

FIRST KENTUCKY SCHOOL

The tide of western emigration bore many Catholics to Kentucky. They came chiefly from Maryland, and were descendants of Lord Baltimore's colonists. Catholics were among the first settlers in Kentucky, and to a Catholic must be credited the honor of establishing the first Kentucky school. Among the emigrants who came out in 1775, were a Catholic Marylander named William Coomes and his wife. They settled at Harrod's Town, and Mrs. Coomes, at the urgent request of the townspeople, opened a school for the education of the children. So far as is known, this was the first school established within the limits of the present State of Kentucky.[1]

FATHERS BADIN AND NERINCKX

The first Catholic church in Kentucky, which was no more than a rude log chapel, was built in 1790. Three years later, the Rev. Stephen T. Badin, the first priest ordained within the United States, came to Kentucky, to make it the center of a half century's missionary career which extended

[1] Spalding, Sketches of the Early Cath. Missions of Ky., p. 24; Dexter, Hist. of Ed. in the U. S., p. 125.

to Ohio, Indiana, Illinois, and Michigan. In 1805, he was joined by the Rev. Charles Nerinckx. Both of these men had been driven to America by the French Revolution; both were finely trained ecclesiastics, and combined with an heroic cast of character a priestly zeal that was truly apostolic;[1] both were ardent advocates of education, and profoundly convinced that Catholic schools were not less necessary than churches for the preservation and spread of the Catholic faith. It was their steadily cherished plan to establish parochial schools for both boys and girls in every permanently established parish.

TRAPPIST SCHOOL

It is probable that several Catholic schools were started in Kentucky under the auspices of Father Badin, during the early years of his ministry there, and were taught by lay teachers, both men and women; but these schools were more or less temporary in character, like the school of Mrs. Coomes. It was not till 1805 that the era of permanent schools and regular teaching was ushered in. In the fall of that year, a community of Trappists—exiled from France—came from Pigeon Hills, Pa., and settled on Pottinger's Creek. Although not a teaching Order, they immediately

---

[1] Father Badin was a fine classical scholar, and notwithstanding the rough missionary work to which he devoted himself, he retained his scholarly tastes all through life, and found time occasionally for the composition of Latin poems, which have been highly praised. Several of these are to be found in the appendix to Spalding's Sketches of Kentucky. See also Webb, op. cit., pp. 454, 466. For evidence of Father Badin's interest in higher education, see Diocese of Bardstown, chap. viii.

opened a school for boys. The teaching was gratuitous, and the youth of the district flocked to the school to acquire, together with a thorough catechetical instruction, the elements of secular knowledge. This was the first Catholic school of any note in Kentucky. It continued to flourish until the Trappists left the State, about three years and a half later.[1]

DOMINICAN SCHOOL

The year following the arrival of the Trappists in Kentucky witnessed the coming of another religious Order, one which was destined to exert a wide educational influence throughout the West. Father Edward Fenwick, a native of Maryland, and three other Dominicans, after having been driven from Belgium by the French revolutionary movement, established themselves in Washington County, Ky., and founded the Convent of St. Rose. In 1807, they opened a school, with about a dozen pupils, the institution taking the name of St. Thomas' College.[2] Father Fenwick was soon succeeded by Father Thomas Wilson as Superior, and under this erudite and able man, who had previously been President of the English College of the Dominicans in Flanders, the number of students rapidly increased, Protestants as well as Catholics attending from the neighboring settlements.[3] The curriculum comprised the elementary studies, be-

[1] Spalding, Sketches, p. 168.
[2] Maes, Life of Rev. Charles Nerinckx, p. 169.
[3] Webb, Centenary of Catholicity in Ky., p. 208; Spalding, Sketches of Kentucky, p. 160.

sides the classics. The method of paying tuition fees, etc., was characteristic of the primitive character of Kentucky life at the time, payment being ordinarily made in farm produce. Another feature also was common to the early Kentucky schools. The pupils were required to devote four hours each day to manual labor. By this means the cost of schooling was reduced, and young and willing hands were obtained in abundance for the necessary work of constructing buildings and cultivating the school farm. About 1820, this school was closed, the services of the Dominicans engaged in teaching being needed for the numerous missions of which the Order had taken charge.[1] In the meantime, however, other Catholic schools had sprung up around St. Rose's. Father Fenwick became the first bishop of Cincinnati, and the founder of the first Catholic educational institutions in Ohio.

VINCENNES

When Benedict Joseph Flaget, an exiled French Sulpician, afterward first bishop of Bardstown, arrived at Vincennes on December 21, 1792, one of his first acts was to reopen the school, the parish having been, since the departure of Father Gibault three years before, without a priest and probably also, during much of this time, without a school. Father Flaget taught the school himself, and his idea was that the pupils, while learning the common branches, should be trained up to agriculture and various trades. Both as pastor and school-

[1]Spalding, op. cit., p. 160.

master, Father Flaget was eminently successful, and his recall to Baltimore, in 1795, was a sad blow to the inhabitants of Vincennes.[1] The following year, Bishop Carroll sent the Rev. John Francis Rivet to Vincennes, where he labored until his death during the winter of 1803-4. Father Rivet had been, like his predecessor at Vincennes, a professor in France, and, like him also, he devoted much of his care to the instruction of the children in the school. Vincennes at this time contained about 50 houses.[2]

DETROIT AND MICHIGAN

POPULATION

As has been shown, a school was established at Detroit shortly after the foundation of the settlement. The school appears to have been continued all along, and to have been in existence when the city passed under American control in 1796.[3] At this time, the place contained from 1,500 to 2,000 people. In the whole region now comprising the Middle Western States there were only about 5,000 inhabitants. When it came under American control, Detroit fell under the jurisdiction of Baltimore. In June, 1798, the Rev. Gabriel Richard was sent there as assistant to Father Levadoux, and, upon the departure of the latter, three

[1] Spalding, Life of Bishop Flaget, p. 34 seq.; Alerding, Hist. of the Diocese of Vincennes, p. 61 seq.; Shea, vol. ii, p. 486 seq.
[2] Alerding, p. 73; Shea, p. 487. See Volney's description of his visit to the place in 1802, Tableau du Climat et du Sol des États Unis, p. 400.
[3] Amer. Cath. Hist. Res., vol. xiii, p. 82.

years later, Father Richard became pastor, with the Rev. John Dilhet, another Sulpician, as his assistant.[1]

FATHER RICHARD

Father Richard was a remarkable man in many respects. He left a deep impress upon Catholic educational policy in the United States, and deserves to be looked on as one of the founders of the existing system of Catholic schools. At a time when, speaking with reference to the country as a whole, Catholic educational thought and policy was still in an uncrystallized state, he set to work to establish a complete system of Catholic education, comprising elementary schools, high schools or academies, and an institution for higher education under Catholic auspices to a certain extent. His position as pastor in the largest city west of the Alleghenies, and the unique distinction he attained to in being elected as a member of Congress —being the only Catholic priest who was ever a member of that body—together with his universally recognized ability, patriotism, and uprightness of character, tended to make his school system known throughout the country, and to give to his educational work a great and wide influence. Father Richard, indeed, merits a distinguished place among American educators, even beyond the recognition that is his due as a champion of distinctively Catholic schools. He was a friend of education in the broadest sense, and his plans comprehended a system of education for the whole people, notwith-

[1]Bertrand, Histoire Littéraire de la Compagnie de St. Sulpice, vol. ii, pp. 35, 109.

standing denominational differences. He was the pioneer in almost every kind of educational work in Michigan. If his ideas for a broad scheme of education, under state jurisdiction, which would be satisfactory to people of all denominations as well as to those of none, failed of permanent realization, they still point the way to a solution of a problem in American education which is assuredly not less pressing now than it was then.

Gabriel Richard was born at Saintes, France, October 15, 1767, and is said to have been related on his mother's side to Bossuet.[1] Becoming a priest, and a member of the Sulpician Society, he was for a time in charge of the famous Seminary at Issy, and professor of mathematics.[2] Like so many other Sulpicians, Father Richard took refuge in America during the French Revolution. Arriving in Baltimore on June 24, 1792, he was sent to Prairie du Rocher, Ill., where he labored for six years, until his appointment to Detroit.[3]

The pastoral jurisdiction of Father Richard at the time of his appointment, and for years afterward, embraced not only the city of Detroit and its vicinity, but also the territory extending from the head waters of Lake Erie on the east to Sault Ste. Marie and Prairie du Chien on the west, including Lower and Upper Michigan, northern Indiana, Illinois as far as the present site of Chicago, and eastern Wisconsin.[4] From time to time during

[1]Michigan Biographies, Gabriel Richard, p. 552; Bertrand, op. cit.; O'Brien, Hist. Rec. and Studies, vol. v, part i, p. 78.
[2]Dionne, L'Abbé Gabriel Richard, p. 6.
[3]Bertrand, op. cit., p. 108.
[4]Richard R. Elliott, Sketch of Father Richard in Amer. Cath. Hist. Res., vol. xvi, p. 155 seq.

his pastorate, he visited the mission stations throughout this vast region.

ESTABLISHES HIGH SCHOOLS

Father Richard's coming at once infused new life into the parish in Detroit. Almost immediately he turned his attention to the question of education. Foreseeing clearly the future greatness of the new Republic and the growth of the great West, he realized that the future of the Church in America depended upon the sound Catholic education of the rising generations.[1]   With a view to raising the standard of education in the city, which was almost entirely Catholic at the time, he established an academy or high school for boys and young men, confining the work of the existing school to the instruction of the younger children, both boys and girls. These two schools were in existence by 1802.[2] In the beginning, Father Richard probably did much of the teaching in the academy himself. At the same time he was casting about for means to afford a higher education to girls.

TRAINS TEACHERS

Here the problem was more difficult.   There were no teachers, and no prospect of getting them from without.   The only teaching sisterhood in the country at the time was that of the Ursulines in New Orleans, and the number of teachers there was insufficient for the need.   Father Richard was

---

[1]Michigan Biographies, p. 552.
[2]Amer. Cath. Hist. Res., vol. xv, p. 87.

not a man to be balked by difficulties, however insuperable they might seem; and he courageously set to work to train up teachers for his proposed young ladies' academy, turning his pastoral residence into a kind of normal school for the purpose, with himself and Father Dilhet as teachers. The latter, a learned priest, of amiable manners, who had been a professor in France, shared fully Father Richard's educational zeal.[1] Four young ladies of high social standing, who showed an aptitude and a willingness for the work, were selected to be trained as the first teachers. The names of these four noble women were Monique Labadie, Elizabeth Lyon, Angelique Campau, and Elizabeth Williams, the latter being the sister of General John R. Williams. Father Richard believed in specialization, and each of the young teachers was prepared for a particular department of school-work.[2] After two years of preparation in this way, the young ladies' academy was opened in 1804. About the same time he established another primary school, separating, apparently, the boys and girls.

Within six years, he thus succeeded in building up in the city an almost complete educational system which embraced both elementary and academic work, and counted a primary school for boys and another for girls, a higher school for boys, and an academy for young ladies. The system in its

[1] Amer. Cath. Hist. Res., vol. xiii, p. 110; Bertrand, loc. cit. Father Dilhet later returned to the east, where we find him, while assisting Father Barth at Conewago, reopening the school there, and, in 1807, helping to start the Sulpician school at Pigeon Hills, Pa., which developed into the famous college of Mt. St. Mary's, Emmittsburg. See Shea, Hist. of the Cath. Church, vol. ii, p. 609; Bertrand, loc. cit.
[2] Amer. Cath. Hist. Res., vol. xv, p. 87.

completeness and co-ordinative arrangement was far in advance of the educational ideals of the time, and seems more like the municipal school organizations of our day. The teachers trained by Father Richard and his assistant were highly successful in their work. Miss Williams and Miss Lyon continued the work of teaching for about forty years, and Miss Campau for more than twenty-five years.[1] Miss Labadie married, but retained a strong and practical interest in school-work all her life, and did much for the higher education of women in Detroit.

TECHNICAL TRAINING

Father Richard was a strong believer in industrial education, holding that the work of the academies or high schools for both young men and young women, in addition to the teaching of the cultural branches, should include a practical training in the arts and sciences which were connected with the occupations of the pupils in after-life. He brought from the east spinning wheels, looms, and carding apparatus, with coloring materials, and in the

[1] Ibid. Miss Williams taught in Detroit for many years. Later, in 1829, we find her teaching in the Indian school at Arbre-Croche, under circumstances involving great personal hardships. Her life there is characterized by Father Badin as "truly an heroic act of virtue and religion—to go and bury oneself in an immense forest among savages, without any human consolation or succor." In 1837 she was again in Detroit, where she opened a female charity school, which was supported by Monique Labadie (Mrs. Antoine Beaubien). Her death occurred in 1843. See Diocese of Detroit, chap. viii. Miss Campau also taught in Detroit for many years. In the year 1830 she went to the Pottawatomie Mission, at St. Joseph's River (Bertrand, Mich.), to assist Father Badin, and took charge of the Indian school there. See Diocese of Vincennes, chap. viii.

girls' schools sewing and spinning and other household arts of the time were taught along with the ordinary subjects of study. In the boys' academy, he set up an electrical machine and physical apparatus of various kinds, and aimed at developing a practical bent toward mechanics and physics, together with a thorough grasp of mathematics.[1] His plans here went far beyond what his material resources enabled him to realize. He also established a school for Indian girls, in which the instruction was almost entirely industrial.[2] In this matter of industrial training, again, Father Richard was far ahead of his time. The idea was unheard of in the east, and it is only within our own days that American educators generally have come to realize its importance and advantages.

THE GREAT FIRE

The striking educational development inaugurated by Father Richard received a severe setback when, in June, 1805, the city was destroyed by fire. The destruction of both church and schools was a heavy blow, and to an ordinary man would have meant a delay of many years in restoring the educational system to the condition of efficiency in which it had been before. Nothing, however, in the whole career of this extraordinary man exhibits so clearly the indomitable energy of his character and his passionate zeal for education as the way in which he met this crisis. Three miles down the Straits was a large warehouse belonging

[1]Farmer, Hist. of Detroit and Michigan, p. 720.
[2]Amer. Cath. Hist. Res., vol. xvi, p. 155 seq.

to the United States Government, and near by was a spacious old homestead, two stories in the center, with one-story wings.   Securing a lease of these buildings, Father Richard remodeled the warehouse for use as a church and school, and established himself in the homestead, devoting the wings to educational purposes, together with certain other buildings on the grounds.[1]   The place, then known as Spring Hill, is now within the city limits.   Here he set up his schools, primary and advanced, and in a short time the work was going on as regularly and as thoroughly as before the fire.   He remained at Spring Hill for fifteen years, and kept up his educational establishment there, until the schools were transferred back to the city, as it was gradually rebuilt.[2]   On October 3, 1806, as the work of laying out the new city was going on, a petition was presented to the Governor and Judges of Michigan, from Angelique Campau and Elizabeth Williams, asking for the donation of a lot on which to erect an academy for girls, and another from Father Richard, asking for a lot for an academy for boys.   Both petitions were granted.[3]   In the fall of 1808, he refers to the opening of a young ladies' academy in the city by Elizabeth Williams in a house purchased by him for the purpose.

OUTSIDE OF DETROIT

Father Richard's educational work was not confined to Detroit, but extended also to other Catholic settlements along the Straits and the Great Lakes.

[1]Ibid., vol. xiv, p. 108; vol. xvi, p. 155 seq.
[2]Ibid.
[3]Sheldon, Early History of Mich., p. 383.

Three miles above the town, at Grand Marais, a school was founded, and another at River Hurons, several miles below Spring Hill.[1] In 1802, a school was opened at the settlement on Mackinac Island, by Angelique Adhemar, a young lady from Detroit, and although it did not continue very long, it educated some who afterward became schoolteachers at Mackinac.[2] Paul Malcher, a wealthy bachelor who died in 1809, left his farm to build a church and school at Côte-du-Nord-Est, or Hamtramck, several miles from Detroit, the parish being attended by Father Richard.[3] The school was built, and in time a flourishing college was also established at the place. At Monroe,[4] on the Raisin River (La Rivière aux Raisins), a school was probably established by Father Dilhet shortly after he took up his residence there as pastor, July 1, 1798. The school was held on Sunday, in the pastoral residence, and included the teaching of "reading, writing, oral recitation of the catechism and of the Holy Gospels, and other useful and moral subjects." Taught only one day a week, the school was naturally lacking in interest and failed to draw many children; in May, 1821, an effort was made to reorganize it, although still confined to Sunday.

THE MEMORIAL

While, however, Father Richard did not allow his educational work to be discontinued or even

---

[1]Hist. of Detroit and Mich., Memorial of Fr. Richard, p. 720.
[2]Wisconsin Historical Collection, vol. xiv, p. 20.
[3]Amer. Cath. Hist. Res., vol. xiii, p. 83.
[4]Maes, Hist. of the Cath. Ch. in Monroe, U. S. Cath. Hist. Mag., vol. ii, p. 148.

seriously interrupted by the disastrous fire of 1805, the event occasioned him no little financial embarrassment, and in the long run, no doubt, seriously interfered with the carrying out of his broad educational plans. He was so poor, in fact, that one year he was unable to pay the United States Government the rent of $200 for the place at Spring Hill, and court proceedings were begun against him.[1] It was while struggling against the financial difficulties incident to carrying on his educational work under such circumstances that Father Richard drew up the following Memorial to the Governor and Judges of the Territory of Michigan. Besides acquainting us with the number and character of his schools at the time, it throws considerable light upon his educational ideas and plans. It is dated October 22, 1808.

"Besides the English Schools in the Town of Detroit there are four primary schools for boys, and two for our young ladies, either in Town or at Spring Hill, at Grand Marais, even at River Hurons; three of these schools are kept by the natives of the country who had received their first education by the Rev. Mr. Dilhet. At Spring Hill, under the direction of Angelique Campau and Elizabeth Lyon, as early as the 9th of Sept. last, the number of scholars has been augmented by 4 young Indians, headed by an old matron, their grandmother, of the Pottawatomie tribe. In Detroit, in the house lately the property of Capt. Elliott, purchased by the subscriber for the very purpose of establishing an academy for young ladies under the direction of Miss Elizabeth Williams, there are

[1] Amer. Cath. Hist. Res., vol. xiv, p. 108.

better than 30 young girls who are taught, as at Spring Hill, reading, writing, arithmetic, knitting, sewing, spinning, etc. In these two schools there are already 3 doz. of spinning-wheels and one loom, on which 4 pieces of linen or woolen cloth have been made this last spring or summer. To encourage the young students by the allotment of pleasure and amusements the undersigned have these 3 months past sent orders to N. Y. for a spinning-machine of about 100 spindles, an air pump, electrical apparatus, etc. As they could not be found, he is to receive them this fall, also an electrical machine, a number of cards, and few colors for dyeing the stuff already made, or to be made, in his Academy.

"It would be very necessary to have in Detroit a similar Academy in which the high branches of mathematics, most important languages, geography, history, natural and moral philosophy, should be taught to young gentlemen of our country, and in which should be kept the machines the most necessary for the important and useful arts, for making the most necessary physical experiments, and framing the beginning of a Public Library.

"The undersigned, acting as administrator for the said Academies, further prays that one of the 4 Lotteries authorized by the Hon. Leg. on the 9th day of 7ber 1806 may be left to the management of the subscriber.

"GABRIEL RICHARD.[1]

"DETROIT, 8ber, N S 1808."

---

[1]Farmer, Hist. of Detroit and Mich., p. 720. "God knows," Father Richard wrote later on, "how many projects, great and small, of schools and of missions occupy my mind, for the savages, for the deaf-mutes, for the children of the poor. . . . But the means are lacking in a country where it is necessary, so to speak, to create everything with nothing."—Dionne, L'Abbé Gabriel Richard, p. 27.

The date of the lottery act was placed a year too late. None of the lotteries, however, went into effect.

TEXT-BOOKS

Another phase of educational work in which Father Richard was a pioneer was the publication of school-books. In 1808 or 1809, while on a visit to the East, with the view of soliciting aid for the rebuilding of his church and schools, he obtained as a gift a printing press and a font of type, and he brought these back with him, and set them up in the Spring Hill establishment. He also brought a printer with him, who instructed his assistant sacristan in the art.[1] This was the first printing press in Michigan.[2] In 1809, he began the publication of a newspaper called "The Michigan Essay or Impartial Observer."[3] At the same time, he was preparing a series of text-books for the schools. The series, as published, consisted of the following works:

"The Child's Spelling Book," 1809, pp. 250.
"La Journée du Chretien," 1811, pp. 350.
"Les Ornemens de la Mémoire," 1811, pp. 130.
"Journal des Enfants," 1812, pp. 196.
"Petite Catéchisme Historique," 1812, pp. 300.[4]

The full title of the third in the list ran as follows: "Les Ornemens de la Mémoire; ou les Traits Brillons des Poètes Francais les plus Célèbres; avec des Dissertations sur Chaque Genre de

[1] Amer. Cath. Hist. Res., vol. xvi, p. 155 seq.
[2] McLaughlin, Hist. of Higher Education in Mich., p. 13.
[3] Ibid.
[4] Amer. Cath. Hist. Res., vol. xvi.

Style, pour perfectioner l'Education de la Jeunesse." As the titles indicate, the books were in French, with the exception of the first, of which there were two editions, one in French, and the other in English. The teaching in the schools was naturally in French, as the great majority of the inhabitants of Detroit in Father Richard's time spoke only that language. English made its way but slowly into the schools, with the gradual influx of emigrants from the east.

The publication of the series of text-books planned was interrupted by the War of 1812. Father Richard's outspoken patriotism made him hateful to the French Tories. As a penalty he was seized by the British when they gained possession of the city, and was kept in confinement across the river until the close of the war.[1]

THE CATHOLEPISTEMIAD

One of Father Richard's educational ideas, as the Memorial shows, involved the establishment of a higher school or college for young men. This idea found its realization, in time, in the famous plan of the "Catholepistemiad, or University of Michigania," which was founded by the Governor and Judges of the Territory in 1817. The Act establishing this institution, which subsequently developed into the University of Michigan, was drawn up by Judge Woodward, and is generally credited to him. But there can be no doubt that Father Richard had a great deal to do with it, although direct evidence of the fact is lacking. He

[1] Amer. Cath. Hist. Res., loc. cit.

was the first to broach publicly the subject of an institution for higher education in Michigan; he was the leading authority in educational matters in the territory at the time, and had prepared the ground for the establishment of the institution by the system of primary and secondary schools he had organized in Detroit; he was one of the two men to whom the control and administration of the Catholepistemiad was intrusted at its foundation. The broad scope of the institution, moreover, and the importance attached to scientific and professional studies in the scheme, show unmistakable traces of the hand of Father Richard.

Notwithstanding its pedantic title and phraseology, the Act constituting the university embraced "certain principles which were of the very highest importance, and which from this time became incorporated in the polity of the territory, and subsequently of the State also."[1]   Connected with the university, and under its jurisdiction, there was to be established throughout Michigan a complete system of primary, secondary, and higher education, including "colleges, academies, schools, libraries, museums, athenæums, botanic gardens, laboratories, and other useful literary and scientific institutions."   The officers and teachers in all these institutions were to be appointed by the university, and to be paid out of the public treasury.   Fifteen per cent. of the public taxes was to be set apart for the purpose.[2]

[1] Cooley, quoted in Putnam's Primary and Secondary Education in Michigan, p. 7.
[2] Act of 1817, Hist. of Higher Ed. in Mich., p. 30.

John Monteith, the Presbyterian minister at Detroit, was made president, and Father Richard, vice-president, of the university. They were also, at first, the only professors. The former held seven of the thirteen professorships, and the latter six. The salary for each professorship was fixed at $12.50 a year. A site was secured in Detroit, a building erected, and in a year from the date of the Act, the lower story was occupied by an English school, a portion of the second story by a classical school, and another with a library.[1] At Detroit, Mackinac, and Monroe, schools were established in accordance with the provisions of the Act, and instructions were issued as to the subjects to be taught. In the college at Detroit, it was provided that the Scriptures should constitute a part of the reading throughout the entire course. By the law of 1821, the Catholepistemiad became the University of Michigan, Father Richard being named as one of the trustees. He was also one of the charter members of the Michigan Historical Society.[2]

CATHOLIC SCHOOLS AND THE STATE

In the organization and character of the Catholepistemiad and its administrative policy during the first years of its existence, taken together with the Memorial of 1808, we have evidence of what Father Richard's views were on the subject of the relation of Catholic schools to the State. It must be remembered that, the population of Detroit be-

[1] Ibid., p. 32.
[2] Ibid.; O'Brien, loc. cit.

ing almost entirely Catholic at the time, the school
system established by Father Richard was practically the school system of the city of Detroit.   It
was really a public school system, although supported mainly by tuition fees and private contributions.   Up to 1820, there was usually not
more than one English or non-Catholic school in
the city, and there were no State-supported public
schools in Detroit until 1830.[1]   There can be no
douĎt that Father Richard expected his Catholic
schools in Detroit and elsewhere to be recognized
by the State and their teachers to be paid from
the public educational funds.   His petition to the
territorial authorities in the Memorial was a petition for a share of the funds to be derived from
the publicly authorized lotteries, for the benefit of
his schools.   The wide powers conferred upon the
administrative authorities of the Catholepistemiad,
in the Act of institution, enabled them to give official recognition to primary and secondary schools
of all denominations throughout Michigan; and
the primary and secondary schools which were to
be established in every county, in accordance with
the Act, were doubtless to be denominational
schools.   The idea of undenominational, or, as the
phrase is to-day, "non-sectarian" teaching, found
scant favor anywhere at the time.   As a matter of
fact, the early public schools in Michigan, as in all
other States, were distinctly Christian in character,
and to a great extent they were denominational
also.[2]

This view of the hopes entertained by Father

[1]Farmer, Hist. of Detroit and Mich., p. 715.
[2]Putnam, Primary and Secondary Ed. in Mich., p. 200 seq.

Richard is confirmed by the grant made to the Territory of Michigan jointly with the Catholic Church, by the Catholic Indian tribes of Michigan, at the very time of the organization of the university. In 1817, at the instance, very likely, of Father Richard, the Ottawas, Pottawatomies, and Chippewas, in the treaty of Fort Meigs, granted six sections of land for educational purposes, half of the grant to go to the Catholepistemiad, and the other half to the Catholic Church at Detroit. The funds derived from the sale of these lands were used subsequently for the benefit of the university and the Catholic schools, as specified in the grant.[1]

In the university itself, which was to be under the joint control of men representing various denominations, the plan was to have the teaching strictly undenominational. Under the administration of the Rev. Mr. Monteith and Father Richard, as we have seen, the reading of the Scriptures was prescribed in the university college which they opened. In respect to religious instruction, therefore, the general educational scheme, so far as can be gathered from the facts, comprehended a central university, of a strictly undenominational character, but under joint denominational control, and linked to it, a system of schools, academies, and colleges throughout Michigan, more or less denominational in character, while recognized as State schools and under State control. In one of the early reports of the regents of the university, it was shown that, of the seven branches or departments established, five were under the direction of clergymen, and two

[1]McLaughlin, Hist. of Higher Ed. in Mich., p. 20.

of laymen.[1] Father Richard's belief in the feasibility of establishing institutions for higher education whose spirit should be free from sectarian bias, and in the conduct and control of which Catholics should have a share as well as non-Catholics, reminds us of a similar idea cherished for a time by Bishop Carroll, of Baltimore, in the years immediately following the Revolution.

The hopes of "the apostle of education in Detroit," as Father Richard has been deservedly called,[2] for the recognition and financial support of the Catholic schools in Michigan by the State, were not permanently realized. Yet he continued to be held in as high esteem by the non-Catholics of the city as when, in 1807, at the invitation of the Governor and others, he had held services for non-Catholics in the Council-house, and lectured on the great religious principles which were common to both his faith and theirs. His election as a delegate to Congress in 1823 was a graceful recognition of the distinguished services he had rendered to the people of Michigan. It is interesting to record that, among his achievements in Washington, he succeeded in getting a grant for the establishment and maintenance of Indian schools for the tribes under his spiritual jurisdiction.[3] Father Richard's end was worthy of his holy calling, and of his noble life. When the Asiatic cholera visited the city, he stood at his post, ministering to the sick and dying, until he himself fell a victim to the dread disease, on September 13, 1832.[4]

[1] Putnam, op. cit., p. 201.
[2] Amer. Cath. Hist. Res., vol. xv, p. 87.
[3] Ibid.
[4] Michigan Biographies, p. 552; Bertrand, loc. cit.

RESULTS

Yet his educational influence did not die with him. It would undoubtedly have been much greater and more lasting had he been able to give an institutional organization to the band of teachers he had trained for the work of the Catholic schools of Detroit, by the formation of a religious community. But the seeds he planted sprang up, nevertheless, and yielded a bountiful harvest in after-years. Several of the schools he started continued to exist and to flourish, and were really the nucleus of the great Catholic educational system of the Michigan of to-day. Three of the young ladies he trained devoted their lives to the work of education, and, while teaching in Detroit and elsewhere, helped to keep alive his educational ideals in the minds of the Catholics of Detroit and Michigan. A fourth, Monique Labadie, having married a French landed proprietor named Beaubien, who was very wealthy, devoted a large share both of her time and means to the interests of Catholic schools. She brought the Nuns of the Sacred Heart to Detroit, to establish a school for the higher education of her sex, and made over to them a property and endowment of $100,000.[1] The little country school at Hamtramck, near Detroit, which was begun in an old farmhouse, developed, under Bishop Résé, into St. Philip's College, which for many years served as a nursery of the higher life to the Catholics of Detroit and Michigan, and trained many of the men, priests and laymen, who were instrumental in building up the Church and her educational institu-

[1] Amer. Cath. Hist. Res., vol. xv.

tions in the State in after-years.   The spirit and the high ideals of Father Richard thus became a precious educational heritage to the Catholics of Michigan, and an evidence of the lasting influence of his work as an educator may be seen in the fact that there is scarcely a Catholic church in Detroit to-day which has not alongside of it a flourishing parish school.

CHAPTER VII

THE EARLY TEACHING COMMUNITIES

EARLIEST PUBLIC NORMAL SCHOOLS

UP TO the time of the Revolution, the idea of a special preparation of teachers for the work of the schools was practically unheard of in America. The belief was universal that the teacher needed no more than a knowledge of the subjects that were to be taught; and as the subject-matter of instruction in elementary schools was confined to the "three R's," it will be seen that the standard of qualification for the office of teaching in such schools was exceedingly low. Nevertheless, the getting of teachers who possessed even the limited qualifications required, was largely dependent upon chance. It was not until 1789 that the subject of giving a more thorough training to teachers was even broached, and it was many years afterward before anything practical in the matter was done.[1] The evolution of the idea came about only gradually. The Lancasterian or pupil-teacher system was introduced into this country in the early years of the nineteenth century. The normal school idea began to be discussed about 1820, the discussion springing from the general re-awakening of interest in popular education which followed the War of 1812.[2] A school for the training of teachers was set up in Vermont in 1823,[3] but the

[1]Gordy, Rise and Growth of the Normal School Idea, p. 9.
[2]Ibid., op. cit., p. 22.
[3]Ibid., p. 12.

first normal school properly so called—outside of the religious Orders—was founded only in 1839, its opening, at Lexington, Mass., marking the beginning of the great educational movement led by Horace Mann.[1]

EARLIEST CATHOLIC NORMAL SCHOOLS

In regard to the preparation of teachers for their work, Catholic schools fared much better than the State public schools or those of other denominations, during the period following the Revolutionary War. Catholic opinion on this subject was far in advance of the general educational views of the time. The first Catholic normal school in the United States antedated by at least twenty years the normal school established at Lexington by Horace Mann. There were several causes that led to this. Chief among them was the fact that Catholic educators were in closer touch with Europe and more readily influenced by educational conditions and movements there, than non-Catholic educators. Another factor, closely connected with the preceding, was the tendency of Catholics to turn the work of teaching in the schools over to religious communities. This tendency was due partly to a religious motive, and partly to a financial one. In Europe, the work of teaching was largely in the hands of the religious Orders, and it was natural that the leaders of the Church in America should seek the solution of educational problems in the experience of the Church in the various Catholic countries and States of the Old World. The priests

[1]Gordy, p. 47.

and religious who were exiled to America by the French Revolution, carrying with them the educational ideas and ideals of the countries from which they came, exercised a powerful influence in this direction.

From an educational standpoint, the Catholic teaching community or Order is simply a permanent organization of teachers, living a common life, under conditions approved by the Church. One of the indispensable conditions is the spending of at least one year, by the candidate for admission, in an establishment wherein active preparation is made for the work of teaching by study and religious training. This establishment is commonly called a novitiate, and is usually nothing more than a normal school, in which professional training in the teaching of secular branches is combined with religious exercises calculated to nourish and develop the spiritual life. Most of the teaching communities in the Church date from a time subsequent to the founding of the Brothers of the Christian Schools by La Salle, in 1684, who was also the founder of the first normal school.

It was to the religious teaching Order that the leaders of the Catholic educational movement in the United States turned, in order to solve the problem of getting teachers for the schools; and while American educators generally were still wrestling with the idea of normal school training in a theoretical way, Catholics had already carried out the idea in practice in several parts of the country, by establishing religious Orders with their novitiates or training-schools. The first effort in this way appears to have been made by Father Charles Neale, in bringing four Carmelite Nuns from Antwerp to found a convent at Port Tobacco, Md., in 1790. Bishop Carroll was anxious for them to open an academy for girls; so anxious was he, in fact, that when it was seen that, being cloistered nuns, they were restrained by the rules of their order from doing this, he wrote to the Holy See and obtained the necessary permission. The Sisters, however, were loath to change their mode of life, and did not act on the permission. It was not until 1830 that they consented to do so, and then the school was opened in Baltimore, the Sisters, twenty-four in number at the time, removing to that city.[1]

THE POOR CLARES

In 1792, three nuns of the Second Order of St. Francis, commonly known as the "Poor Clares," arrived from France, and, after attempting to establish a house at Frederick, Md., settled in Georgetown. In 1801, they purchased from John Threlkeld a lot on Lafayette Street, and opened an academy. This was the first Sisters' school in the English-speaking States. The institution did not prosper, however, owing to the rigid rule of life led by the nuns and their unfamiliarity with the language and customs of the country. They found it very hard to support themselves, and on the death of the abbess, in 1804, the other Sisters returned to Europe.[2]

[1] Shea, Hist. of the Cath. Church in the U. S., vol. ii, p. 385; vol. iii, pp. 53, 427; Rec. Amer. Cath. Hist. Soc., vol. i, p. 214 seq.
[2] Shea, op. cit., vol. ii, p. 412; Lathrop, A Story of Courage; Annals of the Georgetown Convent of the Visitation, p. 150.

VISITATION ORDER

FIRST FOUNDATIONS

Yet the school established by the Poor Clares at Georgetown was destined to continue, and to develop eventually into one of the most important educational establishments for women in the country. Finding it difficult to induce the religious Orders from Europe to take up educational work in America, Bishop Carroll and others who were interested with him in Catholic school development turned their attention to the foundation of religious Orders of women at home. Father Leonard Neale, afterward Archbishop of Baltimore, had given the subject a great deal of thought, and while pastor in Philadelphia, he had under his spiritual direction a young lady named Alice Lalor, who had come from Ireland in 1795. Miss Lalor had long desired to enter the religious life, and Father Neale saw in her a providential instrument for the carrying out of his cherished educational plans. Under his direction, Miss Lalor, with two widows of like religious inclinations, Mrs. McDermot and Mrs. Sharpe, who had joined her, opened an academy. A young American postulant soon joined them. But the yellow fever, which scourged Philadelphia in 1797-8, was fatal to the infant institution. The postulant fell a victim to the plague, and the school was closed.[1]

Father Neale, after having been appointed President of Georgetown College in 1799, invited Miss Lalor and her two companions to come to Georgetown, in the hope of being able to inaugu-

[1]Shea, op. cit., p. 415; Lathrop, A Story of Courage, p. 147 seq.

rate the projected religious community under more favorable auspices. Proceeding to Georgetown, they were domiciled for a time with the Poor Clares, but on June 24, 1799, they opened a school of their own, near the academy of the Poor Clares. Their school was taught gratis, and was the first free school in the District of Columbia. It was situated on the grounds of the present Convent of the Visitation, Georgetown. The first free public schools in the District of Columbia were opened in 1805.[1]

EARLY STRUGGLES

When the Poor Clares returned to France, their property was purchased by Father Neale and turned over to Miss Lalor and her companions. For many years, however, they had a severe struggle against poverty and discouragements of every kind. The convent consisted of a two-story house, containing six or eight rooms. To this was attached a schoolhouse, with dormitory upstairs, and assembly-room and refectory on the ground floor. Both buildings were of frame, roughly built, and uncomfortable in the extreme. None of the rooms in the school-building were plastered until, in 1811, one of the Sisters lathed and plastered the assembly-room with her own hands. Vocations were very scarce, only four postulants joining them between 1801-10. To make matters worse, Mrs. Sharpe (Sister Ignatia), their best teacher, died in 1802. For a time, the school de-

[1] Shea, loc. cit.; The Ave Maria, "An American Community," vol. lxi, p. 585. This Catholic free school is still in existence, counting, in 1906, about 100 pupils.

clined, only the commonest branches, reading, writing, arithmetic, and geography, being taught, and the number of pupils being scarcely more than a dozen.[1]

The little band was as yet unorganized as a religious community, and this was one reason so few postulants came to join them. Several efforts were made to get members of religious Orders in Europe to come and train them in the ways of the religious life, but without success. It was their own desire to become members of the Visitation Order, founded by St. Jane Frances de Chantal. In 1812, a novitiate was established, and Bishop Neale permitted them to make simple vows, to be renewed annually. When he became Archbishop of Baltimore, he petitioned the Holy See for power to erect the community into a convent of the Visitation Order. The petition was granted in 1816, and the following year the Sisters were admitted to the making of the solemn vows. They then numbered 35.[2]

INCREASING PROGRESS

The turn of the tide in the affairs of the community came with its approval by Rome and its recognition as a branch of the Visitation Order. The number of Sisters rapidly increased, fourteen being received in the four years following the approbation. A free day-school was opened again and it soon counted over 100 pupils.[3] The obliga-

[1]Lathrop, A Story of Courage, pp. 154, 160.
[2]Shea, op. cit., vol. ii, p. 617; Lathrop, p. 184.
[3]The Ave Maria, loc. cit.

tion of educating a certain number of poor children
(7) gratis every year in the academy was assumed
by the Sisters, as an offset to the permission granted
them, in view of conditions in this country, to
charge for board and tuition.[1]

With the increasing number of Sisters, the course
of training in the novitiate was enlarged and made
more thorough, and by this means the curriculum
of the academy was gradually added to and advanced. Mathematics, philosophy, chemistry,
physics, together with literature, the ancient and
modern languages, and instrumental music, were
taught. In 1832 the number of pupils had risen to
100, and within a decade after the formal organization of the religious community, the academy
became one of the best known schools for girls in
the country. Protestants as well as Catholics
patronized it. Many men prominent in public life
sent their daughters there to be educated, the situation of the institution at the national capital giving
it a special advantage in this respect. There are
indeed few schools for girls in the United States
which can boast of so long a list of distinguished
alumnæ as this venerable school—the oldest of our
English Catholic academies.[2]

BRANCH HOUSES

The educational influence of the institution has
not been confined to the work at Georgetown. Colonies of Sisters were sent out from time to time, and
new houses, with academies and schools, established

---

[1]Lathrop, op. cit., p. 201.
[2]Lathrop, p. 366 seq.

at various places, both in the east and in the west. Chief among these may be mentioned Mobile, St. Louis, Baltimore, Brooklyn. The establishments in the last three cities became, in turn, centers from which in time bands of Sisters went forth to found other houses and schools in various parts of the country.[1] The work of the Order has been chiefly in the field of secondary education, but the elementary branches are taught also, and in most cases the boarding-school, or academy, is supplemented by an elementary day-school.

ESTABLISHMENTS FOUNDED BY THE VISITATION SISTERS OF GEORGETOWN, UP TO 1850 [2]

Place	Kind of School	Date of Founding	No. of Sisters Sent
Georgetown, D. C.		1799	
Mobile, Ala.	Boarding and day-school	1833	9
Kaskaskia, Ill.	Boarding-school	1833	8
St. Louis, Mo.	Sisters removed there from Kaskaskia	1844	
Baltimore, Md.	Day-school	1837	
Frederick, Md.	Boarding and day-school	1846	12
Washington, D. C.	Day-school	1850	5

MOTHER SETON AND THE SISTERS OF CHARITY

FATHER DUBOURG

The first American community of women devoted to Catholic education was founded by the president of Georgetown College, and grew up under the shadow of that venerable mother-school of Catholic higher education. The second com-

[1] Ibid.; The Catholic Directory for 1907, p. 728.
[2] Archives of the Visitation Convent, Georgetown, March, 1906.

munity of women was connected in its origin and early growth no less closely with St. Mary's Seminary, Baltimore, the first Catholic seminary in the United States. In the foundation of the Sisters of Charity, by Mother Seton, Rev. William Valentine Dubourg played a part analogous to that taken by Archbishop Neale in the founding of the Order of the Visitation. Father Dubourg was a Sulpician, who had come to this country in consequence of the French Revolution, and was an eminent scholar, as well as a man of affairs. Like Father Richard of Detroit, he was quick to realize that education was the key to the future success of the Church in this country, and he at once set about laying foundations for an educational system that included in its scope schools, colleges, and seminaries. Appointed by Bishop Carroll as president of Georgetown College in 1796, he was, after two years, sent to Havana, to build up the newly started college there. Returning to Baltimore the following year, he commenced, on the seminary grounds, the erection of St. Mary's College, which in a short time achieved great popularity and success under his able direction, and was chartered by the State.[1] Subsequently, he was made Bishop of Louisiana, and later on was promoted to the archiepiscopal see of Besançon, in France.[2]

Such was the man who, in 1806, while on a visit to New York, chanced to meet Mrs. Elizabeth A. Seton. Mrs. Seton entertained the hope of consecrating herself to the religious life, but, seeing no prospect of doing so in accordance with her wishes

[1]White, Life of Mrs. Elizabeth A. Seton, p. 202.
[2]Barberey, Elizabeth Seton, vol. i, p. 72.

in this country, she was thinking of going to Canada, to join a religious community in Montreal.

MRS. SETON

Mrs. Seton was a convert to the Church, born in 1774, of a well-known and highly respectable New York family, her father, Richard Bayley, being a famous physician and a member of the medical faculty of Columbia University.[1] Her early education, obtained in a private school in New York, was brief and slight, though quite as good as could be had by girls in the schools of the time. She received her real education after she quit school, in the years she devoted to reading in her father's excellent library and under his direction.[2] Her favorite books were, she tells us, the Bible, Thomson, and Milton. In her recollection of a visit she made to the country when eight years old, we are enabled to catch a glimpse of her inmost soul and its yearnings. "I delighted to sit alone by the water-side," she says, in her "Remembrances," "wandering hours on the shore, singing and gathering shells. Every little leaf and flower, or insect, animal, shades of clouds, or waving trees, were objects of vacant, unconnected thoughts of God and heaven."[3]

After her reception into the Church in 1805, Mrs. Seton found herself, a widow, penniless in

[1] White, op. cit., p. 39.
[2] Ibid.
[3] Memoir, Letters, and Journal of Eliz. Seton, vol. ii, p. 149; Sadlier, Elizabeth Seton, p. 7.

New York, with five young children to support, and all her former co-religionists bitterly turned against her. She underwent a terrible struggle against poverty on the one hand, and the inner trials resulting from her abandonment, or persecution, by her former friends on the other. The attempt to gain a livelihood for herself and her children by boarding the pupils of a school kept by a certain Mr. Harris was not very successful. Such was the condition of things when Father Dubourg, his mind filled with great educational plans, met Mrs. Seton in New York, and, with his penetrating vision, recognized in her talents and culture, joined to her strong leaning to the religious life, a chosen instrument of God for the development of Catholic education. It has sometimes been said that the absence of all visible means of success, in starting a work that is undertaken for God's honor and glory, is a sign that it is destined divinely to succeed. If this be so, the divine blessing was surely upon the work of Father Dubourg and Mother Seton from the very beginning, for never was an enterprise undertaken with a more complete lack of material means, and under circumstances so little likely to lead to the hoped-for results. By the advice of Father Dubourg, Mrs. Seton removed with her family to Baltimore in June, 1808, and rented a two-story brick house on Paca Street, near the seminary. The house was capable of accommodating eight or ten boarders, besides Mrs. Seton's family, and the plan was to open a boarding-school for girls. Father Dubourg's hope was, that other pious ladies, animated with the same spirit, might in time join Mrs. Seton, and that thus a religious community devoted to the work of teaching might be formed.[1] A gift of a thousand dollars was supplied for the enterprise by some friends of Mrs. Seton's, chief among whom were the Filicchi family, of Leghorn, Italy, who soon afterward donated another thousand dollars for the same purpose. Mrs. Seton's two boys were received by Father Dubourg into his college, and educated gratuitously. Her three daughters she retained with her.

BALTIMORE SCHOOL

The school was accordingly opened about the beginning of September, 1808, and the little house was soon filled. Only Catholic pupils were admitted, the idea being to give to the school a strong religious tone. "There are in the country enough, and perhaps too many, mixed schools," wrote Father Dubourg, when outlining his plans, "in which ornamental accomplishments are the only objects of education; we have none, that I know, where their acquisition is connected with and made subservient to *pious* instruction."[2] The subjects of instruction were, besides Christian doctrine, reading, writing, arithmetic, plain and fancy needlework, English and French. Morning and evening prayer was in common. There was daily attendance at Mass, and the recitation of the rosary, besides other devotions. Some of the pupils were quite young, being under 12 years of age.[3]

[1] White, op. cit., p. 210; Memoir, Letters, and Journal of Eliz. Seton, vol. ii, p. 34.
[2] White, Letter to Mrs. Seton, op. cit., p. 210.
[3] Ibid., p. 220.

ORGANIZATION OF THE COMMUNITY

Mrs. Seton was assisted in the work of the school by her eldest daughter, at this time about 14 years of age, but on December 7, 1808, she was joined by Miss Cecilia O'Conway, of Philadelphia. In the spring other aspirants to the religious life came—Miss Maria Murphy, a niece of Matthew Carey, of Philadelphia, and Misses Mary Ann Butler and Susan Clossy, of New York.[1] Several young ladies in Baltimore and other places were also ready to join the proposed community. The time was thus come, when, in the judgment of Bishop Carroll and Father Dubourg, the little band of devoted women should be invested with the privileges of the religious life to which they aspired. As a first step, Mrs. Seton was admitted to annual vows, and this was shortly followed by the taking of the religious habit. Provisional rules were also adopted. The Sisters at first called themselves Sisters of St. Joseph, but they decided before long to take the name of Sisters of Charity, after the religious Order founded by St. Vincent de Paul.[2] At a later date, the community organized by Mother Seton was formally affiliated to the original institute in France.

EMMITTSBURG

In the early summer, two other postulants arrived, Mrs. Rose White, a widow, of Baltimore, and Catherine Mullen, making six now under Mrs. Seton's direction. The need of larger quarters for

[1] Sadlier, Elizabeth Seton, p. 98.
[2] Ibid., p. 116.

the school and the growing community became imperative. By a providential coincidence, a convert at the seminary, named Mr. Cooper, who was studying for the priesthood, was inspired at this time of need to devote his means to the advancement of the noble enterprise undertaken by Mrs. Seton. Mr. Cooper purchased for the Sisters a farm near Emmittsburg, on which stood a small stone cottage, and began the erection of a new house on the property for the community.

By this generous gift, a home suitable to the needs of the rapidly growing band was provided, and the future of the community assured. For a time, indeed, the Sisters had to endure great hardships at Emmittsburg. During the first winter, while awaiting the completion of their house, they suffered extremely from cold, hunger, and sickness. For many years, as has been the case of almost all religious communities in America, there was a veritable struggle for existence. But when the spring of 1810 opened, the Sisters at Emmittsburg were cheered by the arrival of some boarding-pupils, a day-school for the children of the village and the surrounding country having been opened during the winter. Before the close of the year, the boarding-pupils numbered fifty, and the day-scholars had also greatly increased.[1]

THE CONSTITUTIONS

In 1812 the rules framed by St. Vincent de Paul for the Daughters of Charity in France were formally adopted by the Sisters at Emmittsburg,

[1] Sadlier, op. cit., p. 131.

with the approval of Archbishop Carroll. A brief glance at the scheme of organization of this typical American teaching Order will not be out of place. The government of the community was vested in a council, at the head of which was the Mother-Superior. The other members of the council were the assistant-mother, the treasurer, and the procuratrix. There was also an ecclesiastical superior, who was to be a clergyman. The Mother-Superior and the members of the council were to be·elected in the general assembly of the Sisters for a term of three years. The Mistress of Novices, and the Superior of each branch-establishment, were appointed by the council. Candidates for admission to the society had to be not under 16 years of age nor over 28. If accepted, they entered the novitiate, and after spending at least two years in study and prayer, were allowed to make the vows of poverty, chastity, and obedience.[1] The constitution of the new society was thus essentially democratic, although the element of autocracy also enters largely into the governmental framework. The constitutions of most religious communities of women engaged in educational work in the United States resemble more or less that of the Sisters of Charity of Emmittsburg.

THE NOVITIATE

The adoption of the rules and the election of the governing officers proved a great stimulus to the growth of the organization, and under the superiorship of Mother Seton, and the wise counsel of the

---

[1] Sadlier, op. cit., p. 155; White, ibid., p. 282 seq.

Rev. John Dubois, president of the preparatory Sulpician Seminary at Emmittsburg, the new institute soon gained a strength that enabled it to attempt new educational enterprises. When a novitiate was formally established, during the summer of 1813, there were ten novices, nine of whom had come the preceding year.[1] A regular course of studies was appointed for the novices, such as was thought best calculated to fit them for the work of teaching afterward. These studies consisted chiefly of the common branches. Needlework was also taught, as well as history and French. One of the features of the novitiate training was the conferences of Mother Seton. These covered a wide range of experience, but bore chiefly upon the future work of the novices as *religious teachers*. Mother Seton's work in this way was not confined to the novitiate. One of her habits was to visit the classes frequently, either in person or by deputy, in order to "witness the capacity, mode of teaching, attention, and success of the different teachers."[2] Notes were taken of these visits, and through conferences with the Sisters, both in private and public, the deficiencies and faults of young teachers were corrected. The purpose of this system of inspection and supervision was identical with that of the modern "practice" or "model" school.

EDUCATIONAL AIMS

The bent of the educational aims of the community was toward the establishment of free

[1] Sadlier, p. 177.
[2] Regulations for the Sisters, in the community archives.

common schools for the poorer classes, rather than of academies for the daughters of the well-to-do. At Emmittsburg itself, a free school for the poor children of the neighborhood was, as we have seen, started even before the academy. This school began with twenty pupils, the instruction being entirely gratis. It is worth recording, too, that not only were text-books furnished the pupils free, but their dinner each day as well.[1] Lessons and practice in sewing and household economy also formed part of the regular instruction. In 1820, a two-story brick building was erected for this school. If Mother Seton could have had her way, it is likely that the educational work of the community would have been altogether confined to free schools for the poor.[2] The rules framed by St. Vincent de Paul did not allow the Sisters of Charity to engage in any educational work except that of the gratuitous instruction of poor children. But in America new conditions had to be faced. Schools for the well-to-do were as much needed as schools for the poor. Besides, the institution at Emmittsburg was heavily in debt, and the Sisters found it impossible to carry on educational work, except on the condition of receiving payment from the pupils of the academy. The original rule was thus modified to meet the new conditions, as in the case of the Visitation Nuns at Georgetown. But Mother Seton and her Sisters always retained the noble ideal of free instruction, and this ideal, successfully carried into practice in numerous schools they were soon enabled to establish outside the mother-house, gave an im-

[1]White, p. 384.
[2]Ibid., p. 231.

petus that was felt everywhere to the growing movement in favor of the establishment of *free* schools for the poor.

NEW SCHOOLS

In 1814, Sister Rose White, with two companions, was sent to take charge of St. Joseph's Orphan Asylum, in Philadelphia. This was the first establishment opened by the Sisters outside of Emmittsburg. There was a demand on every side, however, for them to take charge of schools and orphanages, as well as hospitals, and as fast as the community increased new schools were opened. In 1817, the Sisters modestly began their work in New York City—a work which was destined to grow to such vast proportions—by opening an orphan asylum and pay school. The next year, a free school was begun for the German Catholics in Philadelphia, and two years later, a free school was opened in New York City.

MOTHER SETON AS AN EDUCATOR

Mother Seton thus saw her work extending on every side, with the promise of still greater growth in the future. She had herself actively engaged in the work of teaching in the early days, in Baltimore and at Emmittsburg, but feeble health, and the multiplying cares incident to the organization and government of the fast-increasing community, forced her in time to confine her eager interest in education to the task of superintending the teaching of the other Sisters, and the training of the novices.

She was still a constant visitor to the class-rooms. She gave frequent spiritual conferences to both pupils and Sisters. She was, in fact, the life and soul of the whole institution at Emmittsburg, especially on the religious side, and the Sisters who went forth to found new schools and provinces of the Order carried with them the two most prominent characteristics of the spirit of Mother Seton, as far as education is concerned, which were, zeal for religious instruction and devotion to the poor. Mother Seton's letters and journal afford abundant evidence of these two characteristics, although they throw little light upon her views on education in general. She wrote much and beautifully, translated several ascetical works from the French, and composed a number of poems. The institute of the Sisters of Charity itself is perhaps the best evidence of her educational genius, as well as of her educational views and policy.

EDUCATIONAL INFLUENCE

Mother Seton was only in her forty-seventh year when she died, in 1821.[1] The community numbered nearly fifty members at the time, and the number was rapidly increasing. The list of schools given below, with the dates of their foundation, shows how quickly the sisterhood grew and how far its educational influence reached. In studying the list, it must be remembered that, wherever there was an orphan asylum kept by the Sisters, there was usually a school also for children outside the asylum. In these schools, which were sometimes

[1]White, op. cit., p. 442.

taught in the asylum-building and sometimes outside of it, the children of the poor were received gratis.

But the list, long and far-reaching, geographically speaking, as it is, does not give a complete idea of the influence of Mother Seton and her community upon Catholic education. The schools in several of the localities mentioned developed in time into strong provincial centers of the work of the sisterhood, and these eventually became independent sisterhoods, while retaining the name and the rules of the Sisters of Charity as founded by Mother Seton. One of the principal factors in this movement toward independent existence was the tendency on the part of the Emmittsburg community, after the death of Mother Seton, to copy more and more after the original Sisterhood of St. Vincent de Paul in France, with the view of being admitted into the organization of the French sisterhood as a province. This union was actually achieved in 1850.[1] It was achieved, however, only at the sacrifice of several features of the life and rule of the sisterhood, which, in the opinion of many of the Sisters themselves as well as of the bishops in whose dioceses they were laboring, tended to diminish the field of their educational utility. Such was, for instance, the prohibition, enacted in 1846, against the Sisters conducting orphan asylums for boys. It was this that led to the withdrawal of the Sisters in the State of New York from the Emmittsburg community the same year. Upon the protest of Archbishop Hughes against this prohibition, the ecclesiastical Superior

[1] White, op. cit., p. 463.

of the Emmittsburg Sisters, Father Louis Delual, of St. Mary's Seminary, Baltimore, granted permission for the formation of a new community to those of the Sisters in New York who preferred to remain there. Out of forty-five Sisters then in the State, thirty-five remained,[1] and these at once organized the new community of the Sisters of Charity whose mother-house came afterward to be located at Mt. St. Vincent's, on the Hudson. The splitting-up of the various provinces of the Emmittsburg sisterhood to form independent sisterhoods or communities, furnishes a typical illustration of the causes that have operated to produce the division of so many other religious teaching Orders in this country, both of men and of women. Generally speaking, it has been due either to the desire to break away from European influence and constraint, or to the temptation to profit by the advantages, real or fancied, of carrying on educational or other work with diocesan limitation and under direct diocesan control.

Besides the direct educational influence of Mother Seton and her sisterhood in the ways above indicated, the indirect influence upon the growth of religious teaching bodies has been very great. This indirect influence has been exercised by the stimulus given to the formation of new religious communities, as well as in the shaping of their constitutions and educational ideals. An illustration is afforded by the foundation of the Sisters of Charity of Nazareth, Ky. This teaching Order was founded by Bishop David, who had been chaplain to the Sisters at Emmittsburg, and sought to

[1]Sadlier, op. cit., p. 271.

reproduce for the benefit of the Catholic schools of Kentucky and the west the essential features of the religious teaching organization founded by Mother Seton. The Kentucky sisterhood was so much like the Emmittsburg one, that the proposition of Bishop David to unite the two met with little objection on the score of their respective rules and constitutions, and only failed of realization because of difficulties raised in connection with the question of government and practical administration, in view of the distance between them.[1]

ESTABLISHMENTS FOUNDED BY THE SISTERS OF CHARITY OF EMMITTSBURG, MD.,[2]
1809-1850

Place	Kind of School	Date of Founding[3]	No. of Sisters Sent
Emmittsburg, Md.	St. Joseph's Academy	July 31, 1809	8
Philadelphia, Pa.	St. Joseph's Orphan Asylum	Oct. 6, 1814	3
New York, N. Y.	New York Orphan Asylum and Pay School	Aug. 13, 1817	4
Philadelphia, Pa.	Free School for German Catholics	Oct. 10, 1818	1
New York, N. Y.	Free School	May 13, 1820	1
Baltimore, Md.	St. Mary's Asylum and School (Free)	July 4, 1821	2
New York, N. Y.	The Lancasterian School	April 30, 1822	2
Frederick, Md.	St. John's School and Asylum	Dec. 23, 1824	2

[1] White, loc. cit., p. 356.

[2] Copied from the archives of the mother-house at Emmittsburg, February, 1906.

[3] The dates given here sometimes refer to the formal acceptance of the school by the community or the naming of the Sisters to be sent, and sometimes to the opening of the school or the Sisters' arrival there—generally the former. The interval between the naming of the Sisters and the opening of the school, however, was usually not much greater than sufficed for the journey from Emmittsburg to the place of the school.

Place	Kind of School	Date of Founding[1]	No. of Sisters Sent
Washington, D. C...	St. Vincent's School and Asylum	Oct. 4, 1825	3
Harrisburg, Pa....	Free School and Asylum	March 4, 1828	3
Albany, N. Y.......	St. Mary's School	Sept. 8, 1828	3
Cincinnati, Ohio...	St. Peter's Asylum	Oct. 8, 1829	4
Philadelphia, Pa...	St. John's Asylum and School	March 8, 1830	4
Wilmington, Del...	St. Peter's School and Asylum	April 14, 1830	3
New Orleans, La...	N. O. Female Orphan Asylum	Oct. 4, 1830	2
Washington, D. C..	St. Paul's Academy	April 21, 1831	4
Brooklyn, N. Y....	Brooklyn Asylum and Free School	March 29, 1831	3
Georgetown, D. C..	Establishment of Mrs. Iturbide, School and Asylum	June 3, 1831	2
Boston, Mass......	St. Vincent's Asylum	Feb. 28, 1832	3
Alexandria, Va.....	St. Francis Xavier's School	March 2, 1832	2
Philadelphia, Pa...	St. Joseph's Church School	March 28, 1832	3
New York, N. Y....	Half Orphan Asylum	Oct. 30, 1832	2
Philadelphia, Pa...	St. Mary's School	Jan. 29, 1833	3
New York, N. Y....	St. Joseph's Pay School	Aug. 21, 1833	3
New York, N. Y....	St. Mary's School	Aug. 21, 1833	3
Conewago, Md.....	Day School	June 19, 1834	2
Utica, N. Y........	St. John's Asylum and School	Sept. 11, 1834	2
Richmond, Va......	St. Joseph's Asylum and School	Nov. 22, 1834	3
Philadelphia, Pa....	St. Joseph's Male School	Jan. 20, 1835	3
Pottsville, Pa......	St. Ann's School	May 15, 1836	2
Norfolk, Va.......	Norfolk School	Sept. 1837	3
Martinsburg, W.Va.	Martinsburg School	Jan. 1, 1838	3
Vincennes, Ind.....	St. Mary's School	March 20, 1838	4
New York, N. Y....	St. Patrick's Free School	Aug. 1, 1838	2
Brooklyn, N. Y.....	St. James' Free School	Nov. 1, 1839	3
Brooklyn, N. Y.....	St. Paul's Asylum	March 25, 1841	4
Baltimore, Md.....	St. Vincent's Male Orphan Asylum	Aug. 12, 1841	2
New York, N. Y....	Rose Hill College	Sept. 5, 1841	3
Mobile, Ala........	St. Mary's Orphan Asylum	Nov. 9, 1841	4
Cincinnati, Ohio....	German Male Asylum	Aug. 26, 1842	3
St. Louis, Mo......	St. Mary's Orphan Asylum	May 1, 1843	3

[1] See note 3, p. 221.

Place	Kind of School	Date of Founding[1]	No. of Sisters Sent
St. Louis, Mo......St.	Vincent's School.....	May 3, 1843	3
Near Mt. St. Mary's College..........St.	Francis Xavier's School	Aug. 12, 1843	2
Washington, D. C...Male	Asylum...........	Oct. 29, 1843	3
Donaldsonville, La..St.	Vincent's Asylum and School..........	Nov. 12, 1844	6
Rochester, N. Y....St.	Patrick's Asylum....	Apr. 10, 1845	4
Albany, N. Y.......St.	Vincent's Asylum and School..........	Aug. 11, 1846	5
Milwaukee, Wis....Cathedral School........		Aug. 25, 1846	3
St. Louis, Mo.......St.	Philomena's School..	Aug. 25, 1846	
Baltimore, Md.....St.	Vincent's School....	Sept. 20, 1846	3
Washington, D. C..St.	Joseph's School......	Jan. 1847	6
Natchez, Miss .....St.	Mary's School.......	Nov. 9, 1847	3
Baton Rouge, La...Select School............		Jan. 1848	3
Norfolk, Va.......St.	Mary's School and Asylum	Jan. 29, 1848	3
Troy, N. Y.........St.	Mary's School and Asylum	Mar. 20, 1848	3
Boston, Mass......St.	Mary's School.......	Mar. 20, 1848	2
Buffalo, N. Y......St.	Patrick's School.....	June 3, 1848	3
Baltimore, Md.....St.	Peter's School.......	Aug. 26, 1848	2

There are five independent branches of the Emmittsburg sisterhood, the mother-houses of which are located in New York, New Jersey, Ohio, Pennsylvania, and Kansas. In the year 1904-5, the mother-community, at Emmittsburg, counted 1,694 Sisters, 1 academy, 5 industrial and 33 parochial schools, with 9,223 pupils; and had establishments in Maryland, Massachusetts, New York, Delaware, Pennsylvania, Michigan, Indiana, Illinois, Missouri, Wisconsin, California, Virginia, Alabama, Mississippi, Tennessee, and Texas.

The community founded by Mother Seton, together with the branches connected with it in origin, comprises to-day about 5,500 Sisters in all, with over 120,000 pupils—about one-tenth of the

[1] See note 3, p. 221.

total Catholic school attendance in the country.[1]
The relatively small number of pupils credited to
the Emmittsburg community as compared with the
large number of Sisters, is due to the fact that
the community now devotes itself to hospital-work
more than it formerly did. The mother-community has, in fact, tended to revert more and
more to the original ideal of St. Vincent de Paul.
All the branches of the Sisters of Charity, however,
conduct hospitals and charitable institutions of
various kinds, as well as schools, as indeed do
nearly all the teaching Orders of women in the
United States.

FATHER NERINCKX AND THE SISTERS OF LORETTO (KY.)

EUROPEAN INFLUENCE

While the problem of providing teachers for
Catholic schools was being successfully solved in
the east by the foundation of the sisterhoods described, the same problem was engaging the attention of the leaders of Catholic thought and work in
the west. About the same time that Mother Seton,
with the advice and aid of the Sulpicians of Baltimore, was laying the foundations of the great institute of the Sisters of Charity in America, Father
Nerinckx, aided by Father Badin, was laboring to
found a teaching sisterhood in Kentucky. The
coincidence is worthy of note. There is no evidence that the Kentucky priests were influenced by
the foundation of the Sisters of Charity at Emmittsburg, or of the Visitation Nuns at Georgetown. Indeed, the *first* attempt of the Kentucky

[1] Catholic Directory, 1906.

missionaries to found a teaching Order antedated
Mother Seton's establishment by several years.
The movement in Kentucky, like that in the east,
sprang spontaneously from the innermost life of
the Church, to meet a pressing external need.
That the movement, in both instances, took the
form of a religious society, was due to the influence
of European ideas. If the Catholics in even the
backwoods settlements of the west were able successfully to solve the problem of providing trained
teachers for their schools, a quarter of a century
before the establishment of the first public normal
school in the east, it was owing to the fact that,
even in the west, Catholics were in closer touch
with European educational movements than were
non-Catholic educators throughout the country generally. The priests who were driven to America
by the French Revolution must be chiefly given the
credit for bringing to American Catholics this
important advantage. Father Nerinckx, like
Father Dubourg, sought to meet the need of the
hour in the same way as it had been met in his native land. Yet the religious society founded by
Father Nerinckx, while modeled upon religious
communities in Europe, was not allied to, or
copied after, any one of them in particular. Its
rules and constitutions were original with him, and,
in this sense, it might lay claim to the privilege of
being the first distinctively American community.

FIRST ATTEMPTS

Father Nerinckx's first attempt to organize a
religious community to provide teachers for Cath-

olic schools was made as early as 1805.[1] The attempt was renewed in 1807, a Catholic gentleman named James Dent having generously offered to donate 400 acres of land to the institute, another hundred acres being given by his brother. A convent schoolhouse was erected by Father Badin, and six or seven young ladies had applied for admission to the community. Unfortunately, just as everything was ready, a fire broke out accidentally and reduced the building to ashes.[2] The accident left the missionaries penniless, and the design had to be abandoned.

THE FOUNDATION

Father Nerinckx's zeal and courage, however, were superior even to such a calamity. Several years later, conditions in the Catholic settlement at Hardin's Creek, in Marion County, seemed to him to offer another opportunity. This was early in 1812. Miss Mary Rhodes, lately come from Maryland, had, in a spirit of generous zeal, started a little school there, and the school, although taught in a dilapidated abandoned cabin, was a great success. Shortly afterward she was joined by Christina Stuart. Miss Rhodes had been educated in a convent, and cherished the ideal of the religious life. With this end in view, the two took up their residence in a rude hut which adjoined their schoolhouse.[3] Three other young ladies soon came to join them—Nancy Havern, Nellie Morgan, who was teaching a little school in

[1] Maes, Life of Rev. Charles Nerinckx, p. 135.
[2] Ibid., p. 142.
[3] Ibid., p. 242.

the neighborhood, and Nancy Rhodes, a sister to
Mary. The small tract of land on which the
cabins stood was bought for $75 plus a negro slave
owned by Nancy Rhodes. With their own hands,
the energetic little group set about repairing and
remodeling the wretched, floorless hut in which
they had taken up their abode. The leaky roof
was patched; a layer of boards was thrown across
the upper joists, so as to form a sort of an attic,
to be used as a common sleeping-room; a parti-
tion was put up, to divide the kitchen and refectory, a dining-table being formed by boards nailed
to a tree-stump which had been left standing within
when the structure was built. Improvements of
the same rough character were made in the schoolroom, for the accommodation of day-scholars and
pupil-boarders who soon crowded this pioneer con-
vent-school, the first west of the Allegheny Moun-
tains.[1]

Such were the rude beginnings of the Sisterhood
of Loretto and of their first academy and school.
The conditions could hardly have been poorer or
more unpromising, so far as regards the material
elements of success. It is a story of supreme self-
sacrifice and courage, recalling the conditions surrounding the foundation of the Visitation Convent
at Georgetown and Mother Seton's establishment
at Emmittsburg. But the story has been repeated
again and again since then, in the history of the first
foundations of other religious communities, witness-
ing to the educational zeal of Catholics, and to the
heroic work of the teaching Orders, especially the

[1]Maes, loc. cit.; Flintham, Sisters of Loretto, p. 7; Spalding,
Sketches of Kentucky, p. 203.

Orders of women, in the development of Catholic education in the United States.

With the approbation of Bishop Flaget, the little group of teachers were formed into a religious community, taking the name of "The Friends of Mary at the Foot of the Cross," although they came to be called most commonly the "Sisters of Loretto," from the name of their convent home. A sixth young lady, Sarah Havern, had in the meantime come to join them. The formal investiture of the three first candidates with the religious habit took place on April 25, 1812. The institute received the approbation of the Sovereign Pontiff April 1, 1816.[1]

THE FIRST ACADEMY

The organization of the teachers into a religious community, and the replacement of the original cabins or huts by a group of new and larger log buildings, the money for which was raised by subscription, and in the erection of which good Father Nerinckx labored with his own hands, gave a great impulse to the school and to Catholic education in Kentucky. By October, 1812, there were between 30 and 40 pupils—nearly all that could be accommodated. The program of studies was simple, but substantial: "Reading, writing, needlework, etc., sound morality and Christian politeness," was set forth in the prospectus as the sum of instruction.[2] Tuition was but $5 a year.[3] Boarders paid only

[1] Flintham, Sisters of Loretto, p. 12.
[2] Maes, op. cit., p. 268.
[3] Ibid., p. 269.

$32 a year, orphans being received gratis.[1] It is not surprising to learn that the Sisters had to resort to spinning and weaving for their neighbors in order to provide necessary provisions and clothing for themselves. As late as 1838, the charge for board and tuition was only $41 per annum, and only one month's vacation was allowed, from August 1 to September 1.[2]

GROWTH OF THE COMMUNITY

Nevertheless, the school and the community prospered. The number of pupils increased, and, along with material improvements, the circle of studies was enlarged and advanced. The Sisters studied hard to meet the demands made upon them by their better instructed pupils. Professors of St. Mary's and St. Joseph's Colleges gave special courses to the Sisters, covering the common-school subjects, such as grammar and geography, as well as the higher branches. Professors of art and music were even brought to Loretto from the east. By 1826, the program of studies included drawing, painting, and every kind of needlework, astronomy and mathematics, literature and modern languages, in addition to the primary branches;[3] and pupils came from Alabama, Mississippi, Louisiana, Arkansas, and other States, besides Kentucky. Candidates for the society, too, came from all sides, and the Sisters were enabled before long to open other establishments. The

[1] Ibid., p. 277.
[2] Catholic Advocate, 1838, Advertisement.
[3] Archives of the Loretto Academy.

first of these was at Calvary, Marion County, in 1816. Two years later the Sisters opened an academy and day-school at Gethsemane, Ky. Subsequently, the buildings of this institution were sold to the Trappists, and became the germ of the famous establishment which that austere religious Order has built up there.[1]   In 1825, there were 100 Sisters, with Loretto and four branch-schools in Kentucky, all built of logs, with a total of about 250 pupils.[2]   Besides the regular work of instruction in their schools, the Sisters, wherever they had a school, took charge of the work of preparing the girls of the vicinity for their first communion.   In the decade following their organization as a religious community, they had 8,000 girls under religious instruction in this way.[3]

EDUCATIONAL INFLUENCE

The educational influence of the Sisters of Loretto, while always centered in Kentucky, extended in the course of time far beyond the limits of that State.   Calls for the Sisters came from all parts of the west and south, and, beginning at an early period, the community, as it grew stronger, established branch-houses and schools in a number of neighboring and distant States.   As early as 1823, a colony of twelve Sisters was sent to Missouri, and opened a school at the Barrens, in Perry County.   Other schools were later established in the same State.   Between the years 1838

[1] Flintham, op. cit., p. 13.
[2] Spalding, Sketches of Ky., p. 204; Life of Bishop Flaget, p. 302.
[3] Religious Cabinet, 1842, p. 623.

and 1842, three schools were opened in Arkansas.
In 1847, a colony was sent to southwestern Kansas to labor among the Osage Mission Indians.
In 1852, the Sisters sent a pioneer group of teachers to far-distant New Mexico, to assist Bishop Lamy in the work of restoring Catholic faith and civilization among the Indians and whites of that ancient Catholic mission. The long journey was made chiefly by wagon, and was one of great hardship, three of the Sisters contracting the cholera on the way, one of whom, the Superioress, died.[1] From Santa Fé as a center, the Sisters established a number of flourishing academies and schools throughout New Mexico, Texas, and Arizona. They were also the pioneers in Catholic educational work in Colorado, their school at Denver, begun in 1864, being followed by others at Pueblo, Conejos, Colorado Springs, and Loretto. To the eastward, the educational work of the Order has not extended beyond Ohio.[2]

ATTEMPTS TO FOUND A BROTHERHOOD

In connection with the early history of the Loretto sisterhood, two other projects of Father Nerinckx, which throw light upon his educational views, have to be mentioned. One was the establishment of a brotherhood similar to the Loretto society, which should devote itself to the education of boys and young men. Father Nerinckx was strongly urged in this direction by Bishop Flaget,

[1]Maes, op. cit., p. 594 seq.
[2]The above facts were gathered from the archives at Loretto, Ky. See also Maes, op. cit.

who had likewise long entertained the same project. In 1819, a large farm was purchased near Loretto for about $3,000, the money having been collected for the purpose by a house-to-house canvass. The destruction of the dwelling-house and other buildings on the farm by fire the same year was a great setback, causing a postponement of the beginning of the institute, for which several young men had already offered themselves as candidates. Partly to collect funds, and partly to secure additional candidates for the brotherhood, Father Nerinckx set out for Belgium. During his absence, the Rev. William Byrne, with the consent of Bishop Flaget, occupied Mount Mary's, as the place had been christened, and started a school, which developed into St. Mary's College. When Father Nerinckx returned in 1821, bringing with him three Flemish youths as candidates for the brotherhood, he found the college in a flourishing condition, and was unable to secure possession of the place for the carrying out of its original purpose.[1] The project was consequently postponed, and ended with the zealous missionary's death in 1824. Another attempt to found a religious Order of men was made by Bishop Flaget in 1826. The Order was actually started, but had only a temporary existence.[2]

NEGRO SISTERHOOD

Another educational project of Father Nerinckx, and one which is in itself sufficient to stamp him as a man whose educational ideas ran far ahead of his

[1]Maes, op. cit., p. 385 seq.; Spalding, Sketches of Ky., p. 212.
[2]Spalding, Life of Bishop Flaget, p. 295.

time, was the establishment of a negro sisterhood, for the education of the colored race. The new institute was to be in connection with the Loretto sisterhood, though the precise relation which was to subsist between the two societies does not appear to have been fully defined. His plans in this respect probably contemplated no more than the training of the first negro Sisters by the Loretto community, and the general supervision by the latter of the new community during the period of its formation. The new institute was actually begun. Several young negro children were adopted at Loretto, and, while being educated, were trained in the ways of the religious life. In May, 1824, the good priest was able to announce that three of the negro girls had been admitted to the religious veil, a religious garb having been adopted for them, and special rules framed. But Father Nerinckx's death three months later was fatal to the project, as there was no one at hand who was able and energetic enough to carry out the plan, bright as was the prospect it held out for the education and elevation of the colored race.[1]

INSTITUTIONS ESTABLISHED BY THE LORETTO SOCIETY UP TO 1850[2]

Place	Kind of School	Date of Founding	No. of Sisters Sent
St. Charles, now Marion Co., Ky., transferred to present site, Loretto, Nerinckx P.O., in 1824....	Loretto Boarding and Day School	1812	3

[1]Maes, op. cit., p. 510.
[2]Copied from the official records at the Mother-house, Loretto Academy, Nerinckx, Ky., March, 1906.

Place	Kind of School	Date of Founding	No. of Sisters Sent
Calvary, Marion Co., Ky., closed in 1900	Calvary Boarding and Day School	1816	Sr. Christina Stuart, Supr. Number unknown.
Nelson Co., Ky., sold to Trappists in 1848	Gethsemane Boarding and Day School	1818	6
Spencer Co., Ky., closed 1828	Bethania Boarding and Day School	1821	11
Breckinridge Co., Ky., transferred to Bethlehem Convent, Hardin Co., Ky., in 1831	Mt. Carmel Boarding and Day School	1823	6
Barrens, Perry Co., Mo., transferred to Cape Girardeau, 1838	Bethlehem Boarding and Day School	1823	12
Casey Co., Ky., closed 1828	Mt. Olivet Boarding and Day School	1824	Mo. Dorothea Fenwick, Supr. Number unknown.
Apple Creek, Perry Co., Mo., transferred to New Madrid, Mo., 1831, recalled to Barrens, Mo., 1837	St. Joseph's Parochial School	1831	3
Fredericktown, Mo., left in 1836	St. Michael's Boarding and Day School	1832	6
Ste. Genevieve, Mo., suppressed 1858	Boarding and Day School	1837	8
Near Pine Bluffs, Ark., transferred to Post Arkansas in 1842, recalled to Loretto, Ky., 1845	St. Mary's Boarding and Day School	1838	3

Place	Kind of School	Date of Founding	No. of Sisters Sent
Little Rock, Ark., recalled to Loretto, Ky., 1845	St. Joseph's School	1841	3
Near Louisville, Portland, Ky.	Mt. St. Benedict Academy	1842	3
Osage Mission, Kansas	Manual Labor School for Indian Girls; in 1870 called St. Ann's Academy (Boarding School); later called St. Paul. Novitiate opened in 1891. Buildings burned Sept. 3, 1895, and Sisters withdrawn	1847	4
Florissant, Mo.	Loretto Academy Boarding School	1847	6

SISTERS OF CHARITY OF NAZARETH

ORIGIN

A little later in the same year that saw the birth of the Sisters of Loretto, another teaching community of women originated in Kentucky which was destined to play a prominent part in the development of Catholic education in that State and throughout the Middle West. The Rev. John B. David, a Sulpician, subsequently coadjutor-bishop of Bardstown, who had come to America from France in 1792, while in charge of the diocesan seminary of St. Thomas, near Bardstown, Ky., conceived the design of establishing a sisterhood which should be under the control of the diocesan authorities, and devote itself to works of mercy and the education of the poor.   It is a striking evidence of the vigor of Catholic life in Kentucky in those early days, and of the importance attached to education, that the elements necessary to the success of the enterprise were so readily forthcoming, notwithstanding the foundation of the Sisterhood of Loretto and other educational establishments in the State about the same time.   In November, 1812, Teresa Carico and Elizabeth Wells presented themselves to Father David as candidates for the new society.   In the January following, they were joined by Catherine Spalding, and several months later by Mary Beaven, Harriet Gardiner, and Mary Gwinn.   In June, 1813, the society may be said to have been formally organized, Catherine Spalding being elected Mother-Superior.   Father David had framed provisional rules, covering the object and duties of the institute, and regulating the exercises and life in common.   Two years later, they exchanged these provisional rules for those of the "Daughters of Charity," founded by St. Vincent de Paul.[1]   They were thus brought into relationship with the Sisters of Charity of Emmittsburg, who had also adopted the rule of St. Vincent de Paul. Father David's ineffectual attempt to unite the two institutes has already been related, as also the influence of Mother Seton and her work in the origin and organization of the Kentucky sisterhood, Father David having previously acted as chaplain for the Sisters at Emmittsburg.

[1] Spalding, Sketches of Kentucky; Life of Bishop Flaget; Webb, Centenary of Catholicity in Ky.; Shea, History, vol. iii.

MOTHER SPALDING

Mother Catherine Spalding, a relative of the future archbishop of the same name, was only nineteen years of age when she joined the society. For twenty-four years she occupied the position of Mother-Superior. She was a woman born to command, clear-sighted, firm, broad-minded, gentle and conciliatory in manner and speech, and yet quick to act and inflexible in resolutions once taken. To her more than to any one else, after Father David, is due the credit for the organization and growth of the community during its early years and the shaping of its ultimate development.[1] The institute began in a little log house adjoining the Church of St. Thomas, near Bardstown. The house had only one room below and one above, with a hut near by, which did duty as a kitchen.[2] There was no school at first, the Sisters not considering themselves competent for this office. Father David took in hand personally the work of preparing them to teach, devoting to their instruction all his leisure hours. While studying under his direction, they spun and wove and sewed, making garments for the seminarians and for the families living round about, and supporting themselves thus for two years. With the help of the seminary students, a log building was erected near their dwelling, and here, on September 14, 1814, a school was formally opened, boarders as well as day-scholars being received.[3] The number of pu-

[1] Webb, op. cit., p. 253.
[2] Spalding, Sketches of Ky., p. 230.
[3] Webb, op. cit., p. 247.

pils rapidly increased, and after four years the Sisters were enabled to erect a larger school-building of brick.

SISTER ELLEN O'CONNELL

The early candidates for the sisterhood, although full of educational zeal, were greatly hampered by their lack of school training; but early in 1814 a young lady named Ellen O'Connell, the daughter of a distinguished professor, came from Baltimore to join the community. To the possession of more than ordinary talents, she had added the advantages of a thorough education, and she became thenceforth the guiding spirit in the intellectual development of the institute. Placed at the head of the new school, she at once set to work to raise the standard of studies in the institution, teaching the higher classes herself, while training the young Sisters to become teachers. She acted as mistress of novices, as well as head of the academy, and from the time of her arrival may be said to date the establishment of the novitiate training-school as a regular feature of the institute's life and work.[1] Margaret Carroll, known in religion as Mother Columba Carroll, had also much to do with the educational development of the school and community at Nazareth. She was a pupil of Sister Ellen O'Connell, and practically succeeded her in directing the academic interests of the institution, being directress of studies for many years, and, later on, Mother-Superior.

[1] Webb, op. cit., p. 247.

EARLY SCHOOLS

Under the direction of the little group of able and devoted women at its head, and the prudent supervision of Father David and Bishop Flaget, the infant community grew rapidly. In 1822, they moved to a new site, two and a half miles north of Bardstown, and here on a tract of land purchased through the generous gift of Scholastica O'Connor, a young widow and a convert to the Faith, who joined the society about this time, the mother-house was permanently established, and the building up of Nazareth Academy commenced anew. At this time, the Sisters numbered thirty-eight, and the boarding-pupils twenty-five.[1] Even before this date, however, with the rapid increase of the community, the Sisters were enabled to send out several colonies to found branch schools. The first of these was a parochial school at Bardstown, opened with three Sisters, September 8, 1819. The year following a school was begun at Long Lick, in Breckinridge County, but the difficulties were such that the enterprise had to be soon abandoned. The same year, Sister Angela Spink and two others were sent to Union County, where, although the district was but newly settled and conditions were of the roughest kind, they succeeded by dint of enterprise and patient suffering in founding St. Vincent's academy and parochial school, since become an important center of the community's work in Kentucky.[2] At the time of the removal of

[1] Ibid., p. 249.
[2] Ibid., p. 249; Spalding, Sketches, p. 234 seq.

the mother-house to its permanent site, in 1822, the community had thus, during the nine years of its existence, given Kentucky three flourishing schools. Notwithstanding the drain upon their resources, occasioned by this missionary spirit, the Sisters made extensive improvements at Nazareth, chiefly in the erection of new buildings, spending about $20,000 during the first six years of their residence there.[1]

BRANCH SCHOOLS

The missionary spirit, which is one of the inherent characteristics of the teaching communities, soon carried the influence of the Nazareth establishment beyond the boundaries of Kentucky. In March, 1824, four Sisters, with Sister Harriet Gardiner as Superior, were sent to open a school at Vincennes, Ind. The place had, at the time, a population of from 1,000 to 1,500 inhabitants, most of whom were French, while in the vicinity there were several settlements of families from Kentucky, many of them being Catholic. The Sisters established an academy and day-school at Vincennes, and also, about 1830, an academy and school at St. Peter's Church, Montgomery, then known as Black Oak Ridge, in Daviess County. They also kept a school for a time at the settlement known as St. Mary's, in the same county. The schools at these two latter places were described by Bishop Bruté in 1834 as "plain log houses," the attendance at St. Peter's being given as six boarders and twenty-five day-scholars. But the Sisters were

[1]Spalding, Sketches, p. 239.

no longer there at the time of the bishop's visit.[1]
Their life and work in Indiana was beset with great
difficulties, the patronage their schools obtained was
very scanty, and to the material privations they had
to endure were added the deprivation of Mass and
the sacraments for weeks and even months at a
time. For these reasons, the Sisters were recalled
to Nazareth in 1834, shortly before the arrival of
Bishop Bruté. At the bishop's request, however,
they returned and reopened the academy and school
at Vincennes. The number of pupils after their
return is given as four boarders and about fifty day-
scholars.[2] The Sisters were again recalled to their
mother-house in 1838.[3] Although abandoned by
the Sisters, the schools established at Vincennes and
in the vicinity formed the starting point of the subsequent Catholic school development in Indiana.
It was to St. Peter's that Father Sorin with the
Brothers of Holy Cross came in 1841, and a little
later the Sisters of Providence took up the school
there and in Vincennes—two religious communities
that have had much to do with the development of
Catholic education in Indiana and throughout the
Middle West.[4] After leaving Vincennes, the Sisters took charge of the school at New Albany, Ind.,
replacing the Sisters of Loretto.[5] In 1831, Mother
Catherine, with three other Sisters, opened a school
in Louisville, in the basement of St. Louis' Church,
and two years later an orphan asylum was begun at

[1] Amer. Cath. Hist. Res., vol. xv, p. 77; Alerding, op. cit.,
p. 251.
[2] Bayley, Life of Bishop Bruté, p. 94.
[3] Spalding, Sketches, p. 238.
[4] Trahey, The Brothers of Holy Cross, p. 49.
[5] Shea, op. cit., vol. iii, p. 647.

the same place. An academy was also opened at Lexington. The next important establishment of the community outside of Kentucky was that of an academy and school at Nashville, Tenn., in 1842.[1]

ESTABLISHMENTS OF THE SISTERS OF CHARITY OF NAZARETH, UP TO 1844[2]

Place	Kind of School	Date of Founding	No. of Sisters Sent
Nazareth, Ky	Nazareth Academy	Sept. 14, 1814	7
Bardstown, Ky	Bethlehem day-school	1819	3
St. Vincent's, Ky., Union Co., removed from Breckinridge Co.	St. Vincent's Academy	1820	5
Scott Co., Ky	St. Catherine's Academy	1823	4
Vincennes, Ind	Academy and day-school	1824	4
St. Mary's (Vide-Poche), Ind	Academy and day-school	1830?	
St. Peter's, Ind	Academy and day-school	1830?	
Louisville, Ky	Presentation Academy and free school	1831	4
Louisville, Ky	Orphan Asylum	1833	
Lexington, Ky., removed from Scott Co	St. Catherine's Academy and day-school	1833	4
New Albany, Ind	Day-school	1838	
Nashville, Tenn	St. Mary's Academy and day-school	1842	

EDUCATIONAL WORK OF THE SISTERS OF CHARITY (KY.) IN 1844[3]

Number of Sisters	76
Nazareth Academy, boarding-pupils	120
St. Vincent's, Union Co., boarders	35
Lexington, academy, boarders	22
" " day-scholars	40

[1] Spalding, Sketches, passim; Webb, op. cit.
[2] Ibid., passim; Webb, op. cit.
[3] Spalding, Sketches, p. 240.

```
Louisville, academy, day-scholars..................... 50
    "       free school, day-scholars................. 75
    "       orphan asylum, day-scholars.............. 40
Nashville, academy, boarders...................... 18
    "        "        day-scholars ................. 47
                                                     ───
    Total number of pupils...................... 447
```

SISTERS OF ST. DOMINIC

BEGINNINGS

The beginnings of the Dominican sisterhood of Kentucky were much like those of the other two sisterhoods which originated there. The moving spirit in the foundation of the Order was the Rev. Thomas Wilson, Superior of the Dominican Order, and founder, with Father Fenwick, of St. Thomas' College. Anxious to provide more ample facilities for the education of the girls of his parish and neighborhood, Father Wilson, in 1822, gathered about him a little band of young women desirous of embracing the religious life, whom he had imbued with something of his own educational zeal, and organized them into a religious community in affiliation with the world-wide Order of St. Dominic.[1] The names of these young women, who thus became the pioneer Dominican Sisters in the United States, were Maria Sansbury, known as Sister Angela; Mary Carico, Sister Margaret; Teresa Edelin, Sister Magdalen; Elizabeth Sansbury, Sister Benvenuta; Ann Hill, Sister Ann; Rose Tenley, Sister Frances.[2]

Taking up their dwelling in a log cabin on a

[1] Webb, Centenary of Catholicity in Ky., p. 261; Spalding, Sketches, p. 160.
[2] Webb, p. 262.

farm attached to the Dominican parish of St.
Rose, they began active preparations for the opening of a school, which was inaugurated the following year, an old still-house serving as the school-
building.   The school opened with fifteen pupils.
Unable to support themselves and to make necessary improvements from the revenue of the school,
the Sisters for years were obliged to have recourse
to other means.   They engaged in spinning and
weaving; with their own hands they gathered in
the winter's wood, "tilled the soil, gathered in their
scanty crops, pulled and housed fodder for the
cattle."[1]   It was many years before they were able
to enjoy, even occasionally, the luxuries of wheaten
bread and real coffee.[2]   To raise the money necessary for new and larger buildings, they appealed
to the public interest in the object of their undertaking, tramping the country, two by two, for
miles in every direction, and asking of rich and
poor alike.[3]   Meanwhile, they kept up their own
studies, under the direction of those of the Sisters
who were better instructed, thus gradually raising
the academic standing of the institution and community.   Teachers were also called from without
to instruct the Sisters.   As early as 1829, a professor of drawing and painting from the east was
engaged for this purpose.[4]

EDUCATIONAL INFLUENCE

By the year 1830, the community was strong
enough to send a colony of three Sisters to Ohio,

[1] Webb.
[2] Ibid., p. 264.
[3] Ibid., p. 263.
[4] Ibid.

where they opened a school at Somerset. This school grew rapidly, and by the year 1843 had about 100 pupils.[1] About 1843, a day-school was also opened in the neighboring town of Springfield, Ky.[2] Later on an academy was founded by the Sisters in Louisville. The constitution of the Dominican sisterhood, like that of the Ursulines and the Visitation Nuns, looks to the formation of independent convents, as the result of the Order's growth, rather than to the building up of one wide-spreading, closely knit organization. Several of the schools of the Order which owe their origin, immediately or mediately, to the mother-house in Kentucky, became in time independent establishments and the mother-houses of so many distinct communities, while all following the rule of St. Dominic. This fact must be borne in mind, in estimating the influence which the Kentucky establishment of 1822 has had upon Catholic education in the United States. The number of Sisters there has never been, comparatively speaking, very large. The colonies it has sent out have been few. Yet its direct educational influence has been very considerable. The school at Somerset, for instance, of which it was the parent, and which developed into an independent community, not only became an important center of educational work in Ohio, but gave birth to other establishments which in turn became independent centers of educational activity over wide fields. One of these independent centers, developed from the Ohio convent,

---

[1] Spalding, Sketches, p. 160; Hammer, Edward Dominik Fenwick, p. 120.
[2] Ibid.

was at Nashville, Tenn., another was at Galveston, Tex., a third was at San Rafael, Cal., while four Sisters from Somerset were sent to help found the convent of St. Clara, at Sinsinawa Mound, Wis., which subsequently became the mother-house of one of the most important teaching sisterhoods in the country.[1]   The Ohio institution has, in fact, exercised a much wider direct educational influence than the original mother-house in Kentucky.

[1]Dominican Year Book, 1908, p. 50.

CHAPTER VIII

INFLUENCE OF THE HIERARCHY

1808-1838

A PERIOD OF EXPANSION

IN DEALING with the early religious teaching Orders in the United States, their history has been given, in a compendious form, down to near the middle of the nineteenth century, with a view of showing their educational influence to better advantage. It is necessary now, in order to complete the account, to give a more detailed sketch of the growth of the Catholic school movement throughout the country during the same period. The general characteristic of the period between the year 1808, when the Baltimore diocese was divided, and the year 1838, so far as concerns Catholic educational effort, is that of steady growth and expansion. There was no great influx of foreign educators and teachers, such as distinguished the period following the close of the Revolutionary War. There were no deep stirrings of Catholic life and energy, such as had given birth to the first American teaching Orders. No great educators like Gabriel Richard or Charles Nerinckx appeared. The ideal of Catholic education had been fixed, and the lines of its future growth marked out, by the work that had been already done. The school movement, during this third of a century or so, simply kept pace with the work of expansion and organization which was slowly but steadily going on within the Church. The general division and subdivision of the country into dioceses under episcopal control, which was one of the chief factors in the growth and organization of the Church, stimulated the establishment of schools, and led to their diocesan organization. The bishops who came to occupy the newly created sees were, without exception, champions in a practical way of Catholic schools.

THE DIOCESES

In 1808, the diocese of Baltimore, which had, up to this time, embraced the whole United States, was divided, and the four new sees of New York, Philadelphia, Boston, and Bardstown erected. The diocese of New York comprised that State and the eastern part of New Jersey; the diocese of Philadelphia, the States of Pennsylvania, Delaware, and Western New Jersey; the diocese of Boston, the New England States; while that of Bardstown included Kentucky, Tennessee, and the Northwest Territory. The see of Baltimore retained Maryland, Virginia, the Carolinas, and Georgia. In 1815, Louisiana and the Floridas were erected into a diocese, and this was followed by the establishment of the sees of Richmond and Charleston (1820), Cincinnati (1821), St. Louis (1827), Detroit (1833), Vincennes (1834), and Nashville (1838).

FIRST GENERAL SCHOOL LAW

The first canonical assembly of the members of the hierarchy, known as the First Provincial Council of Baltimore, was held in 1829. Besides Archbishop Whitfield, of Baltimore, the hierarchy was represented by Bishops Flaget, of Bardstown; England, of Charleston; Edward Fenwick, of Cincinnati; Rosatti, of St. Louis; Benedict Fenwick, of Boston; and the Rev. William Matthews, Administrator of the diocese of Philadelphia. Among other eminent ecclesiastics present were Fathers Francis Patrick Kenrick, Simon Gabriel Bruté, Anthony Blanc, and John Clanche, all of whom subsequently became bishops.[1] Several of the decrees adopted related to the subject of education. In regard to the establishment of Catholic schools, the decision arrived at was clear and imperative. The canon declared:

"We judge it absolutely necessary that schools should be established, in which the young may be taught the principles of faith and morality, while being instructed in letters."[2]

The subject of uniformity in the use of textbooks also engaged the attention of the Council. Provision was made for the publication of a standard catechism, and for the revision of such non-Catholic text-books as were being used by teachers in Catholic schools. Subsequent provincial coun-

[1] De Courcy, The Cath. Ch. in the U. S., p. 124; Append., p. 543.
[2] The full text of this important decree, which may be said to be the first canonical enactment of the Catholic Church in America relating to the school question, is as follows:

"Quoniam quamplurimos adolescentes ex catholicis parentibus praesertim pauperibus ortos, in multis provincii hujus locis expositos esse, et adhuc exponi constat magno fidei amittendæ periculo, vel morum corruptelæ, ob inopiam talium magistrorum quibus tantum munus tuto committi possit; necessarium omnino censemus ut scholæ instituantur, in quibus juvenes edoceantur fidei morumque principia, dum litteris imbuuntur." Decreta Conciliorum Provin. et Plen. Balt., n. 33.

cils sought to provide for the more effective carrying out of these decrees. At the Second Provincial Council, held in 1833, the presidents of the three principal Catholic educational institutions, Georgetown College, St. Mary's Seminary, Baltimore, and Mt. St. Mary's, Emmittsburg, were appointed as a committee to supervise the preparation of suitable class-books for Catholic schools and colleges, it being decreed that no text-book should be introduced which did not gain the approval of the majority of the committee.[1]

Efforts had been made to bring about uniformity in the use of the catechism particularly, but without success. Bishop Carroll, after the Revolution, had introduced the excellent little catechism used in England, and this came to be quite generally adopted.[2] Bishop Flaget, however, got out a new catechism in Kentucky, as did also Bishop England, in Charleston, and Bishop Conwell, in Philadelphia. There was some confusion in consequence, and the matter gave rise to a great deal of discussion. Under Archbishop Whitfield, a German catechism was published.[3]

EUROPEAN AID

In the foundation and support of Catholic educational institutions, as well as churches, considerable financial assistance was received during

[1] Decreta, n. 38.

[2] Bishop Carroll's catechism formed the basis of the Baltimore Catechism, which was revised and officially adopted by the Third Plenary Council in 1884.

[3] Three dozen copies of this catechism, ordered by Bishop England in 1830, cost $5. Amer. Cath. Hist. Res., vol. xv, p. 107; Shea, op. cit., vol. ii, p. 96.

this period from two associations founded in Europe. The first was the Association for the Propagation of the Faith, organized at Lyons in 1822, largely through the influence of Bishop Dubourg; and the other was the Leopoldinen-Stiftung, or Association for Aiding Missions, formed at Vienna some years later, through the efforts of Vicar-General Résé, of Cincinnati.[1] Without the aid received from these sources, the development of the Catholic school system would have been impossible in some of the dioceses. The diocese of Cincinnati and the dioceses formed from it are indebted particularly to the Vienna Association for its generous and timely assistance in this way.

ARCHDIOCESE OF BALTIMORE

In 1812 the diocese of Baltimore contained the following Catholic educational institutions: Georgetown College; St. Mary's Seminary and College, Baltimore; Mt. St. Mary's Seminary and College, Emmittsburg; the Visitation Academy and Free School, Georgetown, and the Academy and Free School of the Sisters of Charity, at Emmittsburg.

FIRST "COMMON SCHOOL" IN BALTIMORE

In 1815 the Rev. John Francis Moranville, a native of France, who came to the United States during the French Revolution, opened a school for

[1]Shea, vol. iii, pp. 361, 631; Cincinnati Telegraph, vol. iii, p. 110.

poor children in Baltimore, in connection with St.
Patrick's Church, of which he was pastor.[1] This
was the first "common school" in Baltimore, there
being as yet no public schools in the city.[2] Seeing
the children of the poorer classes growing up in
ignorance, he organized an association of charitable ladies under the name of "St. Patrick's
Benevolent Society," for the purpose of providing
money for the support of a school. The funds
were raised chiefly by the monthly contributions of
the members, and by collections in the church.
Pupils were admitted without distinction of creed,
there being from 60 to 70 in attendance almost
from the beginning. Many of the children were
also clothed by the society, and once a year they
were treated to an entertainment in the pastoral
residence, where they were waited on at table by
the good priest and his charitable co-workers.
The difficulties attending the undertaking were
great, for the parish was very poor, and the
benevolent society, after a time, languished; but
Father Moranville's zeal was superior to all difficulties. He revived the society and kept it up,
securing, besides, the generous co-operation of non-
Catholics in the city. He was a friend and adviser
of Mother Seton in the establishment of her community, as well as of the Sisters of Charity and

[1]Father Moranville reached the United States in 1794.
Arriving at Baltimore soon afterward, he taught for a time
in an academy opened about 1795 by Madame Lacomb, an
exile from San Domingo. The academy was attended by
young ladies of the highest rank. Father Dubourg was also
for a short time an instructor in this institution. Balt.
Cathedral Records, p. 17.

[2]Scharf, Chronicles of Balt., p. 374; Shea, History of the
Cath. Ch. in the U. S., vol. ii, p. 670.

the Lorettines in Kentucky, and was instrumental in sending young ladies with a religious vocation to each of these institutes. He also induced the Trappists to start a school in New York. St. Patrick's School has continued to exist down to our own days, a monument to the charity and educational zeal of Father Moranville and the good ladies of his congregation.[1]

ST. MARY'S FREE SCHOOL

As early as 1795, Bishop Carroll had broached the subject of a free school for the cathedral parish. It was not, however, until the year 1817 that, as the result of the active interest of Archbishop Maréchal in the matter, the plan was successfully carried out, a girls' school being opened in February of that year, and a school for boys the December following. The girls' school was supported by an association of ladies formed for the purpose. An interesting feature of the movement was a "reading school," which was held on Sundays in connection with the girls' school, and to which the young ladies who were the best readers in the parish lent their services. It is an interesting fact also that the association made an appropriation of $200 the first year in order to provide clothes for pupils.[2]

In 1821 Sisters of Charity from Emmittsburg took charge of the girls' school and, in connection with it, opened an orphan asylum. The Catholic Laity's Directory for 1822 states that there were then two free schools in Baltimore, "in which the children are carefully instructed in

[1] Religious Cabinet, vol. i, p. 622 seq.
[2] Cathedral Records, pp. 21, 99.

the various branches of useful knowledge, and at a proper age are apprenticed to such trades as they themselves may incline to, or are supposed to be most advantageous to their future prospects in life. They are generally supported by private donations, and stated collections in the different churches."[1] Among the staunch friends and generous supporters of Catholic education was the venerable Charles Carroll, of Carrollton. In 1824, on returning home from church, after hearing a sermon preached by Archbishop Eccleston, in which he appealed for the support of these schools, he sent a check for $50 for the purpose.[2]

FIRST COLORED SCHOOL

There were four Catholic churches in Baltimore at this time. A congregation of colored Catholics was also being formed, and to provide for the education of their children, Father James Joubert, a Sulpician, founded, in 1825, the colored Oblate Sisters of St. Frances. The first three members were Elizabeth Lange, Frances Balis, and Miss Bogue. A school for colored children was begun, which gradually increased in size and efficiency, as the number of members in the new community grew. By 1834 there were twelve Sisters. Girls were received both as boarders and as day-scholars, and were taught "English, French, cyphering and writing, Sewing in all its branches, embroidery, Washing and Ironing."[3] Board and

[1] Laity's Directory for 1822, p. 83.
[2] Amer. Cath. Hist. Res., vol. xv, p. 77.
[3] Cath. Almanac for 1835 and 1838.

tuition was only $4 a month, the effort being thus made to bring the education offered within reach of the poorer classes, while the work of the school was made largely industrial in character. By 1856 the Sisters numbered seventeen; and there were 135 pupils in the girls' school, with fifty in the boys' school.[1]

NEW SCHOOLS IN BALTIMORE

Archbishop Whitfield, who succeeded to the metropolitan see in 1828, showed himself, like his predecessors, an active friend of Catholic education. A new free school for boys was opened in Baltimore the same year, and the cornerstone laid for a larger and finer building for the orphan asylum and free school in charge of the Sisters of Charity. The new Boys' Free School was erected on a lot given to Archbishop Maréchal by Robert Oliver, Esq. The school, said "The Metropolitan," in 1830, was in charge of "an association of gentlemen who, by their untiring exertions, provide for the support of the teacher, Mr. Shea, who conducts the exercises on the monitorial system." Sunday-school was taught by Mr. Shea in the school. The same writer describes the new school of the Sisters of Charity as "a handsome and spacious building, 45 feet in length and 51 feet in breadth," facing on Howard's Park, near the Cathedral, and says: "To the liberality of our citizens of all denominations, the completion of this asylum is indebted. At two fairs held in its behalf, the sum of $3,000 was made each time. The number of orphans now under its roof is

[1]De Courcy-Shea, op. cit., p. 115; Shea, History, vol. ii, p. 92.

twenty-two; the day-scholars amount to about 400, and are daily increasing."[1]

Archbishop Whitfield succeeded in establishing another school in Baltimore when, in 1830, he induced the Carmelite Sisters, to the number of twenty-four, to remove there from Port Tobacco, Md., and to open an academy for girls. This school was continued until 1852.[2]

WASHINGTON SCHOOLS

While Catholic education was thus making steady and solid progress in Baltimore, under the energetic impulse of the metropolitans, schools were also being built up in other parts of the archdiocese. From the beginning of the nineteenth century, the Sisters of the Visitation, at Georgetown, had conducted a free school for girls, in addition to their academy there, and by 1822 another "charity school," attached to Trinity Church, had been established by the Jesuit Fathers, in which children of both sexes were educated.[3] In the city of Washington, St. Patrick's Church had been built by the Rev. William Matthews in 1804, and this zealous and scholarly priest, who had been president of Georgetown College, although not himself a member of the society, allowed the Jesuits, about 1821, to open a day-school in connection with the newly erected church. The institution was known as the Washington Seminary, and later developed into Gon-

[1] The Catholic Metropolitan, Feb., 1830, p. 66.
[2] De Courcy-Shea, op. cit., p. 142.
[3] The Laity's Directory, 1822, p. 84.

zaga College.[1]   In connection with St. Patrick's
Church, St. Vincent's Free School and Orphan
Asylum for girls was founded in 1825, three
Sisters of Charity taking charge.[2]   The year 1831
saw two new schools begun by the Sisters of Char-
ity in the District of Columbia.   One was St.
Paul's Academy, and the other, a free school and
academy known as the Establishment of Mrs.
Iturbide, in Georgetown.

OTHER PLACES

A free school and orphan asylum was opened by
the Sisters of Charity at Frederick, Md., in 1824,
and a boys' school, known as St. John's Seminary,
was some years later organized at the same place
by the venerable pastor, the Rev. John McElroy,
S.J.[3]   At Bryantown, a school was founded in
1837.[4]

In Virginia, which then formed part of the
diocese of Baltimore, efforts were being made to
afford the scattered Catholics the benefits of a
religious education.   In 1832, the Sisters of Charity opened a school at Alexandria, and this was

[1]History of St. Patrick's Parish, Centenary Celebration,
1904. The college was closed in 1829, and from that time until
1848 a private school was maintained in the building. In the
latter year the college was reopened by the Jesuits, and in 1871
was moved to its present site, on I Street, between North
Capitol and First, N. W.
[2]This institution has continued to exist down to the present. In 1899 the site of the old building, at the southwest
corner of Tenth and G streets, was sold for $450,000, and a
magnificent new asylum erected in the eastern suburb of
Washington.
[3]Catholic Almanac, 1833.
[4]Shea, op. cit., vol. iii, p. 444.

followed by others at Richmond (1834), Norfolk
(1837), and Martinsburg (1838).[1]

Sisters of the Visitation from Georgetown
founded a branch school and academy in Baltimore
in 1837.[2]

SUMMARY

All told, nineteen elementary schools were established in the archdiocese of Baltimore during the
years 1812-1838. The archdiocese contained, at
the latter date, 89,000 Catholics, 61 churches or
chapels, and 74 secular priests.[3] Ten of these nineteen schools were conducted by the Sisters of Charity. The possession of the mother-house of this
rapidly growing teaching Order, as well as the
mother-house of the Visitation Sisters, made the
archdiocese of Baltimore the center of influence,
during this period, in the steadily evolving parish
school system, as Georgetown and the other two
colleges had given it pre-eminence in the field of
higher education. Educationally as well as
ecclesiastically, Baltimore had thus become the
Catholic center of influence in the United States.

DIOCESE OF PHILADELPHIA

EDUCATIONAL PROSPECTS

When the diocese of Philadelphia was established, in 1808, there were three Catholic schools,
attached to the churches of St. Mary's, Holy

[1] Emmittsburg Archives; The Cath. Ch. in City and Diocese
of Richmond.
[2] Records of the Georgetown Convent.
[3] Shea, vol. iii, p. 447.

Trinity, and St. Augustine's, besides the orphan asylum founded in 1797. In 1814, the Sisters of Charity began their work in the diocese by taking charge of this asylum, under the direction of Sister Rose, this being the first mission accepted by the Sisters. Philadelphia offered a promising field for educational work, and the Sisters followed up this first step by taking charge of a free school for German Catholics in October, 1818. A Catholic Sunday-school was organized in 1816 for the benefit of such children as had to work on weekdays; Matthew Carey was one of the founders, and was chosen vice-president, the president being Father Carr, O.S.A. The Sunday-school work included secular as well as religious classes, the hours of attendance being from 8 to 10 A.M., and from 2 to 3 P.M.[1] The following year, the colored Catholics of the city petitioned the trustees of St. Mary's to appoint a teacher for their children to instruct them in the "common English branches, and to teach them the catechism and their morning and evening prayers."[2] The petition was favorably considered, and a teacher promised the following summer.

FACTIONAL TROUBLES

These bright educational prospects were, however, already overclouded by the factional troubles which had arisen in St. Mary's Parish, and which resulted in making the Church in Philadelphia a prey to disorder, strife, and open schism for a

[1] Amer. Cath. Hist. Res., vol. vii, p. 156.
[2] Ibid., p. 186.

period of twenty years. Catholic educational development was completely checked, and even the existing schools were more or less disorganized, where they were not entirely closed. The historian Shea has tersely summed up the disastrous educational effects of the schism in St. Mary's Church by saying that the diocese of Philadelphia, in which Catholics were more numerous and more wealthy than in any other diocese, was, in 1829, "without a seminary, a college, a convent academy for the education of young ladies, with but a single asylum, few schools, and a disheartened people."[1]

BISHOP KENRICK

The turn of the tide came when, in 1830, the Rev. Francis Patrick Kenrick was appointed coadjutor-bishop of Philadelphia.[2] A native of Ireland, Bishop Kenrick had been for nine years professor of theology in the seminary at Bardstown. A profound scholar, as well as an able administrator, the young professor had zealously co-operated with Bishop Flaget in his educational work in Kentucky, and it was to be expected that the Catholic school would be one of the first things to occupy his attention in Philadelphia. The new bishop was fortunate in finding at St. Mary's Church, where he went to reside, a young priest, the Rev. John Hughes, who had been educated at Emmittsburg, and whose ideas on education, as well as on other important matters, were at one with his own. Father Hughes became the bishop's secre-

[1]Shea, vol. iii, p. 260.
[2]Ibid., p. 545 seq.; O'Shea, The Two Kenricks, p. 62 seq.

tary for a while, and for seven years, until his consecration as bishop of New York, he was the right-
hand man of Bishop Kenrick in the carrying out of
the educational policy of Catholic schools for
Catholic children, a policy which had shortly before been enacted into a law by the First Provincial
Council of Baltimore. Bishop Kenrick was keenly
alive to the difficulties that stood in the way of the
establishment of Catholic schools. Indeed, as late
as 1850, he wrote: "I am fully sensible of the importance of Catholic schools, but I do not know
how we are to establish them. Teachers of a religious character are not easily had, and schoolhouses
are wanting."[1]   Nevertheless, his advent to the
diocese marked the beginning of a new era in the
development of Catholic education in Philadelphia,
and proof of this was soon afforded in a practical
way.

LAUREL HILL COLLEGE

In 1829, a select school or preparatory college
had been opened, in a house adjoining St. Mary's
Church, by the pastor, the Rev. Jeremiah Keily,
who, as a Jesuit, had been at the head of the school
attached to St. Patrick's Church, Washington.
Father Keily was ambitious to give Philadelphia
a Catholic college, and in 1835, having removed
the institution to Laurel Hill, in Penn Township,
he secured for it an act of incorporation as Laurel
Hill College. The time, however, was not yet
ripe for the establishment of institutions of higher

[1]From the original letter in the historical collection at
Notre Dame, Ind., copied by Mr. Martin I. J. Griffin.

education in Philadelphia, and the new college was soon obliged to close its doors.[1]

ACADEMY AND SEMINARY

Greater success attended the efforts of Father Hughes, when, in 1832, after just finishing the erection of St. John's Church, he established in connection with it a select school for boys, known as "The Western Academy." Father Hughes acted as principal of the school, and was assisted by two lay teachers.[2] Two years later, the academy was placed in charge of B. Constant, who had succeeded Father Brosius as President of Mt. Airy College.[3] In 1832 also, Bishop Kenrick began a diocesan seminary, the first students being lodged and taught in his own residence.[4]

SISTERS OF CHARITY

Bishop Kenrick was anxious to have the Sisters of Charity take charge of the elementary schools. A new orphan asylum for both boys and girls, St. John's, was established by Father Hughes, and opened by the Sisters in the spring of 1830.[5] Besides being a shelter for orphans, the new asylum was also a free school for day-scholars, who greatly outnumbered the former. On March 28, 1832, three Sisters were named at Emmittsburg for

[1] Shea, op. cit., vol. iii, p. 556; Hist. Sketches of the Cath. Churches in Phila., p. 42.
[2] Amer. Cath. Hist. Res., vol. xiii, p. 140.
[3] Cath. Herald, 1834, adv.
[4] Hist. Sketches of the Cath. Ch. in Phila., p. 167.
[5] Emmittsburg Archives; Hassard, Life of Archb. Hughes, p. 90; Shea, vol. iii, p. 547.

Sacred Heart School, a free school for girls at
10 Prune Street, near old St. Joseph's Church, and
on February 4, 1833, three took charge of St.
Mary's School.[1] The Catholic Almanac for 1834
credits the Sisters with the charge of four schools
in the city, with seventeen Sisters. In January,
1835, another school was opened, St. Joseph's
Male School, a branch of the one already established in connection with St. Joseph's Church.[2]

NEW TEACHING ORDERS

Besides the Sisters of Charity, two other relig-
ious Orders of women were soon engaged in educational work in the diocese. One of these was a
French community called "Les Dames de la Retraite," who opened an academy about 1832 on
Chestnut Street, in "The Gothic Mansion," which
stood on the site of the present Free Library.[3]
There were classes in both French and English.
The other community was the Sisters of Charity of
the Blessed Virgin. They were founded by the
Rev. Terence J. Donaghoe, pastor of St.
Michael's. The parish had just been organized,
and Father Donaghoe had no sooner finished the
church in 1834 when he took in hand the work of
organizing a Catholic school. Several pious young
women whom he had brought from Ireland
formed the first teachers as well as the first religious of the new institute, which was destined afterward to do so much for Catholic education in the

[1] Archives; Amer. Cath. Hist. Res., vol. xiii, p. 140.
[2] Emmittsburg Archives.
[3] Cath. Almanac, 1833; The Cincinnati Telegraph, vol. ii,
p. 31, 1832.

west. Their school and convent was near Second and Thompson streets. Here they remained until 1844, when, after the burning of their convent by the Native American rioters, they removed to Dubuque.[1]

THE CHOLERA

During the cholera scourge of 1832, the Sisters of Charity especially distinguished themselves. The city council voted to present to each of the Sisters a gift of silver plate, in recognition of their services to the city in caring for the sick, but the gift was, with characteristic modesty, declined. The council then voted to give the money the plate would cost to the two orphan asylums and the Sacred Heart free school.[2]

THROUGHOUT PENNSYLVANIA

Outside of Philadelphia, as in that city, the growth and organization of Catholic church work was characterized generally by an effort to found Catholic schools. Schools were undoubtedly kept up, at least in a desultory way, at a number of the old colonial mission centers, such as Goshenhoppen, Conewago, and Haycock. At Lancaster the school was probably continued, and in 1823 a generous Catholic of that place, Robert J. Thomson, made a bequest to secure its permanent endowment, having provided in his will that the sum of $2,400, after the death of his relatives, should go "for the

---

[1]Hist. Sketches of the Cath. Ch. in Philadelphia, p. 57; De Courcy-Shea, The Cath. Ch. in the U. S., p. 252; Cath. Standard, Jan. 23, 1869.
[2]Amer. Cath. Hist. Res., vol. xiii, p. 140.

foundation of a Catholic school in Lancaster," or such other charitable purposes as the pastor might think fit.[1] The money, however, was not used for school purposes. At Conewago, near which was a Catholic school in colonial times, two rough-cast, limestone schoolhouses were built by Rev. M. Lekeu, in 1830, on ground near the church. Rev. F. X. Kendeler, a secular German priest, taught school there for many years. Other priests also taught, as it was difficult to get good lay teachers, and among them may be mentioned Father Michael McFaul and the Jesuit Father Sullivan, before 1850, and later on Father F. X. De Neckere.[2]

PITTSBURG

At Pittsburg, where the first Catholic church was built in 1811,[3] efforts were early made to organize a Catholic school. In 1828 two nuns of the Order of St. Clare arrived from Belgium, and established a convent and academy. Two years later, the community numbered fourteen members.[4] Owing, however, to trouble with the ecclesiastical authorities, the community was disbanded in 1835. The same year witnessed the arrival of the Sisters of Charity in Pittsburg, where they took charge of the day-schools attached to the church, and opened an academy for the more advanced pupils.[5] The Sisters of Charity were a great boon to the cause

[1] Rec. Amer. Cath. Hist. Soc., vol. v, p. 315.
[2] John T. Riley, of Conewago, letter to the author; Holy Year Collections, vol. vii, p. 1061; Cincinnati Telegraph, vol. iii, p. 107.
[3] Lambing, The Cath. Ch. in the Diocese of Pittsburg, p. 40.
[4] Ibid., p. 483.
[5] Ibid., p. 485.

of Catholic education throughout Pennsylvania. They opened a school at Harrisburg, in 1828; at McSherrystown, in 1830; at Pottsville in 1836, and two years later they took charge of the orphan asylum at Pittsburg.[1]

At Wilmington (Del.), an academy for boys was opened by the Rev. P. Reilly, about the year 1837.[2] A primary Catholic school undoubtedly existed in Wilmington long before this date.

RESULTS

Although much progress had been made, the condition of Catholic education in the diocese at the close of this period was, on the whole, unsatisfactory. Outside of the seminary, there was no provision for higher education. In Philadelphia, the schools of the Sisters of Charity provided for the education of girls, especially of the poorer classes; but little had been done for the Catholic education of boys, and only a small number, comparatively, attended the catechism classes on Sundays.[3] Catholic boys obtained their education in the public schools,[4] and the public schools, as Bishop Kenrick said, were "everywhere conducted in a way to leave the children without any religious impression, or to impress them with sectarian views."[5]   It was with good reason that Bishop Kenrick described Catholic education in the diocese, and especially in

[1]Lambing, op. cit.
[2]Shea, vol. iii, p. 561.
[3]Bishop Barron, at Philadelphia, to Dr. Cullen, Oct. 7, 1839.
[4]Ibid.
[5]Bishop Kenrick to Dr. Cullen, Mar. 2, 1843, Rec. Amer. Cath. Hist. Soc., vol. vii, p. 309.

Philadelphia, as being "in a sad condition." He had long endeavored to obtain Christian Brothers from Europe to open boys' schools, but without success.[1]

DIOCESE OF NEW YORK

THE MEN AND THE PERIOD

When the diocese of New York was created in 1808, New York had but one Catholic church, St. Peter's, and to this was attached a parochial school. The Catholic population of the city was estimated at 14,000, chiefly Irish.[2] The newly appointed bishop, the Rt. Rev. Luke Concanen, who was in Rome at the time, did not live to reach his see. In the meantime, from 1808 to 1815, Father Anthony Kohlmann, S.J., acted as administrator. Two other bishops occupied the see during the period we are considering, Bishop Connolly, 1815-1825, and Bishop John Dubois, 1829-1842. The latter was the founder of Mt. St. Mary's College, Emmittsburg; he had had a hand in shaping the early growth of the Sisters of Charity; and, at the head of the diocese of New York, as in the back-woods settlements of Maryland, he labored to build up Catholic educational institutions of every class, in the belief that the development of Catholic education was of vital necessity for the growing Church, thinking "the catechizing of the young a more important matter than preaching to the grown."[3] Father Kohlmann was a man of the

[1] Ibid., Letter of Bishop Kenrick to Superior of Christian Brothers, July 3, 1851.
[2] Shea, vol. iii. p. 162.
[3] McCaffrey, Discourse on the Rt. Rev. John Dubois, p. 13.

same stamp—learned, pious, zealous, instinct with
the spirit of the great educational body to which
he belonged. Under his vigorous administration,
New York City, into which an ever-increasing
stream of Catholic emigration was pouring, soon
rivaled Baltimore and Philadelphia in the number
of its Catholic schools, as well as in the educational
influence it exerted. Bishop Connolly was an
Irish Dominican, who also labored earnestly to
build up Catholic schools. Another man whose influence in this direction was very great was the Rev.
John Power, who came to New York from Ireland
in 1819, and was appointed pastor of St. Peter's.
He was administrator of the diocese for a year,
after the death of Bishop Connolly, and both then
and for many years thereafter, his best efforts
were largely devoted to the work of the development of Catholic education.

NEW YORK LITERARY INSTITUTION

Father Kohlmann planned the establishment of
a Catholic college in New York, and while pastor
of St. Peter's, in 1809, he began the work, with
the aid of the Rev. Benedict Fenwick, S.J., and
four Jesuit scholastics. Writing July 6 of that
year, he was able to report that "about thirty-five
of the most respectable children of the city, both
Catholic and of all other persuasions, among
whom four are boarding at our house," were in
attendance at the New York Literary Institution,
as the college was called. The next year, the
school was removed out into the country, to the site
of the present cathedral on Fifth Avenue, and, at

the same time, it appears to have changed its character from a day to a boarding-school. By 1813 there were seventy-four boarders. In November of that year, however, the Jesuits abandoned the enterprise, owing to the difficulty of supplying the institution with teachers, and other causes. The school was turned over to the Trappists, but it did not last long afterward.[1]

ST. PETER'S SCHOOL

St. Peter's School at this time appears to have been in a flourishing condition. A committee appointed by the trustees visited it every month, and in 1810 the minutes of the board-meetings state that the salary of the master, Mr. James Moffatt, in consideration of his good work, was raised to $400 per annum.[2] In 1818, this school adopted the Lancasterian system of teaching, and in December of that year it was visited by Lancaster himself, who was then in this country.

URSULINE SCHOOL

Father Kohlmann was anxious to obtain a religious community of women to provide especially for the education of girls, and through the influence of his Order in Ireland, he secured a colony of Ursuline Nuns from the famous Blackrock Convent, Cork, who arrived April 7, 1812. There were three in the party, Mother Mary Ann Fagan, with Sisters Frances de Chantal Walsh and Mary

[1] Woodstock Letters, vol. iv, p. 143; Shea, vol. iii, pp. 163, 165; De Courcy, op. cit., p. 366.
[2] Hist. Records and Studies, vol. iii, part i, Jan., 1903.

Paul Baldwin.[1]   An academy was opened, and also a free school.   An orphan asylum was also included in the plans of the administrator; but, unfortunately, the Sisters became discouraged, owing chiefly to their failure to obtain novices, and in the spring of 1815, they returned to Ireland.[2] The attempt to found an orphan asylum met with scarcely better results, the Trappist monks who, returning from the west, had been induced to take charge of this, soon growing tired of the work and leaving for France about the time of the departure of the Ursulines.[3]

ST. PATRICK'S SCHOOL

Such was the situation when Bishop Connolly arrived toward the end of the year 1815.   Meanwhile, a second Catholic church, St. Patrick's Cathedral, had been erected, and dedicated before the new bishop arrived.   The church stood on a large plot of ground between Broadway and the Bowery Road, at what was then the upper extremity of the city.   Here, in the basement of the newly built edifice, Bishop Connolly, soon after his arrival, founded the second permanent parish school in New York City.   The school was for both boys and girls, and was taught at first by secular teachers.   The number of pupils soon amounted to 500.[4]   A separate school-building was erected on Mulberry Street, near the cathedral, in 1825.[5]

[1]Shea, vol. iii, p. 164.
[2]Ibid.
[3]Ibid.
[4]Considine, Brief Chron. Account, p. 11.
[5]Ibid.

SISTERS OF CHARITY

Bishop Connolly succeeded in inducing the Sisters of Charity, of Emmittsburg, to come and take charge of the orphan asylum, four Sisters arriving in August, 1817, with Sister Rose White at their head.[1] Their first home was in a small wooden building on Prince Street, near the cathedral. They began with five orphans, but the next year they had twenty-eight.[2] In connection with the asylum, there was also a pay school. Three years later, another Sister arrived, and a free school was established, also in connection with the asylum. In 1822 two more Sisters came, and another institution, known as the Lancasterian School, was opened.[3]

STATISTICS

The Laity's Directory for the year 1822 gives the Catholic population of the diocese as about 20,000. There were only eight priests. The parish schools attached to St. Peter's and the cathedral were supported partly by the funds of the State, and partly by moneys raised twice a year by the two congregations. Outside of the city of New York, there were churches with resident priests at Albany, Utica, Paterson, and Carthage. At the latter place, in the northern part of the State, there was also a school, the church, which had recently been erected, serving also as a schoolhouse.[4]

[1] Emmittsburg Archives.
[2] Shea, vol. iii, p. 180.
[3] Emmittsburg Archives.
[4] Shea, vol. iii, p. 182.

BROOKLYN

The first Catholic school in Brooklyn was opened in 1823, in connection with St. James' Church, the basement being used for the purpose. As an evidence of how fixed in the Catholic mind the idea of education as a function of the Church's work had become at this time, the reference to this event in the parish register may be noted. St. James' was the first church erected by the Catholics of Brooklyn, and the record reads: "August 28, 1823, the church was consecrated by Bishop Connolly, assisted by Rev. Dr. Power." "September 12, 1823, J. Mehaney was appointed schoolmaster and sexton."[1]

DR. POWER

During his administration of the diocese, Dr. Power, in 1826, erected a large three-story brick building on Prince Street, for the orphan asylum and school of the Sisters of Charity, whose original quarters had become entirely too small. The erection of the new building was a bold undertaking, for the diocese was heavily burdened with debt. The money was partly raised by charity sermons and entertainments. The new building, however, was soon filled, as the Sisters had by this time 150 orphans under their care.[2]

BISHOP DUBOIS' PLANS

Under Bishop Dubois, who was installed on November 5, 1826, the educational development

[1] U. S. Cath. Hist. Mag., vol. i, no. 3, p. 300; also vol. iii, no. 11.
[2] Shea, vol. iii, p. 188.

went steadily on. A new church, St. Mary's, then on Sheriff Street, had been opened some months before, and in the basement of this the pastor, Rev. Hatton Walsh, began a school the following year. The school-teacher was a layman named Thomas Harran, and the pupils were charged $3 a month. By 1829 there were 100 in attendance. The school was closed by the incendiary destruction of St. Mary's in 1831, but was reopened when the new church was built on the present site of Grand and Ridge streets, two years later. The Rev. William Quarter, afterward bishop of Chicago, who was then pastor, introduced the Sisters of Charity, August 21, 1833, and made the school free. Sisters Eugene, Mary, and Pelagia were the first to come, and they took up their residence at 447 Grand Street, the house being soon purchased for them. The school was taught at first in the basement of the church and a small sum charged each pupil; but boarders were received, and a select school conducted, in their own house. The revenue from this select school, which soon had over 70 pupils, sufficed for the support of the Sisters, and the school in the basement was thus made free. Within a few years, the daily attendance at the free school, or free schools, according to the current expression, the boys and girls being in separate departments, amounted to over 500.[1] Later on the Christian Brothers took charge of the boys' school. The first schoolhouse was built in 1855. In 1860 the fine building of the Rutgers Female Institute was purchased and opened as the

[1] McGirr, Life of Rt. Rev. Wm. Quarter, p. 41 seq.

parish school for girls, under the title of St. Mary's Female Institute.[1]

Bishop Dubois' plans comprehended the establishment of a complete system of Catholic educational institutions, embracing a college and seminary, like that of Mt. St. Mary's, Emmittsburg; schools for boys in charge of Brothers; and academies and schools for girls, under the care of Sisters;[2] but he did not succeed in fully carrying out his plans, owing to the poverty of his flock, the vicious trustee-system then prevailing, and other causes. The college and seminary was actually started. A building was erected at Nyack, on the Hudson River, but this was unfortunately destroyed by fire in 1834, just as it was ready for occupancy.[3]

A TEACHING BROTHERHOOD

The bishop's efforts to secure teaching Brothers to establish boys' schools and academies at one time appeared quite promising. In September, 1828, Brother James D. Boylan arrived from Ireland, and, during the following spring, with some associates, who were also said to be religious, he opened two schools—one at 208 William Street, where a school had been conducted by a Mr. McGowan, and the other at 262 Mulberry Street, in a dwelling-house procured for them by the bishop, in the rear of the cathedral.[4] Brother Boylan's

[1]Considine, Brief Chron. Account; Emmittsburg Archives; Shea, vol. iii, p. 498.
[2]Shea, vol. iii, p. 198.
[3]Shea, op. cit., vol. iii, p. 502; De Courcy-Shea, Hist., p. 400; Bayley, Hist. Cath. Ch. in N. Y., p. 116.
[4]Truth Teller, vol. v, p. 103; Shea, p. 203; De Courcy-Shea, p. 400; Bayley, p. 117.

plans contemplated the formation of a teaching community, and the establishment of a *model school* in New York, wherein the young religious might be trained and given practice in teaching before being sent to establish branch schools in other parts of the country. The idea had the bishop's cordial approval, and elicited a ready and generous response from the Catholics of the city. Meetings were held, and considerable money subscribed. An association was formed under the title of "The Education Assistant Society," the members of which were to pay an entrance fee of $1 and monthly dues of 12½ cents. The community took the name of "The Brothers of Charity in the City of New York for the Education of the Poor." Opposition arose, however, due chiefly to doubts cast on the character and motives, as well as the credentials, of Brother Boylan, in respect to which there appeared to be good ground for suspicion. Divisions appeared also within the newly-formed community. Brother Boylan resigned, and, on September 13, 1829, the brotherhood was dissolved.[1]

DR. VARELA

A high-grade boys' school was organized in 1827 or 1828 by the Rev. Felix Varela in connection with Christ Church, in Ann Street, of which he was pastor. Dr. Varela had been a professor in the University in Havana, Cuba, and reached New York shortly before Bishop Dubois. He was a learned theologian, as well as an author of considerable renown, and becoming pastor of Christ Church in 1827, he soon opened a school for boys

[1]Truth Teller, 1829, vol. v, pp. 103, 174, 212, 228, 238, 245, 260.

and girls, with lay teachers, acting himself as principal. In 1829 the girls' school was removed to 25 John Street, two doors from Nassau Street; the boys' school remained at 31 Ann Street. Bernard McEvoy was teacher in the latter, and Miss Manley and Miss Beckwith in the former.[1] Both were pay schools, the charges ranging from $1.50 to $2.50 per quarter, according to the subjects studied, which were "spelling, reading, writing, grammar, orthography, arithmetic, geography, with the use of maps and globes," and, in addition, in the girls' school, music and ornamental work. The schools appear to have been conducted with great success. How long they continued to exist is uncertain, but for several years their advertisement was regularly published in "Truth Teller," the principal Catholic publication in the city at the time.[2] There was a growing demand for Catholic schools of a high grade in New York, as is evident from the private schools which were started from time to time. The famous Irish prosodist, P. S. Casserly, established an advanced school in the city, in 1829, under the title of the "Chrestomathic Institution."[3]

WORK OF THE SISTERS

It was in the field of the elementary school, however, that Bishop Dubois succeeded most effec-

[1] Truth Teller, 1829, vol. v, pp. 103, 160, adv.; Rodriquez, Vida de Don Felix Varela, p. 311 seq.

[2] For further particulars regarding Dr. Varela, see his life by Rodriquez; also the histories of Shea, De Courcy, and Bayley, already cited; also a sketch of his life in the N. Y. Freeman's Journal, Mar. 19, 1853.

[3] For the prospectus of this school, see the Appendix. Casserly's "Latin Prosody" became a standard text-book in Catholic colleges in the U. S.

tually in extending Catholic education. It was to be expected that, in view of the services he had rendered Mother Seton and the community at Emmittsburg, the Sisters would do all they could to co-operate with him in the work of building up Catholic schools in New York. As a matter of fact, the immense impulse given to Catholic education by the development of the Sisters of Charity was nowhere more clearly evidenced than in New York under Bishop Dubois. Catholic emigrants were pouring into the city, new churches were being opened, and there was an urgent demand for Catholic schools. The great drawback was the lack of professional teachers, and the Sisters were opportunely secured to supply this lack. They were, it is true, unable to send teachers enough to take charge of all the schools offered. But they kept constantly adding to the number of their teachers and schools. They set a high standard, and thus, fostering the ideal of Catholic education, their work stimulated the generosity of the whole Catholic body, clergy and laity, for its practical support.

In 1830 the Sisters replaced the lay teachers in charge of the girls' school at St. Peter's.[1] The same year they opened an academy at 261 Mulberry Street, near the cathedral, thus providing a more advanced grade of instruction for girls than was afforded in the existing parish schools.[2] Connected with the orphan asylum, as has been shown, there was both a pay and a free school; and on October 30, 1832, another branch of this institution

[1]Bayley, op. cit., p. 100; Catholic Almanac, 1834.
[2]Considine, op. cit.; De Courcy, p. 407.

was established by the opening of what was known as the half-orphan asylum, for the children of widows and widowers. This school was situated at the corner of Eleventh Street and Seventh Avenue.[1] On August 31, 1833, three Sisters came to open a school in connection with the new St. Joseph's Church, at the corner of Sixth Avenue and Barrow Street.[2] The same year, as already stated, the Sisters took charge of St. Mary's School. By 1834 they thus had three parish schools in New York, St. Peter's, St. Mary's, and St. Joseph's, besides St. Patrick's Academy in Mulberry Street, and the orphan asylum, with its several branch schools, which engaged the services of thirteen Sisters, there being altogether about twenty-five Sisters in the city.[3] In 1838 they took charge of a free school at the cathedral, independent of the orphan asylum.

THROUGHOUT THE STATE

Outside of the city, the Sisters opened St. Mary's School at Albany, in 1828; an asylum in Brooklyn, in 1831, taking charge, at the same time, of the free school which had been organized there in connection with St. James' Church in 1823; and St. John's Asylum and School at Utica in 1834.[4] The last-named institution was due to the generosity of John and Nicholas Devereux, who erected the building at a cost of $10,000.

[1] Bayley, ibid.
[2] Ibid.; Emmittsburg Archives; Shea, vol. iii, p. 503.
[3] Cath. Almanac, 1834.
[4] Emmittsburg Archives; Mulrenan, Brief Hist. Sketch of the Cath. Ch. on Long Island, p. 11.

There being no means for their support, the Sisters some time afterward were about to be withdrawn, when the same gentlemen came forward and engaged to provide $100 annually for each Sister, and to give the trustees $400 annually in support of the establishment.[1]

Father John Nepomucene Neumann, afterward bishop of Philadelphia, who arrived in the diocese in 1836, did much for Catholic schools while in charge of the missions in the Buffalo district. As it was impossible to get teachers for his schools, he became school-teacher himself, spending several days at each mission in turn, during which he would assemble the children and teach them not only catechism, but reading, writing, and arithmetic. He continued this work of teaching school on weekdays for three years, until his brother Wenceslaus came to his aid in September, 1839.[2]

DIOCESE OF BOSTON

EARLY CONDITIONS

When Bishop Cheverus, in 1810, assumed the direction of the new see of Boston, embracing the whole of New England, the Catholics of Boston were reckoned at 720 souls; there were but three Catholic churches in New England—one in Boston, one at Newcastle, Me., and an Indian log chapel in Maine; and besides the bishop, there were but two priests in the diocese. The smallness of the Catholic population, their scat-

[1] U. S. Cath. Hist. Mag., vol. iv, p. 66.
[2] Catholic Standard and Times, Jan. 25, 1908.

tered condition, and their poverty, made the progress of the Church in New England for some years appear very slow. Catholic schools had to wait for the growth of the infant Catholic body, for it was not until toward the end of the second decade of the century that the advance waves of the great tide of Irish emigration swept over New England,[1] and churches and schools began to multiply. In New England, as elsewhere, Catholics instinctively realized the necessity of religious education in the schools; and as soon as church or chapel was built, priests and people turned their attention to the building of parish schools, as though this were a matter of course.[2]

FIRST SCHOOL

The first Catholic school in New England, if the school for the Indians which was in existence at an earlier period be excepted, was the Ursuline school which was opened in Boston in 1820.[3] A brief sketch of this institution will throw light upon the attitude of both Catholics and the non-Catholic public in respect to Catholic schools. The school owed its origin to the Rev. John Thayer, a Yale graduate, subsequently a convert to the Church, and Boston's first native-born priest. One of the great objects of his life was the establishment of a teaching Order of women in Boston. The savings of a lifetime were carefully put aside

[1] McCoy, Hist. of the Cath. Ch. in the Diocese of Springfield, p. 9.
[2] Ibid., p. 13.
[3] Walsh, Hist. Sketch of the Cath. Par. Schools in the Archd. of Boston, p. 1.

and dedicated in advance to this purpose. Seeing no prospect of securing teachers in this country, he went to Ireland in 1811, and after applying in vain to several religious Orders in that country and England, he sought to prepare candidates himself who might form the nucleus of a new community. In Limerick, two young ladies, Mary and Catherine Ryan, who had been educated by the Ursulines, offered themselves for the work. Before they set sail, however, Father Thayer was stricken by death, leaving near $10,000 in care of the pastor in Boston for the carrying out of the design. Judicious investment of this fund resulted in almost doubling it within a few years. Bishop Cheverus was thus enabled to purchase a lot and erect a convent building adjoining his church or cathedral on Franklin Street, Boston; and here on June 16, 1820, the Misses Ryan, who had in the meantime completed their novitiate in the Ursuline convent at Three Rivers, Canada, and had been joined in Boston by two other young ladies from Limerick, took possession of the first convent in New England.[1] Two others soon applied from Boston as lay Sisters. School was opened, and before the end of the year more than 100 girls were in attendance as day-scholars, half in the morning and half in the afternoon. One of the first cares of Bishop Fenwick, when he arrived in the diocese, was the procuring of a larger building, in a more healthful location, for the convent and school, and in July, 1826, the six Sisters moved

---

[1] Shea, op. cit., vol. iii, p. 125 seq.; U. S. Cath. Mag., vol. ii, no. 7, p. 261 seq. (1889); Life of Cardinal de Cheverus, p. 109.

to a newly purchased place in Charlestown, on
Ploughed Hill, west of Bunker Hill. Boarders, as
well as day-pupils, were now received, and by 1834
the boarders numbered fifty-five. The total destruction of this flourishing school, so full of
promise for the future of Catholic education in the
diocese, by a mob of savage bigots on the night of
August 11, 1834, left a dark stain upon the fair
name of Massachusetts; but the event, although
it resulted in the closing of the school and the dis-
solution of the rising community, does not appear
to have retarded much the general development of
Catholic education in the diocese.[1]

BISHOP FENWICK

As a Jesuit, who had founded the New York
Literary Institution, and had been twice president
of Georgetown College, it is not surprising to find
that Bishop Fenwick was occupied from the very
beginning of his administration with the problem
of Catholic education.[2]   Coming to the diocese

[1] For a full account of this event, see Shea, vol. iii, p. 473 seq.,
and the numerous references given there, especially the Jesuit,
vol. v; also Rec. Amer. Cath. Hist. Soc., vol. v, p. 476; The
Burning of the Convent (pamphlet).

[2] The importance Bishop Fenwick attached to Catholic
schools is shown by an anecdote related by Father Stone-
street, S.J., a contemporary. Coming once to Georgetown,
he inquired about the "poor school." Being informed that the
school was discontinued, he spoke of the matter in the church
at Georgetown on the following Sunday, and strongly emphasized the duty of parents in respect to the Christian education
of their children, ending with the practical exhortation: "Up
with the school, up with it!" In response to his eloquence, the
school again sprang into existence, and soon had over 100
pupils.—Discourse on the Rt. Rev. Benedict J. Fenwick, in
St. John's Church, Frederick, 1846, p. 23.

toward the close of 1825, his first educational achievement, after securing the removal of the Ursulines to Charlestown, was to establish a day-school in Boston for boys and girls. This was in 1826.[1] The same year, a seminary was begun in his own house, the bishop himself doing much of the teaching.[2] The cathedral having been enlarged, the basement was prepared for school purposes, and in this a classical department for boys was opened in 1829.[3] There were thus, at this early date, two schools in Boston, besides the seminary and the Charlestown establishment. The classical school in the cathedral was the germ out of which developed Holy Cross College, Worcester, and the cathedral school was practically closed in 1837, when the college was opened at Worcester.[4] In 1829 another Catholic school was established at Charlestown, at a place called Craigie's Point.[5] On May 2, 1832, a project that the bishop had long cherished was realized, when three Sisters of Charity arrived in Boston, to found St. Vincent's Orphan Asylum, on Hamilton Street, near Fort Hill.[6] The first Sisters were Sister Ann Alexis, Sister Blandina, and Sister Loyola. In accordance with their custom, the Sisters took charge also of the free school, and before the middle of May the number of pupils amounted to 250.[7]

[1] Walsh, Hist. Sketch, p. 2.
[2] Shea, op. cit., vol. iii, p. 144.
[3] Ibid., p. 159; Walsh, ibid.
[4] Shea, ibid.
[5] Ibid., pp. 159, 463.
[6] Emmittsburg Archives.
[7] Shea, vol. iii, p. 468; Cath. Almanac, 1838.

OUTSIDE OF BOSTON

Outside of Boston and its immediate vicinity, other schools were rising, too, as the Catholic population increased and parishes grew up. The first of these was a Catholic academy which was opened by Rev. Virgil H. Barber, S.J., a convert to the Faith, in his church at Claremont, N. H., in 1823.[1] This school was probably closed in 1828. The following year, however, Father Barber reopened the Indian school at Old Town on the Penobscot, Me., which was one of his missions.[2] At Hartford, Conn., where the first Catholic church had been opened in 1829, a classical school for boys was started November 2 of the following year. It was held in the basement of the church, and was conducted by a convert named Joseph Bridgen, who was an experienced teacher, the pastor being the Rev. Bernard O'Cavanagh.[3] An elementary school also appears to have been established at Hartford about the same time.[4] Bishop Fenwick was careful to organize Sunday-schools for the Catholic children wherever it was practicable, and the Sunday-school was often the first step toward the establishment of a parochial school. At Salem, a school was organized in 1831

---

[1]Shea, vol. iii, pp. 119, 128, 153; de Goesbriand, Cath. Memoirs and Biog. of Vt. and N. H., pp. 56, 72; O'Donnell, The Diocese of Hartford, p. 124 seq.

[2]Shea, ibid., p. 159; de Goesbriand, op. cit., p. 76.

[3]O'Donnell, op. cit., pp. 3, 186; Religious Cabinet, vol. i, p. 191.

[4]Centennial Celebration of the First Mass in Conn., p. 27. The basement of the church served the purpose of Sunday-school and day-school, printing-office, quarters for the teacher, printer, and missionary.

by Father Wiley, the builder of the first church, the first teacher being a young lady by the name of Miss Sharp.[1]

THE LOWELL PLAN

A chapter of great interest in the history of Catholic education in the United States was opened when the first Catholic school was founded in Lowell, Mass. This was probably in 1823 or 1824, when Irish emigrants were settling there.[2] A room was rented for the school, and an Irish schoolmaster placed in charge, the pupils being charged six cents a week, a not uncommon tuition charge in those days.[3] As yet Lowell had no permanent Catholic pastor or church, and for this reason, probably, the school for several years had only a desultory existence. In the year 1830, however, events took a new turn, for at the annual town meeting held in May, a committee was provided for, "to consider the expediency of establishing a separate school for the benefit of the Irish population."[4] The committee reported favorably, and in April, 1831, it was agreed to appropriate $50 annually, according to the old district plan, for the maintenance of a separate district school for the Catholics. It must be remembered that at this time church and State were united in Massachusetts, and that the State-supported schools were all professedly religious, belonging either to the Congregationalists, the dominant church, or to

[1] Walsh, Origin of the Cath. Church in Salem, p. 101.
[2] Walsh, The Early Irish Cath. Schools of Lowell, p. 7.
[3] Ibid.
[4] Ibid.

other religious bodies. The new provision was thus only the extension˙to the Catholics of the rights enjoyed by the various other churches under the accepted educational policy.

CATHOLIC PUBLIC SCHOOLS

For several years the school went on under this plan, being only indifferently successful, however, chiefly because of the fewness of Catholics and their poverty. Meanwhile, the Catholics had built a church, and˙received as their pastor Father Mahoney, another priest, Father Conelly, soon coming as his assistant. With the steady influx of Irish, two parochial schools had been established before 1835, one under St. Patrick's Church, and another at a place called Chapel Hill. Application was made for public aid for these schools, with the result that, on June 14 and September 14, respectively, of that year, the two schools were formally adopted into the school system of the town, to be thenceforth supported out of the public funds.[1] The terms of the agreement, on the part of the town committee, were as follows:

"1. The instructors must be examined as to their qualifications by the committee, and receive their appointments from them.

"2. The books, exercises, and studies must all be prescribed and regulated by the committee, and no other whatever must be taught or allowed.

"3. These schools must be placed, as respects the examination, inspection, and general supervision of the committee, on precisely the same footing with the other schools of the town."

[1] Walsh, op. cit., p. 10.

On the part of Father Conelly, who represented the Catholic body in the negotiations, the conditions laid down were, that the instructors must be of the Catholic faith, and that the books prescribed should contain no statements unacceptable to Catholics, nor remarks reflecting upon Catholic belief.[1] As a matter of fact, the books in use in the other public schools, when submitted to Father Conelly, were accepted as satisfactory. The schoolrooms or buildings were to be provided for by the Catholics. Nothing was said about religious instruction.

The plan was promptly put in operation, and appeared to work very well. Patrick Collins was appointed teacher of the school at St. Patrick's, at a salary of $450 per annum, as this was a "writing and grammar school." Daniel McIlroy was named as teacher at Chapel Hill. A primary school was also established at each of the two places, in charge of an assistant teacher. In 1838, the two principal schools were consolidated under the name of the "Fifth Grammar School."[2]

In 1837 the school committee reported that the plan had proved "eminently successful," the total attendance that year in the Catholic schools having been 469. The following year, there were three grammar and two primary schools, with a total attendance of 752. In 1844, there were one grammar and five primary schools, and the average attendance was 638.[3] These figures, taken in conjunction with the school committee reports,

[1] Ibid., p. 9.
[2] Ibid., p. 10.
[3] Ibid., p. 12.

prove the success of the plan. The problem of the Catholic school, in so far as its relation to the State was concerned, appeared to have been satisfactorily solved. Had the plan adopted been continued, the Lowell system would probably have been copied elsewhere, and might eventually have come to prevail generally throughout the United States, as Massachusetts has had a predominant influence in shaping the growth of educational sentiment and policy throughout the country.

The arrangement, however, did not last, being abrogated by the town in the year 1852, after sixteen years of trial, although it was not because of failure to achieve the educational results hoped for. As late as 1850, Secretary Sears, of the State Board of Education, after a visit to the principal Catholic school in Lowell, wrote: "I have seen no school of the kind to equal it in all my visits to schools."[1] The immediate occasion which led to the abrogation of the agreement was the bringing of the Sisters of Notre Dame to St. Patrick's Parish, in 1852, to take charge of a free school for girls. The tide of religious bigotry known as the Know-Nothing movement was rising high, and the bringing in of the Sisters had the effect of focalizing the anti-Catholic sentiment in Lowell. Catholics claimed for the Sisters' school the same right to public support, under the existing agreement, as their other schools enjoyed. It is clear that, back of the action of the pastor of St. Patrick's, in introducing the Sisters, there had existed for some time a feeling of dissatisfaction among Catholics about the religious instruction and

[1] Walsh, op. cit., p. 13.

training given in their schools. There had been trouble in 1844 and in 1848, because of the fact that in nine schoolrooms there were only four Catholic teachers.[1] This was probably due mainly to the difficulty of securing competent Catholic teachers for the schools, rather than to any desire on the part of the education board to discriminate against Catholics. Nevertheless, the fundamental purpose of the Catholic school was thus being neglected, and it was only natural that Catholics should seek to remedy the difficulty by the introduction of professional religious teachers. Looked at in a broader light, the incident evinces the practical superiority of the religious over the lay or secular Catholic teacher in the parish school, and it was typical of a great movement which was in progress throughout the country at the time the Sisters came to Lowell, and which involved the replacement of secular teachers in Catholic schools by members of the teaching Orders.

BISHOP FENWICK'S VIEWS

It is of interest to note the views of Bishop Fenwick on the questions raised by the Lowell experiment, particularly in respect to religious instruction in school, and the right of Catholic schools to support out of the public taxes. The bishop's views on these subjects are expressed very clearly in a letter he wrote to a Catholic gentleman in Lowell shortly before the first school-agreement was arrived at. The letter is dated March 26, 1831:

"I see no impropriety in the Catholic school in

[1] Walsh, op. cit., p. 14.

your town receiving aid from the school fund,
especially if the Catholics of Lowell have contributed their portion, by the payment of taxes or
otherwise, toward the support of said fund.   Common justice would entitle them to something out of
it, for the payment of their Master.   But I really
do not understand how, in this liberal country, it
can be made a condition to their receiving anything,
that they, the Catholics, shall be in that case de-
barred from having a Catholic teacher, learning
out of Catholic books, and being taught the Catechism of the Catholic Church.   We can never
accept such terms. . . . I would not give a straw
for that species of education which is not accompanied with and based upon religion."[1]

DIOCESE OF CHARLESTON (S. C.)

BISHOP ENGLAND

The diocese of Charleston was formed in 1820,
and comprised the States of South Carolina, North
Carolina, and Georgia.   The Rt. Rev. John England, who was named as the first bishop, was a distinguished Irish priest, who had been president and
professor at St. Mary's Diocesan College, in the
county of Cork.   He was a vigorous writer, deeply
versed in classical as well as theological knowledge,
and an eloquent speaker.   His fame as an orator
was such that, notwithstanding the prevailing prejudice against the Catholic religion, he was accorded the privilege, several years after his arrival,
of addressing the Congress of the United States in
the Hall of Representatives.   Bishop England was

[1] Walsh, op. cit., p. 8.

an earnest advocate of Catholic educational institutions of every kind. His voice was frequently heard in their behalf, and the "United States Catholic Miscellany," the first Catholic newspaper published in the country, which he founded in 1822, exercised a potent influence in shaping Catholic opinion in regard to education. He took a prominent part in the proceedings of the First Provincial Council of Baltimore, in which the position of the Church in America in respect to the school question was authoritatively fixed, and in his own infant diocese he struggled heroically against difficulties of every kind to rear an educational system that should comprise a seminary, a college, and elementary schools for both boys and girls. His educational efforts, it is true, met with only partial success, but this was due to causes which were altogether beyond his control. The stream of emigration was westward, and the Church in the south continued to be poor and weak. The bishop, however, accomplished much, and what he effected for education in South Carolina had an important influence throughout the rest of the United States.

THE "CLASSICAL SEMINARY"

When Bishop England reached Charleston, he found only two priests and two occupied churches in the whole of his vast diocese.[1] One of his first acts was the foundation of "The Philosophical and Classical Seminary of Charleston," an institution which was opened on January 8, 1822, and upon which the bishop based the brightest hopes

[1] Works of the Rt. Rev. John England, vol. iii, p. 254.

for the future of Catholic higher education in the south.[1]   Although the college which had previously existed in Charleston had been closed for lack of support, the new academy sprang at once into popularity, and counted sixty-three students, only twelve of whom were Catholics.   The number of students soon rose to 130.[2]   A seminary for the education of candidates to the priesthood was opened about the same time.   The bishop himself was president of the two institutions, and in the beginning did most of the teaching besides, although he was gradually enabled to employ for the work of teaching in the academy the more advanced of the candidates for Holy Orders.   The popularity of the academy, however, did not last long.   The spirit of religious prejudice was aroused, and as the result of the active hostility of leading members of the other denominations, the non-Catholic students were withdrawn.   Although the attendance was thus greatly reduced, and the institution ceased to be paying, it continued to be maintained, together with the seminary, and to bear a high reputation among the educational institutions of the State.[3]

SISTERS OF MERCY

Bishop England's plans for the development of schools and academies were more difficult of realization, but in 1830 three pious ladies of Baltimore, Misses Mary and Honora O'Gorman and Teresa Barry, natives of Cork, proposed to devote

[1] England, op. cit., p. 255; Shea, op. cit., vol. iii, p. 318.
[2] Shea, loc. cit.
[3] Works of Bishop England, vol. iii, p. 256; Shea, loc. cit.

themselves to educational and charitable work in his diocese, and on December 8 of that year they took their vows, being organized as a religious community under the name of Sisters of Our Lady of Mercy. Another lady, Miss Julia Datty, a native of San Domingo, soon joined them. The Sisters opened an academy and a school for girls, as well as an orphan asylum. Although their life was a struggle for existence for a number of years, the new sisterhood increased in numbers, there being ten members in 1832, and twenty-one by 1844. In the course of time they extended their work to North Carolina, Georgia, and Alabama.[1]

Another community, Les Dames de la Retraite, also came to Charleston about this time, and began an academy. These Sisters were French, and had opened an academy in Philadelphia; but their lack of English and other circumstances proved an obstacle to the success of their work, and their stay in the diocese was only temporary.[2]

THE URSULINES

In 1834, a third sisterhood, the Ursulines, from the Blackrock Convent, Cork, came to engage in the work of education in the diocese. The bishop counted much upon the acquisition of these devoted and experienced teachers. There were four

[1] Cath. Directory, 1906; Works of Bishop England, vol. iii, p. 261; Shea, op. cit., p. 580; U. S. Cath. Mag., vol. iii, p. 743; vol. v, pp. 52, 168; Amer. Cath. Hist. Res., vol. x, p. 44; O'Connell, Catholicity in the Carolinas and Georgia, p. 64. The Sisters still conduct an academy and several schools in the city of Charleston, besides educational institutions in other places.

[2] Cath. Almanac, 1834; Shea, p. 588.

in the party, Mother Mary Charles Maloney, Sister Marie Borgia McCarthy, Antonia Hughes, and Miss H. Woulfe, a postulant.[1] For their passage-money and part of the cost of their house in Charleston, the bishop was indebted to the Leopoldine Association in Vienna.[2] The legislature at first refused to charter the Ursuline school; some of the bishop's friends, however, procured him an invitation to preach to the legislators, and on the day following the sermon the bill was passed without division.[3] The Sisters' house adjoined the cathedral on Broad Street, and here they at once opened an academy, their house and garden costing about $12,000.[4]

COLORED SCHOOL

Early in 1835, a school was opened in Charleston for free colored Catholic children. It was quickly filled; but the attempt, though so full of promise for the elevation of the colored race in the diocese, was far in advance of the educational ideas which held sway in the South at the time; a storm of opposition arose, and, in view of threatening legislation, the bishop regretfully closed the school.[5] The number of Catholics in Charleston about this time was estimated at 5,000; in the whole diocese the number was only 11,000, in a population of nearly 2,000,000.[6]

[1] Shea, loc. cit.
[2] Ibid., p. 585.
[3] Religious Cabinet, July, 1842, p. 375.
[4] Rec. Amer. Cath. Hist. Soc., vol. viii, pp. 203, 221; Shea, vol. iii, p. 588.
[5] Works of Bishop England, vol. iv, p. 354.
[6] Shea, p. 586.

BISHOP ENGLAND'S PLANS

Bishop England was not less anxious to provide for the Catholic education of boys. For this purpose he was hoping to secure a community of teaching Brothers, or to establish a new one in the diocese. The breadth of his educational plans may be gaged from the following words, addressed to the Fifteenth Convention of the Church in South Carolina, November 25, 1838:

"In order to effect the religious education of the children properly, nothing could be more useful than to have schools in which the sciences may be taught and the lower branches of education attended to, at the same time that the children belonging to our congregations could therein receive the proper religious instruction. I have made efforts for this purpose at different times, hitherto with but little success as regards the male department. You will not need any reasoning from me to convince you of its necessity. The only question is, respecting its practicability, and every day more urgently presses upon us the necessity of its consideration. . . . The neglect of proper education for our male children is too serious an evil to permit our longer overlooking it."[1]

It was very difficult, however, to secure teaching Brothers in those days, and the extreme poverty of the diocese often made impossible the carrying out of Bishop England's large educational plans. He did not live to see the realization of this project, expiring in 1842, at the age of 56.

[1] Works of Bishop England, vol. iv, p. 374.

ALABAMA AND FLORIDA

BISHOP PORTIER

Rev. Michael Portier, who was appointed vicar-apostolic of the newly created vicariate of Alabama and the Floridas in 1826, was a native of France, who had come to this country some ten years earlier, with Bishop Dubourg. At the time of his appointment, he was at the head of a college which he had founded in the old Ursuline Convent in New Orleans.[1] Soon after his arrival in Mobile, the vicar-apostolic framed plans for the foundation of an institution of higher education for the scattered Catholics of his diocese, which resulted, about the first of May, 1830, in the establishment of Spring Hill College and Seminary.[2] Three years later, Bishop Portier secured a colony of Visitation Nuns from Georgetown, who opened an academy at Summerville, three miles from Mobile. Although the number of his flock at this time was only about 8,000, out of a population of 350,-000, the bishop was eager to establish Catholic schools. With the restoration of the church at Pensacola, he opened a school for boys, and also re-established the boys' school at the ancient Catholic settlement of St. Augustine.[3] Previous to the cession of Florida to the United States in 1819, a free school, supported by the King of Spain, had existed from 1785 at St. Augustine, being taught by the Franciscan friars. Contrary to the pro-

[1]Shea, vol. iii, p. 403.
[2]"Spring Hill College," 1830-1905, p. 11.
[3]Shea, op. cit., p. 699.

visions of the treaty of cession with Spain, the schoolhouse, together with other parochial property there, was taken possession of by the United States Government.[1] Les Dames de la Retraite also came to the diocese, and about 1838 attempted to establish an academy in Mobile, but they soon removed to Pensacola.[2] St. Mary's orphan asylum and free school, Mobile, was begun by the Sisters of Charity in 1841, four Sisters coming for this purpose from Emmittsburg.[3] Shortly before this a day-school for boys was also opened by the bishop in Mobile.[4]

LOUISIANA AND ST. LOUIS

BISHOP DUBOURG

When Rev. William Dubourg was appointed to the see of New Orleans, August 18, 1812, that diocese comprised, in addition to Louisiana proper, Mississippi, and Alabama, the whole of the vast territory lying west of the Mississippi River and included in the old French province of Louisiana. Catholic settlements were few and small, outside of New Orleans, and the whole diocese contained only about ten priests.[5] At the time of his appointment, Father Dubourg was at the head of St. Mary's College, Baltimore. As president of Georgetown College, founder and president of St. Mary's College, and the active friend and adviser

[1]Amer. Cath. Hist. Res., vol. xiii, p. 15.
[2]Shea, p. 701.
[3]Emmittsburg Archives.
[4]Catholic Almanac for 1840.
[5]Shea, History, vol. iii, p. 356.

of Mother Seton in the founding of the Sisters of Charity, this brilliant Sulpician priest had exercised a large influence in the development of Catholic education in the east, and some of the first measures he took in meeting the responsibilities that were now thrust upon him showed that he counted on education, more than upon anything else, to secure the permanent growth and progress of the Church in his new field of labor. Proceeding to Europe in 1815, he spent two years there, being occupied chiefly in gathering and organizing resources for the development of his diocese. The formation of the celebrated "Association for the Propagation of the Faith" was partly due to his efforts in France at this time.[1] Besides collecting money and church ornaments, he busied himself in securing priests for his churches, and teachers for his projected seminaries, colleges, and schools. The result was that, when he embarked at Bordeaux, June 28, 1817, he had engaged some fifty-three persons for work in his diocese—priests, seminarians, Brothers, and Sisters, many of whom accompanied him on his return. Among these were representatives of four religious teaching Orders, the Lazarists, or Congregation of the Mission, founded by St. Vincent de Paul; the Brothers of the Christian Schools, the Ladies of the Sacred Heart, and the Ursulines. The colony of Ursulines was destined for the Ursuline Convent, New Orleans, and consisted of nine young ladies whom the bishop had secured in his journeys through France.[2]

[1]Clarke, Lives of Deceased Bishops, vol. i, p. 228.
[2]Shea, vol. iii, p. 362; Clarke, op. cit., p. 231.

CONDITION OF THE DIOCESE

At this time, the number of Catholics, as indeed the total number of inhabitants, in the immense region under the jurisdiction of Bishop Dubourg, was very small. Churches also were few. In New Orleans itself there was only one, that of St. Louis, besides the little frame chapel for English-speaking Catholics, and the chapel attached to the Ursuline Convent.[1] St. Louis was a town of about 4,000 inhabitants, most of whom were Catholics. It contained, however, but one poor frame chapel, with not even a resident priest, and was visited occasionally from Florissant. In the whole of Upper Louisiana, comprising the western part of Illinois, besides all the territory to the west and northwest of Illinois across the Mississippi, there were only seven small wooden chapels, four priests, and about 8,000 Catholics.[2] Probably the only permanent Catholic schools in the diocese were the Ursuline establishment in New Orleans and the school at St. Louis.

EDUCATIONAL CONDITIONS

Such were, in bare outline, the conditions which Bishop Dubourg had to face in his educational work. Difficulties of a different kind which he had to contend against, such as the schismatical attitude of the clergy in New Orleans, led by the notorious Father Sedilla, may be passed over here. It was

[1] Sketches of the Life of the Very Rev. Felix de Andreis, edition of 1861, p. 235.
[2] Ibid., p. 237.

to this remote western wilderness that he brought bands of devoted teachers, to set up schools and colleges alongside of the rough log churches that existed or that were soon to be built. A striking characteristic of the growth of all the great Catholic educational institutions and societies is, that they were cradled in the most abject poverty. Strong in faith, and inspired by their own loftiness of purpose, their founders struggled on under a leaden load of debt, striving to repair as best they could the loss of subjects occasioned by hardship or disease, until the increase of the Catholic population and the resulting increase of pupils lifted them above the hard necessity of laboring in order simply to continue to exist. This was the case with the teaching Orders which were now brought to the trans-Mississippi region. The little colonies which came with Bishop Dubourg were destined to grow into great organizations, to spread over the greater part of the United States, and to influence powerfully the movement for Catholic education. But for many years they were, like a newly planted tree, occupied chiefly in fastening their roots in the soil. Whatever may be the judgment of history with regard to the qualifications of Bishop Dubourg, from the standpoint of purely ecclesiastical administration, for the episcopal office, there can be no doubt that he stands pre-eminent among the great bishops of his day as a master of educational organization. At a time when the bishops in the east were sorely handicapped in the carrying out of their educational plans by the lack of efficient teachers, he had, by a happy stroke, supplied his diocese with the nuclei of organizations which were able not only to supply it with sufficient teachers for its present and future needs, but also to help in the solution of the same problem in many other parts of the country.

THE LAZARISTS AND BISHOP ROSATTI

The party of Lazarists consisted of nine persons, at the head of whom was the Rev. Felix de Andreis, as Superior; another member of the band was Rev. Joseph Rosatti, who subsequently became the first bishop of St. Louis.[1] The party arrived at Baltimore, July 26, 1816, whence they proceeded to Bardstown, Ky., to await the arrival of Bishop Dubourg. Arriving at St. Louis, October 17, 1817, the Lazarists, in the spring of the following year, began the erection of a church and seminary for their own society at the Barrens, in Perry County, Father Rosatti being placed in charge.[2] Meanwhile, Father de Andreis remained at St. Louis, where the bishop soon after his arrival, December 29, 1817, had founded a seminary for clerical students as well as a college for seculars, devoting part of his own house to the purpose.[3] Father de Andreis was made director of both these establishments, and most of the burden of teaching in the beginning fell upon him. The severity of the strain to which he and his fellow-laborers were subjected is revealed in a letter written at the time. "I assure you," he wrote, "that when I think of Italy, it appears to me an

[1] Sketches of the Life of Very Rev. Felix de Andreis, p. 80 seq.; Shea, vol. iii, p. 361.
[2] Sketches, p. 163.
[3] Sketches, pp. 137, 141, 153, 164.

earthly paradise, in comparison with America. . . .
I know that were it not for the glory of God and
the salvation of souls, I would not stay where I am
for all the gold in the world."[1]   He died, a victim
to his ardent zeal, October 15, 1820.   In spite of
the death of Father de Andreis, the college in St.
Louis was kept up.   The two-story brick building
erected for it in 1820 stood near the site of the old
log church, and here, under the direction of Father
Neil, the institution continued to struggle bravely
for existence until 1826, when it was finally discontinued.[2]

Bishop Dubourg early turned his attention to the
establishment of parochial schools.   In 1819 he
opened a school in the Alvarez residence, a one-
story stone house he had rented for the purpose,
which stood on the north side of Market Street,
between Second and Third streets.

In 1823, a college and preparatory school was
begun at the Barrens; it was continued there until
1842, when it was transferred to Cape Girardeau,
Mo., the theological seminary at the Barrens being
transferred the same year to St. Louis.[3]   St.
Mary's College and Seminary at the Barrens, as
the institution was called up to the time of this
transfer, was a great boon to the Church in the
west, furnishing a constantly increasing supply of
educated and zealous priests, who labored to build
up Catholic schools and educational institutions of

---

[1] Sketches, p. 153.
[2] Hill, Hist. Sk. of St. Louis Univ., p. 5; Sketches of V. Rev.
F. de Andreis, p. 268; Deuther, Life and Times of the Rt. Rev.
John Timon, p. 28; Clarke, Lives of Deceased Bishops, vol. i,
p. 358 seq.
[3] Sketches, p. 259 seq.

every kind. From the Barrens, the educational work of the Lazarists gradually extended to other parts of the country. In 1837, the Seminary of La Fourche was established in Lower Louisiana.[1] Beginning with the year 1841, their work was extended to the States farther east, colleges and seminaries being founded, as the membership of the Order increased. Each of these institutions, in turn, exercised a far-reaching influence in support of the movement for the establishment of elementary schools. The Lazarists, like the other Orders of priests, did not engage in parochial school work directly, their field being that of higher education. But their influence, like that of the Jesuits and other religious Orders, was always favorable to the establishment of schools. Around the college or the seminary of the religious Order, there usually grew up a school or a cluster of schools of various kinds, whose origin is traceable in some way to the institution of higher grade. An influence like that which Georgetown and St. Mary's Seminary had upon the development of Catholic elementary education in the east was exerted by the colleges of the Lazarists, the Jesuits, and other religious Orders of priests upon the development of schools in the west.

When the diocese of Louisiana was practically divided in 1823, Bishop Dubourg found a worthy successor, for the upper portion, in the Rev. Joseph Rosatti, the head of the seminary and college at the Barrens, who had become Superior of the Lazarists on the death of Father de Andreis. Bishop Rosatti was an experienced educator as well as an able administrator. Possessing all his pre-

[1] Ibid., p. 262.

decessor's enthusiasm for the cause of Christian education, he was able, thanks to the rising tide of emigration, to carry out the broad plans of Bishop Dubourg more successfully than that prelate had been able to do himself, and he shared fully the conviction of his predecessor, that the progress of Catholic education would be the measure of the permanent progress of the Church in the United States.

THE JESUITS

In the year 1823, Bishop Dubourg secured a band of Jesuits from Maryland, at the head of which was the active and zealous Father Van Quickenborne. The Jesuits settled at Florissant, where, two years later, Father Van Quickenborne opened a school for Indian boys.[1]   In 1828, there were about fifteen white pupils, from St. Louis and elsewhere, in the "Indian Seminary," as it was called, and this fact, together with the discontinuance of the college in St. Louis in 1826, offered an opportunity to the Jesuits to open an institution of higher education there. With the approval and co-operation of Bishop Rosatti, a building was begun in 1828, and classes were opened November 2 of the following year.[2]   Such was the origin of St. Louis University, the first permanent educational institution established by the Jesuits beyond the Mississippi, and which has continued to be the center of all their educational and missionary work in that region. In the year 1837, St.

[1] Shea, vol. iii, pp. 88, 385; Hill, Sketch of St. Louis Univ., p. 34.
[2] Hill, Hist. Sk. St. Louis Univ., p. 27 seq.

Charles College was founded by the Jesuits at Grand Couteau, in Lower Louisiana.[1]

COLLEGE IN NEW ORLEANS

By the year 1820, a college had been established at New Orleans, by Father Martial,[2] and about the same time a school for boys was opened in the city by the Rev. Michael Portier. Father Portier had charge of the school himself, but was assisted by pupil-teachers, according to the system of Lancaster, which was then so popular in the country. The Laity's Directory refers to it as a "numerous Lancasterian school."[3] The college was at first located outside the city, on property belonging to the Ursulines, upon which, in 1824, they erected their new convent and academy.[4] When the Ursulines moved to the new site, the college was transferred to the city, the old Ursuline building becoming the bishop's residence, and part of it being used for the college. The institution was conducted by the priests of the cathedral, who were assisted by secular professors. The Rev. Michael Portier was at the head of the college when he was made vicar-apostolic of Alabama and the Floridas, in 1826, and upon his departure Father Martial again assumed charge.[5] A school for boys was also established at St. Gabriel's, in 1827, by the pastor, the Rev. Eugene Michaud.[6] Within a few years, three Catholic institutions of higher educa-

[1]Sketches of V. Rev. F. de Andreis, p. 239.
[2]Shea, p. 371.
[3]Laity's Directory for 1822, p. 113.
[4]Shea, p. 383.
[5]Biog. Sketch of Bishop Dubourg, Cath. Almanac for 1839, pp. 63, 64.
[6]Shea, vol. iii, p. 397.

tion for the laity had thus been established in the diocese.

LADIES OF THE SACRED HEART

While in France, Bishop Dubourg had, as has been stated, secured a band of the Ladies of the Sacred Heart, consisting of Madame Philippine Duchesne, as Superioress, Mesdames Berthold and Audé, and two lay Sisters.[1]   The Sisters arrived at St. Louis in August, 1818, and began their work by opening an academy and parochial school at the Catholic settlement of St. Charles.   They soon removed, however, to Florissant or St. Ferdinand, a village fifteen miles north of St. Louis, where, by 1821, they had "a novitiate, with five novices and several postulants, a thriving seminary for the daughters of the wealthy of this and the neighboring States, and a day-school for girls of the poorer class."[2]   Toward the close of the same year, a party of four of these Sisters, under Madame Audé as Superioress, proceeded south to Grand Couteau (Opelousas), within the present State of Louisiana, where they founded an academy, free school, and orphan asylum.   A generous convert, Mrs. Mary Smith, carrying out the wish of her deceased husband, donated 400 arpents of land for the purpose, to which both clergy and laity of the district also generously contributed.   The school and convent building was of brick, ninety-five feet long by sixty in width.[3]   Soon afterward, another academy

[1] Shea, vol. iii, p. 366.
[2] Laity's Directory for 1822.
[3] Laity's Directory for 1822; Rec. Amer. Cath. Hist. Soc., vol. ix, p. 343; Shea, p. 367; De Sennegy, Une Paroisse Louisianaise, p. 46.

and school was opened by the same Order at St. Michael's, in the same State.[1] In 1834 this latter institution counted 115 young ladies, with twenty-three Sisters; while the academy at Grand Couteau had eighty young ladies, with fifteen Sisters.[2] The Sisters also established an academy and school in the city of St. Louis, in 1835, on land donated for the purpose by Judge Mullanphy.[3] The academy and school at St. Charles was also re-established, and in 1838 counted twenty-five boarders and thirty day-pupils, with six Sisters.[4] At this time, then, the Order had three academies and the same number of schools in Missouri, with two of each in the State of Louisiana. From these two States, the work of the Order was in time extended to Philadelphia, New York, and other sections of the country, the sisterhood becoming in the course of time one of the strongest and most influential of the many Catholic religious teaching organizations in America. The work of the Sisters has been mainly in the field of secondary education; they have continued to conduct parochial schools, but the number of these has been inferior to the number of their academies.

SISTERS OF LORETTO

By direction of Bishop Dubourg, Father Rosatti, in 1823, applied to the Rev. Charles Nerinckx, Superior of the Loretto sisterhood in

[1]Sketches of the V. Rev. Felix de Andreis, p. 235.
[2]Catholic Almanac for 1834. Both of these institutions are still in existence, and conducted by the religious of the Sacred Heart.
[3]Sketches, p. 239.
[4]Cath. Almanac for 1838.

Kentucky, for a colony of Sisters to establish an academy and school for girls near the seminary at the Barrens. In May of the same year, twelve Sisters, under Mother Benedicta Fenwick, arrived, after a voyage full of hardship and peril, and soon were enabled to begin a school and an orphanage in their log house. The institution, which was called Bethlehem, was transferred to Cape Girardeau in 1838. St. Joseph's parochial school was opened by these Sisters in the Catholic settlement of Apple Creek, Perry County, in 1831; but the new establishment was transferred to New Madrid before the close of the year, where the Sisters continued their work until 1837. St. Michael's academy and school was organized at Fredericktown, in 1832, with six Sisters. This institution was closed in 1836.[1]

SISTERS OF CHARITY

The Sisters of Charity, of Emmittsburg, commenced their work in the diocese by opening a hospital in St. Louis in the year 1827. An orphan asylum and day-school was later established, the first building being a small frame house, which was afterward changed for a larger building near the cathedral.[2]

VISITATION SISTERS

In 1833 Bishop Rosatti was able to establish an academy and school in that portion of his dio-

[1] Archives of the Loretto Sisterhood; Cath. Almanac, 1833; Hill, Hist. Sk. St. Louis Univ., p. 4; Shea, History, vol. iii, p. 382.
[2] Sketches of V. Rev. F. de Andreis, p. 240; Ann. Prop. de la Foi, vol. iii, p. 539.

cese which lay east of the Mississippi and comprised the western part of Illinois. For this purpose, a band of Visitation nuns were brought from Georgetown, the names of these pioneer Visitandines in the west being Mother Agnes Brent, Sister Genevieve King, Sister Josephine Barber, Sister Helen Flanigan, Sister Gonzaga Jones, Sister Isabella King, Sister Ambrose Cooper, and Sister Rose Murry. The party left Georgetown April 17, 1833, and arrived at Kaskaskia on May 3, the long journey being made by stage to Pittsburg, and thence by boat down the Ohio and Mississippi.[1] School had been taught at intervals under the French régime in both Kaskaskia and Cahokia,[2] but at this time there was no educational provision for the children of either place, although Kaskaskia counted 150 families. The Sisters were gladly received by the inhabitants, and were soon enabled to begin to teach, the old Kaskaskia Hotel building being made to serve as both convent and school. An academic course was organized, as well as an elementary day-school. Three months after their arrival, there were 30 pupils in the day-school; by 1837 the academy had 40 boarders, and a new building was being erected.[3] Vocations, however, were scarce; the town of Kaskaskia did not profit much by the emigration to the west, and the Sisters saw no means of obtaining additional teachers

[1] Archives of the Visitation Convent, Georgetown; Lathrop, Annals of the Visitation; Life of Mrs. Jerusha Barber (Sister Augustin), by Sister Josephine Barber, in de Goesbriand's Cath. Memoirs of Vt. and N. H., pp. 80, 99; Shea, vol. iii, p. 683: "Estab. of the Visitation Nuns in the West," in Amer. Cath. Quart. Rev., vol. xi, p. 31 seq.

[2] See chap. ii.

[3] Amer. Cath. Hist. Res., vol. vii, p. 110.

to meet the growing opportunities. When Bishop Kenrick of St. Louis therefore invited them to establish a convent and school in that city, they gladly accepted the invitation, and on April 14, 1844, Mother Agnes Brent and five other Sisters took up their residence in St. Louis, occupying a rented house on Sixth Street. A few weeks after their departure, the Sisters left behind were forced to abandon their establishment at Kaskaskia by the great Mississippi flood of that year, and likewise removed to St. Louis. As the house on Sixth Street was too small to accommodate the entire community, another school was opened in the house of Mrs. Biddle, on Broadway; but two years later the Sisters were reunited, when a larger establishment was secured on Ninth Street, near St. Vincent's Church. Here they remained until the erection of a still larger and finer institution on Cass Avenue, at Cabanne Place, in 1858. From St. Louis the Sisters sent out colonies to found new establishments at St. Paul and Dubuque, as well as in other parts of the west.[1]

SISTERS OF ST. JOSEPH

While on a visit to France, in 1834, Bishop Rosatti secured another community of teaching Sisters to labor in his diocese. This was the celebrated Congregation of the Sisters of St. Joseph. The Congregation, founded in 1651, had been destroyed by the French Revolutionists, but was restored under Napoleon, the first establishment

---

[1] Annals of the Visitation, p. 352; Sketches of the V. Rev. F. de Andreis, p. 241; Amer. Cath. Quart. Rev., loc. cit.; Cath. Directory, 1907.

of the new organization being formed in 1807, at Saint-Etienne, in Forez, under the direction of Mother St. John Fontbonne.[1] The development of the institute was so rapid under the new order of things that when Bishop Rosatti appealed for teachers for his growing educational system the community was able to send six Sisters to the New World. The party set sail from Havre January 17, 1836, and arrived at St. Louis March 25, coming by way of New Orleans. The pioneer members of the Order in America were: Sisters Febronia and Delphine Fontbonne, nieces of the Mother-General; Sister Febronia Chapellon, Sister St. Protais, Sister Marguerite or Felicite, and Sister Philomena.[2]

Father Douterligne, pastor of the old Catholic settlement of Cahokia, across the river from St. Louis, invited the Sisters to his parish, and here, soon after their arrival, three of them began the educational work of the Order in the United States. An academy was opened, as well as a parochial school, the teaching being in French.[3] In 1838 there were four Sisters, with twenty-five pupils in the academy.[4] Soon after the establishment of the institution at Cahokia, a convent and school was begun at Carondelet, six miles from St. Louis. Carondelet, at this time, was a collection of wretched-looking log cabins, inhabited chiefly by Creoles, and the first establishment of the Sisters consisted of two log cabins, the one selected for their own dwelling or convent having only one

[1]Rivaux, Life of Mother St. John Fontbonne, p. 110.
[2]Ibid., p. 206.
[3]Ibid., p. 210.
[4]Cath. Almanac, 1838.

room.   The poverty and destitution of these
valiant women, in this their first mother-house in
America, might well be likened to that of the Holy
Family at Bethlehem.   Hopeful of the future,
however, they struggled on.   Material means and
several additional Sisters were received from
France, and the following year the daughter of a
prominent St. Louis merchant, Miss Anna Eliza
Dillon, joined their ranks.   With the help of her
instructions, the inability of the Sisters to speak
English, which had been an obstacle to the success
of the school, was soon overcome, and the number
of boarders and day-scholars gradually increased.
Other American-born young ladies followed the
example of Miss Dillon, and with increasing numbers and enlarged resources the missionary spirit
of the community showed itself during the next
decade by the foundation of other academies and
schools.   From St. Louis as a center, in the
course of time, the educational influence of the
community extended in every direction throughout
the United States, the institutions founded in such
cities as Philadelphia, Wheeling, Buffalo, Erie,
Brooklyn, Troy, and St. Paul, becoming in turn
new centers of educational organization and
activity.[1]

RESULTS

By the year 1834 there were in the diocese of
St. Louis, besides the orphan asylum and day-
school of the Sisters of Charity, six convents of
religious women, with six educational establishments adjoining, comprising both academies and

[1]Rivaux, op. cit., p. 215 seq.

elementary schools. The diocese counted thirty-six priests, twenty seminarians, and forty-two churches, with a Catholic population estimated at 50,000.[1]

CHRISTIAN BROTHERS

The plans of Bishops Dubourg and Rosatti, however, contemplated complete provision for the education of boys as well as girls. In primary schools the religious communities of women were counted on for the education of both boys and girls. The three colleges established, with their preparatory departments, afforded opportunities for higher and secondary education for boys and young men. It was hoped, however, through the introduction or establishment of teaching brotherhoods, to provide for the education of boys as amply and as thoroughly as for the education of girls. It has been shown that a preparatory school and college was established, early in Bishop Dubourg's administration, in New Orleans. While in France, in 1816, he succeeded in enlisting the service of the Christian Brothers, or Brothers of the Christian Schools, and the year following three Brothers crossed the water and reached the diocese by way of New Orleans. A boys' school was opened at Ste. Genevieve, Mo.[2] Unfortunately, instead of being kept united until at least one strong central establishment should be formed, the Brothers were separated by the bishop and sent to various missions, with a view to greater educational efficiency. The result was disastrous, for, deprived

[1] Cath. Almanac for 1834.
[2] Shea, op. cit., vol. iii, p. 366.

of the graces of community life, they soon grew disheartened, and withdrew from the Order.[1]

BOYS' SCHOOLS

Besides St. Louis University, with its preparatory school, several schools for boys were established by the Jesuits in the diocese of St. Louis. One of these was at St. Charles, another at Florissant, or St. Ferdinand. The former had in 1837 forty pupils, and the latter twenty, with one Jesuit teacher in each place.[2] The Sisters of Charity, the same year, kept a day-school for boys attached to their orphan asylum in St. Louis, there being twenty-eight pupils from without.[3] Schools for boys were also established in several parishes, with lay teachers, under the supervision of the pastors, who, in some cases, taught certain of the classes themselves. At Ste. Genevieve, a school of this kind was opened by Bishop Dubourg in 1818, in the building which had been erected by the inhabitants of the place for school purposes ten years before.[4] In the year 1838 there was another boys' school at Old Mines, Washington County, with thirty pupils, in the parish of the Rev. Peter Douterligne; another, with forty pupils, was at Westphalia Settlement, under Father Helias; two more were in Illinois, one of which, at La Salle, had forty pupils, under the Rev. Blasius Raho, and the other, at Cahokia, had thirty pupils, under the Rev.

[1]Letter of the Provincial of the Christian Bros., St. Louis.
[2]Cath. Almanac, 1838.
[3]Ibid.
[4]One Hundred and Fiftieth Celebration of the Founding of Ste. Genevieve, July 21, 1885, p. 14 (Pamphlet).

Regis Loisel, with a Mr. O'Flynn as teacher.[1]
An attempt was made, too, by Bishop Rosatti, at
this time, to found a teaching brotherhood for his
diocese.   The Catholic Almanac for 1839 an-
nounces the establishment of the "St. Louis Catholic Day School, containing eighty scholars, under
the care of Messrs. McDonald and Bartlet.   They
have adopted a rule of religious life made for them
by the bishop, and invite other young men desirous
of teaching to join them.   Bishops and priests are
invited to help this infant religious community."
The school appears to have been successful; but
the brotherhood did not last, owing probably to the
difficulty of securing vocations to the religious life.

STATISTICS

In a published Memoir of the year 1840, Bishop
Rosatti has enabled us to see the results produced
by the extraordinary religious and educational activity of which St. Louis had been the center since
the year 1817, and of which the benefits were shared
by non-Catholics as well as Catholics.[2]

DIOCESE OF ST. LOUIS IN 1840

POPULATION.	Total white population, about 500,-000; Catholic population, about 70,000.

[1] Cath. Almanac, 1839.
[2] When Father Francis Neil, pastor of the cathedral in
St. Louis, was setting out for Europe in 1825, for a temporary
absence, he was congratulated by the Protestants of the town
for his efforts "to establish a better system of education in
the place," during his seven years there.—N. Y. Truth Teller,
July 9, 1825; Amer. Cath. Hist. Res., N. S., vol. ii, p. 156.

CHURCHES. **CLERGY.**	Built, 55; being built, 20; planned, 20. Priests, 77: Lazarists, 25; Jesuits, 23; the rest, secular priests, French, Italians, Germans, Belgians, and Irish. Seminarians, 43: Lazarists, 3; Jesuits, 19; seculars, 21.
ACADEMIES AND SCHOOLS FOR GIRLS.	Academies, 12; with the same number of elementary schools, in some of which small boys were also taught. Boarders, 241; day-scholars, 379; orphans, 70. Total, 690.
COLLEGES AND SCHOOLS FOR BOYS.	Colleges, 2; schools, 8; the colleges having also preparatory departments. Boarders, 245; day-scholars, 226; orphans, 69. Total, 540. Seminaries, 2; school for deaf and dumb girls, 1.[1]

At the close of 1841, the population of St. Louis was about 20,000. Fully one-half, if not more, was Catholic.[2]

EDUCATIONAL INFLUENCE

The significance of these figures will be better understood if it is kept in mind that, so far as the diocese of St. Louis was concerned, all that they represent materially, intellectually, and spiritually, as well as in the way of organization, was the result of the work of only twenty years, for, although

[1] Memoir of Bishop Rosatti, in Sketches of V. Rev. F. de Andreis, p. 241 seq.
[2] Life of Archbishop Kenrick, of St. Louis, p. 65.

St. Louis was founded many years before, it had but one little church when Bishop Dubourg arrived in 1817, and there were but one or two priests in Missouri. It is not, however, the mere fact, astonishing as it is, that so great an educational growth was brought about in so short a time, with such a scarcity of means, which gives to these statistics their chief significance for the student of education; their significance lies in what they represented for the future. Within each of these educational institutions mentioned in Bishop Rosatti's Memoir, there was a germ of life and activity that was all the while struggling to develop, expand, and multiply itself; behind many was a religious Order, small in numbers as yet, but possessing an organization which made it necessary for the infant society to develop and expand in order to live; while at the head of many of these pioneer institutions there were men or women who seemed providentially fitted for their opportunities—men and women who were able to foresee the future, or at least prepare for it, and who proved themselves worthy coadjutors of Bishops Dubourg and Rosatti. What the Jesuit missions in Maryland and Pennsylvania had done for the original States, what Kentucky and Ohio had done for the Middle West, St. Louis and Missouri, from 1840 onward, were to do for the Farther West. Chiefly through the growth and expansion of the teaching Orders in the diocese, St. Louis became the center of an educational movement which extended northward as far as Canada and westward as far as the Pacific, and which made itself felt even throughout the east.

ILLINOIS AND IOWA

Even before 1840, this movement had begun. When Father John McMahon was appointed by Bishop Rosatti as first resident pastor of Galena, in 1832, where at this time there were perhaps 500 Catholics, with about 200 more across the river at Dubuque, one of his first acts was "to open a small school," which he taught himself.[1] Dioceses were being created, and others were soon to be created, in the northwest, and it was natural that St. Louis should be applied to for teachers for the schools which arose in many places at the same time as the first frame or log churches. Dubuque was given a bishop in 1837, in the person of the Rt. Rev. Mathias Loras, who had been president and professor at Spring Hill College, Alabama; and although there were only three priests besides the bishop in the diocese, the Catholic Almanac for 1840 significantly states that "a large and commodious brick house has been erected near the cathedral for the bishop and clergy, a part of which is intended for schools."[2] Bishop Loras was an ardent champion of Catholic education, and from the very first he encouraged the establishment of parochial schools. He desired religious teachers preferably, but if these or good lay teachers could not be had, he urged his priests to teach the schools themselves, or to devote at least a portion of their time to this

[1] Kempker, Hist. of the Cath. Church in Iowa, p. 19. Father McMahon was ordained at St. Louis in 1831, at an advanced age. Writing from Galena, Jan. 13, 1833, he says: "I have been obliged to open a small school to enable me to make a living. The people are so poor after the war that they with difficulty can live themselves." He died of the cholera at the same place, June 19, 1833.
[2] Cath. Almanac, 1840, p. 104.

work; and it is a fact to which pioneer Catholics of Iowa have borne witness, that some of the first schools in the older congregations of Iowa were conducted by the missionary priests.[1]

ARKANSAS

The first schools in the State of Arkansas were established by the early Jesuit missionaries, for the instruction of the Indians.[2] Under the administration of Bishop Rosatti, the Sisters of Loretto founded a boarding and day school near Pine Bluffs in 1838, the school being transferred to Post Arkansas four years later. Another school was opened by the Sisters at Little Rock in 1841; but in 1845 both schools were closed for want of support, as the total Catholic population, scattered all through the State, did not amount to more than 700 souls.[3]

DAKOTA

The first attempts at education in the extreme northern part of the Louisiana territory were made by priests from Canada, and although these efforts had no connection with the work of Bishops Dubourg and Rosatti, they are of interest as showing the influence of Catholic missionary work in the es-

[1] Kempker, op. cit., p. 38; see Rec. Amer. Cath. Hist. Soc., vol. ii, p. 135, for an account of Father J. Allimann, who went from the Dominican monastery at Somerset, O., in 1840, to Iowa, where, collecting about a dozen Catholic families at Fort Madison, he built a church 16 x 18 feet, in which he taught school himself for six years, until he was able to get competent Catholic lay teachers.
[2] Shinn, Hist. of Ed. in Ark., U. S. Bur. Ed., Cir. Inf. no. 1, 1900, p. 11; Dexter, Hist. of Ed. in U. S., p. 130.
[3] Loretto Archives; Shea, op. cit., vol. iv, p. 285.

tablishment of schools. In the year 1818, Fathers Provencher and Dumoulin were sent by Bishop Plessis, of Quebec, to the Selkirk colony, on the Red River of the North, where Winnipeg now stands. They were accompanied by William Edge, a young catechist and school-teacher. In September of the same year, Father Dumoulin and Edge went to a settlement called Pembina, now in North Dakota, where a church was built and a school opened. This was the first school in North Dakota. By the beginning of the following year, the missionaries were able to report that the attendance at the school was sixty, and that most of the pupils had learned to read, and "knew the letter of the catechism by heart." Edge was succeeded in 1820 by Mr. Sauvi, a young Canadian, who continued in charge of the school until the summer of 1823, when the Hudson Bay Company, which had brought the missionaries to the country, discovered that Pembina was on American territory, and compelled them to recross the border and remove to St. Boniface (Winnipeg).[1]

NEW ORLEANS

When the diocese of Louisiana was divided, in 1823, Bishop Dubourg remained in New Orleans in charge of the southern portion. Great difficulties were encountered by him in endeavoring to carry out his plans for the development of religion, owing to the schismatic or factional attitude of some of the clergy and laity. The bishop resigned in 1826, returning to France, and became later arch-

[1] Rt. Rev. John Shanley, Bishop of Fargo, in letter to the author, May 26, 1906.

bishop of Besançon.[1] In 1829, he was succeeded in New Orleans by Bishop Neckere.[2] The following year witnessed the arrival of the Sisters of Charity in New Orleans to take charge of the Poydras Orphan Asylum, in connection with which they opened a day-school.[3] In 1834, there were four convents of religious women, with schools attached, in the diocese of New Orleans, viz., one of the Ursulines, two of the Ladies of the Sacred Heart, and one of the Sisters of Charity. The diocese had twenty-two priests, twenty-seven churches, and an estimated Catholic population of 150,000. The Ursuline Convent had thirty Sisters and upward of one hundred pupils. The Sisters of Charity had fifteen Sisters with 110 orphan girls, and over one hundred pupils in the free school.[4] In 1838, the Sisters of Our Lady of Mt. Carmel established a boarding and day school for colored girls in New Orleans, on Claude Street.[5]

DIOCESE OF BARDSTOWN

(INCLUDING OHIO, MICHIGAN AND WISCONSIN TILL 1821, AND INDIANA AND EASTERN ILLINOIS TILL 1834)

BISHOP FLAGET

The Rt. Rev. Benedict Joseph Flaget, who was appointed bishop of Kentucky in 1808, was a Sulpician, and previous to his coming to this country he had been a professor in several seminaries in

[1] Sketches of the V. Rev. F. de Andreis, p. 246.
[2] Shea, vol. iii, p. 666.
[3] Emmittsburg Archives; Sketches, p. 236.
[4] Cath. Almanac, 1834.
[5] Cath. Almanac, 1839.

France.[1] After his arrival in America, he had been sent to Vincennes, where, as has been seen, he started an industrial school for the children of the parish, becoming himself their instructor.[2] Subsequently, he was for three years a member of the faculty of Georgetown College. Bishop Flaget warmly seconded every effort looking to the establishment of schools and the diffusion of knowledge, and took the initiative in several important movements which have left a lasting impression upon Catholic educational development in the west. He infused his own zeal for education into the minds of the clergy of his diocese, and Kentucky became, during the early years of his long episcopate, the educational center of all the region west of the Alleghenies and east of the Mississippi. One of the first objects of the solicitude of Bishop Flaget after his consecration was the founding of an ecclesiastical seminary. This institution was established at Bardstown in 1811, and placed in charge of the Sulpician priest, Father David, who had been brought from St. Mary's Seminary, Baltimore, for the purpose.[3]

ST. JOSEPH'S COLLEGE

The establishment of schools and colleges for lay students also occupied the attention of Bishop Flaget. In 1819, under the direction of the Rev. George A. M. Elder, St. Joseph's College was opened in the basement of the seminary at Bards-

[1]Spalding, Sketches of the Early Catholic Missions in Ky.; ibid., Life of Bishop Flaget.
[2]See chapter on Colonial Schools in the French Possessions.
[3]Spalding, Sketches, p. 221.

town. The next year a separate building was erected
for the college, but for several years the elementary department continued to be conducted in the
seminary basement.[1] The college was for some
time, in fact, little more than an ordinary school.
Gradually, however, the curriculum was enlarged,
until, in course of time, the institution came to hold
a high rank among the colleges of the west. A free
school for poor Catholic boys was also established
in connection with the college, the pupils devoting
half of the day to farm work. "With fifty schools
like this," wrote the bishop enthusiastically, in
1820, "we could renew the face of the whole diocese."[2]

ST. MARY'S COLLEGE

A second elementary school and college was
started in Marion County, Ky., in the year 1821,
under the name of St. Mary's Seminary or College.
The institution was organized by the Rev. William
Byrne, at that time in charge of several missions in
Marion County. Like Father Elder, he had been
a student of Mt. St. Mary's, Emmittsburg, and the
Sulpician Seminary at Baltimore. He was a born
educator, as well as a man of extraordinary energy.
Seeing the boys of his parishes growing up in ignorance, he opened a school in an old stone distillery-
building. The school was quickly filled, and after a
few years it became necessary to erect new and
larger buildings. It was a boarding and day school,
and, like St. Joseph's, included the common
branches as well as the classics. At first, Father

[1]Webb, The Centenary of Catholicity in Kentucky, p. 278.
[2]Ibid., p. 342.

Byrne was the sole member of the faculty, acting as president, prefect of discipline, prefect, treasurer, and professor, but he soon trained up a number of the brighter and more advanced pupils to be his assistants. Under his energetic direction, the school became very popular throughout Kentucky, and during the twelve years it was under his immediate control, the attendance averaged about 100. Twice it was ravaged by fire during this period, but each time the buildings destroyed were replaced by others that were larger and finer. In 1831, the institution was turned over to the Jesuits.[1] Father Byrne had conceived the idea of founding a school and college at Nashville, similar to St. Mary's. We have an evidence of the heroic quality of his educational enthusiasm, as well as of the primitive character of these early educational foundations, in a letter he wrote to Bishop Flaget concerning this project, in which he observed that all he needed to found the new college was his horse, and $10 to meet his traveling expenses. He died, however, before he could put the project into execution, having contracted the cholera while on a pastoral visit to a person stricken with that dread disease.[2]

EDUCATIONAL CONDITIONS

There had thus been established in Kentucky, by 1821, if we include the Dominican institution, four schools for boys, and at least three of them had full preparatory and collegiate courses, as well as the elementary common branches. In the remarkable educational activity which brought

[1] Spalding, Sketches, p. 272 seq.; Webb, op. cit., p. 283.
[2] Spalding, ibid., p. 276.

about this result, the education of girls was not lost sight of; in some respects, they fared even better than boys. This was due to the fact that it was easier to get women to teach than men, and that it was more difficult to found religious teaching Orders of men than of women. The getting of teachers was always the great problem, in Kentucky as elsewhere, during the early days, the support of the school being but a small matter in comparison. Poor as most of the Catholics of Kentucky were, they needed no arguments or urging to be convinced of the importance of a sound Christian education for their children. The leaven, of the old Jesuit teaching in Maryland was still strong within them.[1] They gave with a generous hand all that they had to give, whether in money, provisions, or service, for the support of Catholic schools, wherever these were started; but their generosity, great as it was, could do nothing in the way of supplying that which was the most essential requisite for the school, the teacher.

The problem was one which early engaged the attention of Bishop Flaget, and even before him, it had been taken up by Fathers Badin and Nerinckx, and partly solved. To Father Nerinckx belongs the credit of being one of the first in the country to attempt a solution of this problem by the establishment of congregations of men and of women whose lives should be devoted to the work of teaching in Catholic schools. The result of his efforts in this direction has been already described.[2] It may be added here that his great plans, though partly

[1] See chap. vi, Kentucky.
[2] See chap. vii.

thwarted by circumstances, resulted in establishing
a teaching sisterhood which, together with other
sisterhoods founded near by about the same time,
gave to Kentucky, within a few years, a system of
schools for girls such as no other State in the Union
could boast of at the time. By 1825, almost every
parish of any consequence in Kentucky had its
school for girls and small boys, and a number of
Sisters were engaged in teaching in neighboring
States.

The Catholic educational statistics of Kentucky
for the year 1825 are given in an official report by
Bishop Flaget as follows:

"DIOCESAN SEMINARY AT BARDSTOWN. Seminarians, 19, who also teach in the college. Cost of
the building, $6,000.

"PREPARATORY SEMINARY AT ST. THOMAS.
Young men, 15; priests, 2; teachers, 5. To this
is annexed a SCHOOL FOR BOYS, with 30 students,
who pay annually $35 in federal money, mostly in
produce. Cost of buildings at St. Thomas, $11,400.

"ST. JOSEPH'S COLLEGE. Will cost $20,000
when completed.

"ST. MARY'S COUNTRY SCHOOL. Cost, $4,000.
Charge per session, $6 for tuition, besides board
paid in produce. Very popular. Has 120 boys.
'Application must be made twelve months in advance to secure admission.'

"SISTERHOOD OF LORETTO. Sisters, 100. Convent of Loretto of brick. Cost, $5,000. All their
branch-houses made of logs. Five schools in Kentucky. In 1823, sent out a colony to Ste. Genevieve, Mo.

"SISTERHOOD OF NAZARETH. Sisters, 60; 60
boarders in Nazareth Academy. Three other

schools in Kentucky, and one at Vincennes, Ind. School at Nazareth becoming popular, and patronized throughout the whole western country. "SISTERHOOD OF ST. DOMINIC. Established in 1821. Sisters, 14; boarders, 29."[1]

DIOCESE OF CINCINNATI

(INCLUDING MICHIGAN AND WISCONSIN TILL 1833)

BISHOP FENWICK

Although Ohio was admitted as a State in 1802, and although the population amounted to 230,760 in 1810,[2] the number of Catholics there was very small at the time when, in the year 1814, the Rev. Edward Fenwick, O.P., starting from St. Rose's, Ky., crossed the Ohio River, and made his first missionary journey through the State. Only a few scattered Catholic families were found.[3] It was just about this time, however, that the stream of Catholic emigration began to reach Ohio, and by 1822 the number of Catholics was estimated at 6,000, Cincinnati containing about 200 Catholic families,[4] and little congregations having been formed in various other parts of the State. The appointment of Father Fenwick as bishop of Cincinnati, June 19, 1821, gave a new impetus to the growth of the Church in Ohio and throughout the

[1] Spalding, Life of Bishop Flaget, p. 302.
[2] Niles Register for 1812, Jan. 11.
[3] U. S. Cath. Mag., vol. xii, p. 686; vol. vi, p. 30 seq.; Houck, The Church in Northern Ohio, p. 43; Shea, vol. iii, p. 336; Spalding, Sketches of Kentucky; Hammer, Edward Dominik Fenwick, der Apostel von Ohio, p. 37.
[4] Catholic Miscellany (London), July, 1822, letter from a Dominican at St. Rose's, Ky.

Middle West, and with the spread and development of the Church, there went hand in hand an
educational movement which had for its object the
planting of a Catholic school alongside of every
Catholic church.   Bishop Fenwick had laid the
foundations of the Dominican college in Kentucky;
he was a man of scholarly tastes, as well as a missionary filled with apostolic zeal, and, from the
standpoint of solid educational achievement, he
merits a high rank in the list of great Catholic
prelates who filled the episcopal sees in the United
States during this period.   Bishop Fenwick's jurisdiction for some years comprised not only the State
of Ohio, but also Michigan, with what was then
known as Northwest Territory, now Wisconsin.[1]
Indiana and eastern Illinois remained under the
jurisdiction of Bardstown.   It is important to remember this, in order to trace the progress of the
educational impulse which went out from Cincinnati and Ohio, and traversing the tier of States
south of the Great Lakes made itself felt even in
the pioneer settlements of Wisconsin and Iowa, on
the borders of the diocese of St. Louis.

THE ATHENÆUM

Two years after his consecration, Bishop Fenwick paid a visit to Europe, where he succeeded in
securing priests, as well as material means, for the
development of his diocese.   One of his first acts on
his return, in 1826, was the establishment of a seminary for candidates for the priesthood.   A new
cathedral church was built, and the old chapel con-

[1] Shea, vol. iii, p. 338.

verted into a seminary, which was formally opened on May 11, 1829.[1] In connection with the seminary, a college and preparatory school for boys was also planned, and on October 17, 1831, a building having been erected for the purpose near the cathedral, this institution was opened under the name of the "Cincinnati Athenæum Religioni et Artibus Sacrum."[2] In both institutions, the classes were taught chiefly by the priests attached to the cathedral. The Athenæum prospered for some years, and even Protestants sent their sons to it; but the difficulty of procuring good teachers, in view of the poverty of the diocese, proved a serious obstacle to its growth. In 1840, it was transferred to the Jesuits.

THE POOR CLARES

Bishop Fenwick was anxious also for the establishment of elementary schools. While in Europe, he had induced the Poor Clares in Belgium to send a number of Sisters to his diocese, and in 1826 the Sisters reached Cincinnati, and began an academy or select school. In less than a year they had seventy pupils.[3] The Sisters, however, did not continue long in Cincinnati. Two of them were sent from there to Allegheny City, near Pittsburg, in 1828, where they opened a school, and the rest founded a convent and school at Detroit, in 1833.[4]

---

[1] Hammer, Edward Dominik Fenwick, pp. 57, 65; Shea, vol. iii, pp. 350, 353.

[2] Hammer, op. cit., p. 121; Biog. Sketch of Bishop Fenwick, Cath. Almanac, 1843, p. 67; Cath. Almanac, 1833.

[3] Cath. Almanac, 1843; Shea, vol. iii, p. 351.

[4] Cath. Almanac, 1843, p. 67; also for 1833, 1834; U. S. Cath. Mag., vol. vi, p. 94; Shea, vol. iii, pp. 351, 544, 635; Lambing, Hist. of Cath. Ch. in Dioc. Allegheny and Pittsb., p. 483.

GERMAN SCHOOLS

On October 8, 1829, four Sisters of Charity were sent from Emmittsburg to Cincinnati, to found St. Peter's Free School and Orphan Asylum.[1] Writing August 3, 1831, Father Résé, the vicar-general, describes this institution as highly successful; there were nineteen orphan girls in the asylum and one hundred pupils in the free school, some of the latter being Protestants.[2]   When the Germans organized the second Catholic parish in Cincinnati in 1833 (Holy Trinity), a school was immediately opened also, and at the same time an English school for boys was begun, both of these schools being taught at first by young men from the seminary, until suitable lay teachers were secured.[3] According to the Catholic Almanac for 1838, the school attached to the Holy Trinity parish, known as the Aloysian School, being what was then called both "pay" and "free," had from 300 to 400 pupils, with two lay teachers; St. Peter's Orphan Asylum and Free School had thirty orphans, and from 150 to 200 day-scholars, with five Sisters of Charity; besides which, there was the Athenæum, with Rev. Edward Purcell as president, and the Seminary. The German-Catholic population increased rapidly, and in June, 1838, two additional schools for German children were opened, one a private select school for girls, and the other a parish school for the Catholics who lived north of the canal.[4]   In

[1]Emmittsburg Archives; Metropolitan, Feb., 1830, p. 77; Truth Teller, vol. vi, pp. 274, 399.
[2]Hammer, op. cit., p. 120.
[3]Shea, vol. iii, p. 618; Cath. Almanac, 1838.
[4]Marty, Johann Martin Henni, p. 94.

1842, three more Sisters of Charity arrived and took charge of the German Male Asylum.[1] The Sisters of Notre Dame de Namur established themselves in Cincinnati in 1840, and their institution became in subsequent years the center of an extensive system of schools throughout the Middle West.[2]

DOMINICAN SISTERS

In 1830, three Sisters of St. Dominic came to the diocese from Kentucky, and established at Somerset, near the middle of the State, a free school and orphan asylum, and soon afterward an academy which became in time the mother-house of a number of other schools, academies, and convents of the Order.[3] In 1818, Dominican Fathers from Kentucky founded St. Joseph's Convent, near Somerset.[4] A novitiate and seminary for the Order was also established at the same place, which gradually developed until it became the central establishment of the Dominicans in the United States. Through the labors of the missionaries and pastors it sent out, St. Joseph's has exercised a wide influence in the building up of Catholic schools and academies, especially in the west.

BISHOP PURCELL

Bishop Fenwick died in 1832, and was succeeded in Cincinnati the following year by the Rt. Rev. John B. Purcell, who at the time was president of

[1]Emmittsburg Archives.
[2]Rec. Amer. Cath. Hist. Soc., vol. xi, p. 324 seq.
[3]Hammer, op. cit., p. 120; Spalding, Sketches of Kentucky, p. 160. See chap. vii, Sisters of St. Dominic.
[4]Houck, The Church in Northern Ohio, p. 44; Shea, vol. iii, p. 336.

Mt. St. Mary's College, Emmittsburg.[1] Bishop
Purcell labored with no less zeal than that of his
predecessor in behalf of Catholic education, and,
with the increase of the Catholic population, parishes and schools were gradually formed in all parts
of the State.   By 1833, sixteen frame or log
churches had been erected,[2] and in connection with
most if not all of these schools more or less permanent in character were established, although records
of them all have not come down to us.   There
was a large influx of German Catholics into
Ohio during this period, and the Germans clung
tenaciously to the idea of the parish school, and
showed themselves willing to make any sacrifice in
order to provide sound religious instruction for
their children.   In German parishes in Ohio and
elsewhere, the instruction in the school was given
largely in the German language.   "The first movement of German Catholics in a new settlement,"
says a writer of the time in Ohio, "is to build a
church and schoolhouse."[3]   A mile from Randolph,
Portage County, there was a congregation of forty-
five German Catholics, who, in 1835, had built a
log chapel and schoolhouse.[4]   At Tiffin and
McCutchenville there were also schools about the
same time.[5]   A colony of German Catholics settled
at Glandorf, Putnam County, in 1834, and upon
the completion of the church, in 1837, the pastor,

---

[1]Houck, p. 47.
[2]Cath. Almanac, 1834.
[3]Catholic Telegraph (Cincinnati), Sept. 4, 1835; Houck,
p. 222; see Discourse of Bishop Richter, Golden Jubilee of
Holy Trinity Church, Cincinnati, 1884, in Marty's Life of
Johann Martin Henni, p. 78.
[4]Houck, loc. cit.
[5]Ibid., p. 225.

Rev. W. J. Horstmann, built a school, and for eighteen months, being unable to secure a suitable teacher, taught the school himself, receiving a salary out of the common or public school funds.[1] At Minster and Wapakoneta there were likewise Catholic schools, the teachers being paid from the common school moneys.[2] It was not an uncommon thing for the pastor to teach in the school on week-days, as good lay teachers were almost as scarce in the west in those pioneer days as they had been in the east in colonial times. Cleveland received its first resident pastor in 1835, but it was for long intervals without a priest, until 1840; and the school which was begun in 1837 failed for want of an efficient teacher. The first permanent school in Cleveland dates from the year 1848, when the second church, 30 × 60 feet, was erected on the site of the present episcopal residence, the sanctuary being closed from view by folding doors during the week, and used as a school.[3] The idea that the school was not less essential than the church was shared by laity and clergy alike, and the general conviction of the Catholic mind on this point was aptly expressed by the announcement, in a particular case, that "a schoolhouse and a new church are wanted here. We hope to see the congregation make a successful effort to build immediately the schoolhouse."[4] By 1841, it was estimated, there

[1]U. S. Cath. Hist. Mag., vol. iv, p. 125 seq.; Cath. Telegraph, Dec. 12, 1840; Houck, p. 234.
[2]Cath. Telegraph, loc. cit.; Houck, p. 234.
[3]Rec. Amer. Cath. Hist. Soc., vol. iii, p. 129 seq.
[4]U. S. Cath. Mag., vol. vii, p. 377; Cath. Telegraph, Oct., 1848. Another instance might be cited in the case of the German congregation at Zanesville, in 1848. A correspondent, writing from there to the U. S. Cath. Mag. (vol. vii, p. 544),

were 50,000 Catholics in Ohio, with over forty
churches.[1]

BISHOPS RÉSÉ, RAPPE, HENNI, AND BARAGA

In the carrying out of their educational plans,
Bishops Fenwick and Purcell had the hearty co-
operation of a number of active and scholarly
priests, several of whom became subsequently the
heads of new sees established in the west.   Con-
spicuous among these was the Rev. Frederic Résé,
a native of Hanover, Germany, who was brought
by Bishop Fenwick to Cincinnati, on his return
from Europe in 1826, and made vicar-general of
the diocese, afterward becoming first bishop of
Detroit.[2]   Father Résé did much for Catholic education while vicar-general, not only in Ohio, but
also during his visitations through Michigan and
northern Indiana.   Another zealous laborer in the
cause of Christian education was the Rev. Amedeus
Rappe, a native of France, who arrived in Cincinnati in 1840.   Becoming the first bishop of Cleveland, in 1847, he obliged his priests, wherever possible, to establish parish schools.[3]   Rev. John Martin Henni was another zealous laborer in the cause
of Catholic education.   A native of Switzerland,
he was brought to Cincinnati by Father Résé,
and ordained there in 1829.   As pastor for many
years of Holy Trinity Church in that city, the lead-

says: "The congregation of St. Nicholas find it necessary to
build a new schoolhouse, which in a few days will be commenced; and, this done, they will next—but not this year—
enlarge the church."   The church was still unplastered.
    [1]Cath. Telegraph, Aug. 21, 1841, and Dec., 1842; Houck,
pp. 244, 250.
    [2]Shea, vol. iii, p. 634.
    [3]U. S. Cath. Hist. Mag., vol. ii, p. 225 seq.

ing German parish in Ohio, he displayed untiring energy in founding and organizing schools in the parish, and was actively interested in the development of Catholic educational work throughout the State.[1] Appointed bishop of the new see of Milwaukee, in 1843, he gave to the Catholic school movement in the immensely larger field in which he was then called to labor the same place of fundamental importance as he had done in his position as pastor of Holy Trinity.[2] The Rev. Frederic Baraga, who came from Austria to Cincinnati in 1831, labored for the education of the Indians in northern Michigan, to which he was assigned as his field of labor by Bishop Fenwick soon after his arrival, and of which he became bishop in 1853.[3] Much was accomplished also for education by Bishop Fenwick and Father Résé during their visitation-journeys through Indiana, Michigan, and Wisconsin, and some notice of this will be taken in recording the progress of Catholic education in the dioceses of Detroit and Vincennes.

FATHER MAZZUCHELLI

St. Joseph's Dominican Monastery, at Somerset, Ohio, furnished a number of active missionaries who had an important part in the educational movement which marked the growth of the Church in Ohio and the Middle West during this period. The most active and distinguished of these, after Bishop Fenwick himself, was the Rev. Samuel Charles Mazzuchelli, O.P., an Italian, who was ordained

[1] Marty, op. cit., p. 40 seq.; Die Katholischen Kirchen und Institute in Cincinnati, p. 13 seq.; Shea, vol. iv, p. 250.
[2] Marty, op. cit.
[3] Verwyst, Life and Labors of Bishop Baraga.

in Cincinnati in September, 1830, having been led to come to America through the influence of Bishop Fenwick.[1] Being sent shortly afterward to the extreme northern part of the diocese, he began an apostolate which lasted for thirty-four years, and embraced in its scope the States of Michigan, Wisconsin, and Iowa. When he began his work, this region, which was then the "Far Northwest," contained only a handful of priests, and these were widely scattered. For several years, in fact, he was almost alone in Wisconsin and Iowa. Catholic settlements were very few and small, and separated, in some instances, by hundreds of miles; but Father Mazzuchelli foresaw clearly the future growth of the west through immigration, and was eager to provide for a corresponding development of the Church by the erection of churches and schools, the organization of parishes and teaching communities. The school, in fact, he regarded as even more necessary than the church. "Mass could be said in the schoolhouse until the church was raised, but the children were always first with him."[2] During his long missionary career, he erected more than twenty-five churches, and in each case, it is said, he also established a school.[3] These schools were scattered through the three great States which formed his chief missionary field. Some of them were for the Indians; some were in the French settlements; and others, in the pioneer towns and villages of Wisconsin and Iowa. The total Catholic white popu-

[1] The Life Story of Father Mazzuchelli, in Golden Bells in Convent Towers, p. 19; Wisconsin Hist. Coll., vol. xiv, pp. 117 seq., 155.
[2] Wis. Hist. Coll., vol. xiv, p. 155.
[3] Ibid.

lation of Michigan and Wisconsin in the year 1827 was reckoned at 7,200 souls, with only six permanent churches or chapels.[1] Another Dominican from the monastery in Ohio, Father Van den Broek, a native of Holland, who came to Wisconsin in 1834, and long labored on the missions in that State, established many pioneer schools, both for Indians and whites, following Father Mazzuchelli's policy of opening a school wherever Catholics were numerous enough to build a church.

AT GREEN BAY

From Mackinac, which he made the first base of his missionary labors, Father Mazzuchelli made his way, in 1830, to Green Bay, a village which contained at the time about 1,000 souls, and here, the year following, he set up a school for the Indians.[2] A French school had apparently existed at the place from its first settlement. After Father Badin had finished the building of the second little church there in 1825, he was succeeded by a pretended priest named Fauvel, who employed himself during the week in teaching school.[3] The church having been burned by accident, a schoolhouse was built by the people, and this was used by him for both school and church.[4] Fauvel continued to teach at Green Bay until after the arrival of Father Mazzuchelli.[5] The Indian school which the latter opened at Green Bay, in 1831, had for its object "to inculcate industry, morality, and Christian

[1] Ann. Prop. de la Foi, vol. iii, p. 315 seq.
[2] See Biog. Sketch in Verwyst's Life and Labors of Bishop Baraga.
[3] Wis. Hist. Coll., vol. xi, p. 226.
[4] Ibid., vol. xiv, p. 166.
[5] Ibid., p. 167.

piety, and to teach the art of spelling, reading, and writing, etc." All poor Indians were to be admitted gratuitously.[1] The first teacher was a lady named Mrs. Dousman, the wife of one of the settlers of the place.[2] Bishop Fenwick, who had visited Green Bay in 1829, and again in 1831, encouraged the establishment of the school, and contributed regularly to its support.[3] Sisters of St. Claire came from Detroit in 1834 to take charge of the school, but they did not stay long. In 1836, Miss Elizabeth Grignon, a daughter of one of the most respectable inhabitants of the place, was teacher of the school.[4] Miss Grignon was acquainted with the Indian dialects, and took charge of temporary Indian schools established by Fathers Mazzuchelli and Van den Broek in several other places. In 1833, she taught at Portage and Grand Kakalin (Kaukauna).[5] Her cousin Margarith, in 1835, taught school also at the latter place, where Father Van den Broek, who had charge of the missions in the vicinity, also taught.[6]

SCHOOLS OF FATHER MAZZUCHELLI

It would be tedious for the reader to attempt to follow Father Mazzuchelli in the journeyings and temporary residences that made up the record of his life during the ensuing years. Our knowledge of the schools he established is neither

---

[1] Wis. Hist. Coll., vol. xiv, p. 184.
[2] Ibid., p. 176; vol. x, p. 482.
[3] Ibid., vol. xiv, p. 177.
[4] Ibid., p. 201; Shea, vol. iii, p. 635.
[5] Ibid., p. 183.
[6] Ibid., p. 197. Father Van den Broek's principal residence for many years was at Little Chute, some twenty miles from Green Bay, and when he went there, in 1836, he lived for half

full nor, in many cases, precise; and much remains for the historical collector and editor to do before a satisfactory account and a just historical estimate of his educational work can be given. It is known that as a rule, if not invariably, he established a school wherever he built a church, and there can be no doubt that, either directly or by indirect agency, he established schools at Mackinac, Sault Ste. Marie, Green Bay, Prairie du Chien, Grand Bute, Portage, Galena, Dubuque, Davenport, Iowa City, and many other smaller settlements in Michigan, Wisconsin, and Iowa. It is to be regretted that the exact dates of the foundation of Catholic schools in all these places have not as yet been ascertained; but his educational work at Green Bay is an evidence of his high educational ideal, and also of the almost insurmountable practical difficulties he had constantly to face and overcome. The greatest difficulty was due, nearly always, to the lack of teachers. Father Mazzuchelli steadily cherished the hope of procuring religious teachers in time, and this hope was realized when, toward the close of the year 1848, he was enabled to lay the foundation of the community of Dominican Sisters at Sinsinawa, Wis.

THEIR EDUCATIONAL INFLUENCE

The schools Fathers Mazzuchelli and Van den Broek set up were, of course, of the most primitive

a year in a wigwam fifteen feet long and six feet high, which served as church, dwelling, and school. Subsequently he induced colonies of Catholic Hollanders to settle in Wisconsin, from which they spread into States lying further west. See Verwyst, Biograph. Sketch of the Rev. T. J. Van den Broek, in Life and Labors of Bishop Baraga, p. 424 seq.; see also The Story of Father Van den Broek, p. 44.

kind—a rude log or frame building, a few rough benches or seats, a teacher, either man or woman, whose principal qualifications consisted in the ability to read, write, and "cypher," and who sometimes had to be given instruction in necessary points by the priest himself: this was usually all that was meant by the word "school" in the west in those pioneer days, as it had been likewise in the east a century or so before. Yet, little as the term implied, when interpreted by our present standards, the institution itself, primitive as it was, meant much for the progress of civilization and religion in the west; for when the great stream of emigration a decade or so later swept over this portion of the west, and immense dioceses, with organized school systems, sprang into existence as if by magic, the work of Father Mazzuchelli and his colaborers played a great part in the result. His churches and schools, scattered over the broad prairies, everywhere pointed to a fixed ideal; and the little bands of well-instructed Catholics he left behind him everywhere were as so many living nuclei around which could center the elements that went to form these new and rapid growths of the Church.

DIOCESE OF DETROIT

(INCLUDING WISCONSIN TILL 1843)

SCHOOLS IN THE DIOCESE

When Vicar-General Résé, of Cincinnati, was made first bishop of Detroit, in 1833, two years before Michigan was admitted as a State, there were schools at all the more important Catholic settlements, besides a complete school system in the city of Detroit, consisting of elementary and advanced schools for both boys and girls.[1]   As vicar-general of the diocese of Cincinnati, he had made a visitation of Michigan in the year 1830, and he has left us some interesting information about several of these schools.

At the old mission station of St. Joseph's,[2] on the St. Joseph River, the Pottawatomie Indians turned over to him the Protestant mission-building, and here Bishop Fenwick promptly sent Father Badin, who at once opened a school for the Indian children, Miss Campau, who had been trained by Father Richard, being brought from Detroit to take charge of the school.   Father Deseilles replaced Father Badin there in 1832, and the school appears to have continued until the removal of the Indians to the west in 1838.[3]   This school, as well as the Indian schools at Arbre-Croche and Green Bay, was, on the application of Bishop Fenwick, granted government support, the annuity amounting to $1,000 for the three.[4]

At Monroe, Mich., where there had been a school since 1820, he found that the pastor, Father Smith, and the leading members of his flock were converts to the Faith.   Father Smith had built a

[1] See chap. vi, Detroit.
[2] Later known as Bertrand, Mich.
[3] Golden Jubilee of the Univ. of Notre Dame, p. 32 seq. Miss Campau, who was at this time sixty-eight years of age, acted as interpreter as well as school-teacher. Father Badin says of her that she was "very pious, as zealous for the salvation of the Indians as she is well instructed in religion and eloquent in expressing herself in all that concerns the faith, the customs, the ceremonies, and the discipline of the Church." Ann. Prop. Foi, vi, p. 166.
[4] Cincinnati Telegraph, vol. i, p. 199.

new church, and converted the old chapel into an academy, placing it under the direction of four young ladies. A school for boys undoubtedly existed also at this time at Monroe.[1]

AT ARBRE-CROCHE

During the same visitation, the vicar-general found a flourishing school among the Ottawa Indians at Arbre-Croche (Harbor Springs), forty-five miles from Mackinac.[2] This school was founded by the Rev. P. S. Dejean, a French secular priest, who had come to Arbre-Croche the year before, as the first resident pastor.[3] Father Dejean had previously been stationed at the Huron River Mission, where he established a school for boys and another for girls.[4] At Arbre-Croche, in addition to erecting a church, he put up a log building 46 × 20 feet, with three rooms, the Indians gladly joining in the work. Here school was opened August 23, 1829, and within a month there were thirty-eight pupils, of whom eighteen were girls. There were two teachers from Detroit, Joseph L'Etourneau for the boys, and Miss Elizabeth Williams for the girls, the latter being one of the

[1] Biog. Sketch of Bishop Fenwick, in Cath. Almanac for 1848, p. 78; U. S. Cath. Miscellany, Sept. 4, 1830; Webb, op. cit., p. 455.
[2] Cath. Almanac for 1848, p. 78.
[3] Verwyst, Life and Labors of Bishop Baraga, p. 61.
[4] Annales Prop. de la Foi, t. iii, p. 312. Writing from Rivière-aux-Hurons about 1826, Father Dejean said: "I have established a girls' school kept by a Sister of the Sacred Heart; she has twenty pupils; she comes from a nascent convent near Detroit. I keep school for the little boys three times a week, and at the same time the catechism. Among them I count many savages very industrious; they understand a little French."—Ibid. He was building a church there at the time.

four teachers trained by Father Richard many years before.[1] Twenty-five of the pupils boarded at the school, their parents supplying them with corn and potatoes, and the missionary with lard and salt.[2] Clothing for the pupils was provided for by each Indian family contributing annually a large box of sugar weighing from eighty to one hundred pounds, the sugar being emptied into barrels by Father Dejean, brought down to Detroit, and exchanged for cloth, which was brought back to the school and there converted into garments. Reading, writing, and catechism were taught in French, which was the only language used; but the chief aim of Father Dejean was industrial education. The boys were set to work to clear the land and raise vegetables. The girls were taught cooking and other household duties, the larger boys and girls doing the cooking for the meals.[3] Great stress was also laid upon good manners. Father Dejean took part personally in teaching, visiting the school frequently and superintending the industrial work, besides giving moral instruction.[4] Toward the end of 1830 he left Arbre-Croche on account of poor health, and, on May 28, 1831, he was succeeded there by Father Baraga, who had been sent from Cincinnati by Bishop Fenwick, and who began at Arbre-Croche an apostolate among the Indians and whites of the northwest that was to last for nearly forty years. At this time there was only one other priest in northern Michigan.[5]

[1] See chap. vi, Detroit.
[2] Verwyst, op. cit., p. 62.
[3] Ibid., pp. 62, 63.
[4] Ibid.
[5] Ibid., p. 118.

NORTHERN MICHIGAN

Father Baraga kept up the school at Arbre-Croche and labored to improve it along the lines laid down by his predecessor. His long apostolate, first as priest, and afterward as bishop, in the northern peninsula of Michigan, was characterized by an educational activity which caused schools to spring up everywhere with the churches, it being generally understood that the religious edifice erected at first should serve the double purpose of church and school. Father Baraga's life-purpose was the conversion and civilization of the Indians. A graduate in law of the University of Vienna, the instinct of scholarship was strong within him even amid the exhausting labors and trials of missionary work in the northwest during the '30's and '40's, and his Indian Prayer-Book and Catechism, and famous Chippewa Grammar and Dictionary, among his other works, were of incalculable service in the work of converting the savages, and, still more, in that of educating and civilizing them. In his efforts to educate the Indians, Father Baraga, like Catholic missionaries generally in this country from the very beginning, laid stress chiefly upon the learning of the common arts of civilized life, and especially upon tilling the soil. He gave instruction in these personally to old as well as to young, and often went to the limit of his resources in providing the means for effective object-lessons.[1] Reading, writing, and catechism were, as a rule, the chief schoolroom studies in his Indian schools.[2]

[1] Verwyst, p. 223.
[2] Sometimes grown men and women mingled as pupils with children in these schools. See Verwyst, p. 209.

He established Indian day-schools among the Ottawas at Grand River (Mich.), in 1833, at the Chippewa village of La Pointe (Wis.), probably in 1836, and at L'Anse (Mich.), in 1843, besides opening temporary schools in many other Indian settlements during his missionary journeys and visits.[1] Sometimes, even after he became bishop, he gave instruction to two or more Indian children in his own house.[2] After 1845, as the country began to fill up with immigrants, Father Baraga's labors were naturally directed more to the whites. Where there was an Indian school, with only a few white settlers, it was no uncommon thing for the white children to attend the Indian school; but as the immigrants increased, and the Indians declined in number, schools for white children were gradually established at all the important settlements, as fast as congregations were organized.[3] Father Francis Pierz, a native, like Bishop Baraga, of Carniola, was a most efficient co-laborer of the latter in northern Michigan during this period, having come to the diocese in 1835. He founded

[1] Verwyst, op. cit., pp. 149, 175, 209.
[2] Ibid., p. 287.
[3] Ibid., passim. The schools for the Indians were, however, kept up wherever possible. In 1866, Sisters of St. Joseph, of Carondelet, Mo., took charge of the Indian school at L'Anse. It is interesting to record the fact that, as there was question at the moment as to how the school could be supported, Bishop Baraga forced his silver watch upon the pastor as a contribution to its support. The watch brought $25 in cash. The bishop's intense interest in education was shown no less memorably when, a few days before his death, being visited by Father Terhorst, and making inquiries about the condition of the school, he compelled the father to take, for the benefit of the school, the contents of a tin box, which contained all the money the bishop possessed. The money amounted to $20. Verwyst, p. 353 seq.

an Indian school at La Croix in 1835, and schools at many other places later.[1]

BISHOP RÉSÉ'S INFLUENCE

Bishop Résé reached his diocese early in the year 1834, at a time when emigrants from the east were pouring into Michigan in great numbers, as a result of the opening of the Erie Canal in 1826, and the establishment of steam navigation between Buffalo and Detroit. The population of the territory, which was but 32,000 in 1830, had increased by the year 1837 to 212,000.[2] Bishop Résé's arrival soon resulted in a quickening of Catholic educational activity in Detroit. The Poor Clare Sisters had just opened an academy and school in the city, which were well patronized, and a colony of the Sisters was sent to Green Bay to take charge of the school at that place. Difficulties arose, however, about matters relating to property and administration, between the Sisters and Bishop Résé, who was their ecclesiastical superior, which resulted, about two years later, in the closing of the schools of the Order in Detroit, Green Bay, and Pittsburg, and the breaking up of the community.[3] Soon after his arrival, the bishop started a diocesan seminary in his own house, and, two years later, he erected a four-story building for it adjoining St. Anne's Cathedral. About the same time as he began this building, he established St. Philip's College, at Hamtramck, or Côte-du-Nord-Est, for secular students.[4]

[1] Verwyst, op. cit., p. 381.
[2] Report Commissioner of Ed., 1898-99, p. 389.
[3] Shea, op. cit., vol. iii, p. 636.
[4] Ibid.

SCHOOLS IN DETROIT

Bishop Résé also sought to develop the school system established at St. Anne's by Father Richard, which had, apparently, lacked efficient supervision since the latter's death. Under the direction of Rev. Fr. O'Cavanaugh, a high school for boys was again commenced, about 1835, the principal teacher being William McDonough, who had come from Dublin.[1] The Germans had become sufficiently numerous to form a congregation, and when the German Church of the Holy Trinity was dedicated in 1835, a separate school for the German children was probably organized too.[2] An orphan asylum was also begun by Father Kundig in 1834.[3] The school of the Poor Clares was succeeded in 1837 by a female charity school taught by Elizabeth Williams, and supported by Mrs. Antoine Beaubien, which had an average attendance of forty children. Miss Williams died in 1843, and her place was taken in the school by Miss Matilda Couchais, who taught about a year, and was succeeded by the Sisters of Charity, four of whom arrived May 4, 1844. Under their charge, a free school for boys and girls was opened June 10, the same year, at the southwest corner of Randolph and Larned streets.[4]

CONDITIONS IN 1837

At the time of the resignation of Bishop Résé, in 1837, the Catholic schools of Detroit were thus

[1]Farmer, Hist. of Detroit and Mich., p. 720; Cath. Almanac for 1838; Shea, vol. iii, p. 636.
[2]Shea, p. 635; Cath. Almanac for 1840.
[3]Farmer, pp. 648, 650 seq.
[4]Ibid., p. 721.

in a very flourishing condition. There were elementary schools for the French, English, and German children, conducted in the basement of St. Anne's Cathedral. In the year 1840 the French school counted 200 pupils, the English, 100, and the German school, sixty;[1] and a report made to the common council the following year showed that these schools, together with the high school, embraced nearly all the Catholic children of the city.[2] Throughout the entire diocese, including Wisconsin, there were, in the year 1842, about twenty Catholic schools, not counting mission schools of a more or less temporary character, sixteen priests, twenty-five churches and chapels, with a Catholic population of about 25,000.[3]

DIOCESE OF VINCENNES

(INCLUDING EASTERN ILLINOIS TILL 1844)

BISHOP BRUTÉ

The Rt. Rev. Simon William Gabriel Bruté, who arrived at Vincennes, as its first bishop, November 5, 1834, was known as one of the most learned and distinguished Catholic educators in the United States. Born in France in the year 1779, he joined the Sulpicians, after graduating with highest honors as a doctor of medicine at Paris, and was ordained a priest. Coming to this country in 1810, he became a member of the faculty of Mt. St. Mary's College, Emmittsburg, and after serving as president of St. Mary's College, Balti-

[1]Cath. Almanac, 1840.
[2]Farmer, p. 720.
[3]Shea, vol. iii, p. 639.

more, from 1815 to 1818, he returned to Emmittsburg, where he remained as professor of theology
and philosophy until his selection for the see of
Vincennes.[1] He took a lively interest in the neighboring institution of the Sisters of Charity, and
acted for many years as the spiritual director of
the inmates. As a professor, he was universally
esteemed for his ability and scholarly tastes, and
he had perhaps the largest share in the training of
the group of great ecclesiastics whom Mt. St.
Mary's gave to the Church during those fruitful
years.[2]

EDUCATIONAL CONDITIONS

The population of Indiana, which was only 24,-
127 in 1810, had increased to 343,031 by 1830.
There were several thousand Catholics—principally
Germans and Irish—among the immigrants, but
they were widely scattered through the State, and
this is why, at the time of Bishop Bruté's arrival,
there were neither priests, churches, nor schools,
outside of the old Indian mission stations and the
neighborhood of Vincennes. The period of 1830-

[1]Bayley, Memoirs of the Rt. Rev. Simon Wm. Gabriel
Bruté; Shea, Hist. of the Cath. Ch. in U. S., vol. iii, p. 640
seq.; Alerding, Hist. of the Diocese of Vincennes; McCaffrey,
Discourse on the Rt. Rev. Simon Gabriel Bruté, Emmittsburg,
1839.
[2]Although a native of France, Bishop Bruté, after becoming
an American citizen, was distinguished by his patriotic devotion
to the land of his adoption. During the War of 1812 he had
charge of the parish at Emmittsburg, and when Baltimore was
attacked he made every effort to rouse the patriotism of his
parishioners, delivering an address to those who set out for the
defense of the city, and walking to Baltimore himself in order
to join them and minister to them, should there be occasion, in
the trenches. Bayley, op. cit., p. 54; Memoir, Letters, and
Journal of Eliz. Seton, vol. ii, p. 217.

1840, however, was one of extremely rapid growth for Indiana, the population doubling itself during the decade. Bishop Bruté's painstaking descriptions of his episcopal visitations of the State, which he began soon after his arrival, show us little groups of Catholic families in all the rising towns, with new immigrants streaming in constantly.[1] Besides the bishop, there were but three other clergymen in the diocese. The need of additional laborers was urgent, but the bishop believed that the foundation of Catholic schools was not less necessary. "Without these," he said, "religion can never be firmly established."[2]

Vincennes had a population almost entirely French, of 1,500 souls.[3] A school had existed at the place, at least from time to time, probably from the foundation of the settlement. Father Gibault had taught the children of the parish himself, and Father Flaget had done the same.[4] In 1818 Father Blanc,[5] while pastor, had tried to found a college at Vincennes, but the attempt was unsuccessful, owing to the opposition of a faction of the people.[6] The Sisters of Charity had come from Kentucky in 1824, and opened an academy and school. Some months before the arrival of Bishop Bruté they had been recalled to the mother-house, owing to the hardships of their life in Vincennes. Bishop Bruté showed what importance he attached to Catholic education, and clearly indicated

[1] See letters of Bishop Bruté, signed "Vincennes," in Cath. Telegraph (Cincinnati), 1835, vol. iv, pp. 317, 349.
[2] Bayley, Memoirs of Bishop Bruté, p. 78.
[3] Ibid., p. 81.
[4] See chap. ii.
[5] Subsequently bishop of New Orleans.
[6] Alerding, Hist. of the Diocese of Vincennes, p. 89.

his future policy, by immediately providing for their return. "My first care," he says, "was to secure their immediate return."[1]

Besides the Vincennes establishment, there were several schools in the diocese at this time. At St. Peter's and St. Mary's churches, in Daviess County, under Father Lalumière, school continued to be taught intermittently even after the Sisters' withdrawal.[2] Farther to the south, there were German-Catholic settlements of considerable size, attended by Father Ferneding, at Dover (Cross Roads, M'Kenzie Settlement) and New Alsace, in Dearborn County,[3] and at both these settlements, as was the custom among the Germans, the log buildings which served as churches on Sundays were probably used as schoolhouses during the week. In the northern part of the State, an Indian school existed among the Pottawatomies at St. Joseph River, and among the Chickakos on the Tippecanoe. Such were the conditions when, on July 16, 1835, Bishop Bruté set out for France, to look for men and means for the religious and educational development of his vast charge.[4]

AN EDUCATIONAL DEVELOPMENT

When he landed in New York, July 20 of the following year, Bishop Bruté brought back with him nineteen priests and seminarians, among

---

[1]Bayley, op. cit., p. 94. See chap. vii, Sisters of Char. of Nazareth. The charge for board and tuition at the Vincennes academy in 1833 was only $86, according to the Catholic Almanac for that year.
[2]Golden Jubilee of the Univ. of Notre Dame, p. 17.
[3]Alerding, op. cit., pp. 379, 381.
[4]Shea, vol. iii, p. 644.

whom were the Rev. Celestine de la Hailandière and Rev. Maurice de St. Palais, both destined in turn to occupy the episcopal see of Vincennes.[1] An immediate impetus was thus given the work of religious and educational development in the diocese, and churches and schools began to arise in every section of Indiana. Vincennes was the first place to feel the stir of the new life. With the money he had obtained in France, Bishop Bruté at once established an ecclesiastical seminary, as well as St. Gabriel's College for secular students. The bishop, priests, seminarians, and college students all occupied the same house, and took their meals in the same refectory, the bishop and his clergy constituting the faculty. Two free schools were also opened at the same time, one for boys and the other for girls, besides an orphan asylum under the care of the Sisters.[2] Small as the place was, an educational system was thus set up at Vincennes which comprised complete elementary, secondary, and higher educational provision for both male and female pupils, and which it was intended should serve as a model for the whole diocese.[3] The bishop counted on getting some religious Order to take charge of the college and devote its energies to its development, and this was effected three years later, when Father Hailandière, then vicar-general, secured several members of the Eudist Congregation in France, with Father

[1] Shea, vol. iii, p. 645.
[2] In 1840 the average attendance at the boys' free school was seventy-five and at the girls' fifty-five. Cath. Almanac, 1840.
[3] McCaffrey, Funeral Discourse on Bishop Bruté, Emmittsburg, Aug. 19, 1839; Cath. Almanac, 1843, Biog. Sketch, p. 50; see Cath. Almanac for 1833, 1839; Alerding, op. cit., p. 149; Cincinnati Telegraph, 1839.

Bellier as Superior, to assume the direction of the institution. The Eudists, however, did not long remain, although the college was well attended and its future seemed full of promise.[1] The Sisters of Charity of Nazareth were recalled a second time from Vincennes and the diocese in 1838, their place being taken there during the spring of the same year by four Sisters from the Emmittsburg community.[2]

WORK OF FATHER KUNDECK

German Catholics were coming in large numbers to southern Indiana about this time, and sometimes many families settled together, forming a Catholic parish. A school was probably started at Jasper, Dubois County, in 1838, when Father Joseph Kundeck took charge. Father Kundeck was an active missionary and an extraordinary church-builder, even for those pioneer days, and German schools were no doubt organized in a number of his missions. In 1842 he had drawn a colony of 250 German emigrant families to a place twelve miles south of Jasper, where a town was laid out, a church built, and a school and academy begun by the Sisters of Providence.[3] In 1852, while on a visit to Europe, Father Kundeck induced the Benedictines, of Einsiedeln, Switzerland, to send some of their members to Indiana to found a school and college; the institution was begun two

[1] Alerding, p. 492; Shea, vol. iii, p. 650; Cauthorn, A History of the City of Vincennes, p. 152. The annual charge for board and tuition at the college is given as $100 by the Cath. Almanac, 1838.
[2] Emmittsburg Archives.
[3] Cath. Advocate (Louisville), vol. vii, p. 210, Aug. 6, 1842.

years later, and was known as St. Meinrad's College.[1] It is probable that schools were established at all the more important German-Catholic settlements in southern Indiana which sprang up before 1840, chief among which, in addition to those already mentioned, were Bradford, Harrison County; St. Michael's, Jefferson County; St. Peter's, Franklin County; St. Nicholas, Ripley County, and Enochsburg, Franklin County.[2]

EVANSVILLE AND NEW ALBANY

Evansville received Father Deydier as its first pastor in 1837, and two years later, before a church had been built, this energetic man had opened a Catholic school, bringing a young Irishman named Michael Byrne from the east as the teacher. The latter subsequently became a priest.[3] The Sisters of Charity from Kentucky took charge of the school at New Albany about the year 1838.[4] Fort Wayne, with 150 to 200 families, had erected a church by the year 1836, and probably had also a Catholic school.[5]

AT NOTRE DAME

A few miles south of the old mission of St.

[1] Alerding, p. 546.
[2] Ibid., pp. 346, 351, 382, 399. A frequent arrangement of school and church in the pioneer parishes of Indiana and the west was represented by that at St. Joseph's, nine miles northwest of Evansville. The church at St. Joseph's, built in 1841, was of logs, and divided into two stories; the upper story was used for divine services, while the lower floor was divided into two portions, one half being used for a school, and the other half, subdivided into two small rooms, served as the pastoral residence. Alerding, p. 288.
[3] Ibid., p. 269.
[4] Shea, vol. iii, p. 647.
[5] Ibid., p. 643 seq.

Joseph's (Mich.), a Sisters' school had been established by the venerable Father Badin, and
although it did not long continue, still the project
led to the foundation of an educational establishment at the place which has had an important influence upon Catholic education in the west.
Father Badin had, as has been shown, opened a
school for the Indians at St. Joseph's (Bertrand)
in 1830.[1] Soon after, he built another chapel for
those living about St. Mary's of the Lake, five
miles to the south. Considering the spot as possessing peculiar advantages for an educational institution, he bought from the Government the section of land which included the lake, erected a log

[1]Between the present cities of Niles and South Bend there
appears to have been three villages of the Pottawatomie Indians.
The first was located about half a mile south of Niles, where
a chapel had been built by Allouez, and where had stood,
probably, Fort St. Joseph. About three miles south of this, and
west of the St. Joseph River, was the principal Indian settlement, which was known as Pokagon's Village. Five miles
farther south there was another Indian settlement at a spot
known as St. Mary's of the Lake, which was also probably an
ancient mission station. Across the river from Pokagon's
Village, in 1831, when Bishop Fenwick visited the locality,
was "a small congregation of Canadian Catholics," with a
chapel of their own (Bertrand). For several years following
Father Badin's arrival in 1830, this locality was the missionary center of an immense district, extending from and including Chicago on the west to Ohio on the east, and from
the Grand River on the north to Vincennes on the south, as,
indeed, it had probably been the missionary center of even
a larger area during colonial times. In June, 1832, we find
Father Badin, with his flourishing school at Pokagon, planning
to establish another school among the Indians at the recently
vacated Carey Baptist Mission near Niles, while occupied, at
the same time, with the project of getting Sisters and establishing at St. Mary's of the Lake a teaching Order which
would make that place the educational center of the region
of which the locality was the mission center. See U. S. Cath.
Miscellany, vol. x, p. 182; Cath. Telegraph, vol. i, pp. 14, 199,
311; vol. iv, pp. 62, 317, 334; Cath. Almanac, 1833-1839; Ann.
Prop. Foi, vols. vi, vii, viii.

chapel 24 × 40 feet, and put up a small frame building of two stories to serve as a convent and school for the Sisters, as he appears to have had in view at first a Sisters' school and academy. Some time during 1834 Father Badin secured two Sisters, but the "few Catholic families, Americans, Irish, and French," whom Bishop Bruté reported as living in the vicinity, when he visited the place in the month of May of the following year, were evidently unprepared to support the project, and by the time of the bishop's visit the Sisters were gone and the school was closed.[1] Bishop Bruté entered warmly into the plans of Father Badin, accepting from him the deed for the property, and awaiting a more mature time for the foundation of the institution desired.[2] When Father Sorin with the Brothers of the Holy Cross arrived in the diocese several years later, the property was transferred to them, and upon it was built the mother-house of this Congregation in the United States, as well as the University of Notre Dame du Lac.[3]

CHICAGO

Chicago, when it was visited by Bishop Bruté in May, 1835, had a neat little church, with Father St. Cyr as pastor, and a flock of 400.[4] There was

---

[1]Catholic Telegraph, vol. iv, pp. 62, 334; Bayley, op. cit., p. 85.

[2]Cath. Tel., vol. iv, p. 334.

[3]Golden Jubilee of the Univ. of Notre Dame, p. 18. The mother-house of the Sisters of the Holy Cross was located at first at Bertrand, near Pokagon's Village.

[4]Shea, vol. iii, p. 644. Writing of Chicago as it appeared at this time, Bishop Bruté says: "From a few scattered houses near the fort, it has become in two or three years a place

probably a school of some sort in existence at Chicago from the time of Father St. Cyr's arrival toward the end of the year 1834. Visiting the place again after his return from Europe, in 1838, Bishop Bruté found a thriving little town of seven or eight thousand people, containing near a thousand Catholics, and, convinced of its future importance, he was eager to provide for a corresponding educational development. Writing from Chicago, August 30, 1838, to Mother Rose of Emmittsburg, he said: "I dream of Sisters here! But how so? Colonel Beaubien offers lots, etc. Very well! But Sisters?"[1]

There were several settlements of German Catholics in eastern Illinois at this time, and it is very likely that here, as elsewhere, wherever the Germans had a church, even though the services were only occasional, there was a steadily kept school. The best organized of these congregations was in Jasper County.[2]

BISHOP HAILANDIÈRE

Bishop Bruté's death in 1839 left many of his great educational hopes and plans, which were far in advance of the pioneer period in which his episcopate fell, unfulfilled; but his successor, Bishop de la Hailandière, was thoroughly in sympathy with Bishop Bruté's educational ideas, and continued energetically to develop and perfect the

of great promise. Its settlers sanguinely hope to see it rank as the Cincinnati of the north. Americans, Irish, Germans, French, meet at a common altar."—Cath. Telegraph, vol. iv, p. 333.

[1] Amer. Cath. Hist. Res., vol. xv, p. 96.
[2] Shea, vol. iii, p. 647.

system that had been inaugurated.   It was Bishop Hailandière who induced the Eudists to take charge of St. Gabriel's College, Vincennes, and the Congregation of the Holy Cross and the Sisters of Providence to send over colonies to take charge of boys' and girls' schools respectively, as well as to establish colleges and academies in the diocese.[1]

At the time of Bishop Hailandière's consecration, in August, 1839, there were in the diocese a seminary for ecclesiastical students, and a college for seculars; an academy for girls; about two dozen elementary schools; twenty-three churches; twenty-five priests; fourteen seminarians, with a Catholic population of upward of 25,000.[2]

[1] Shea, vol. iii, p. 650.
[2] Catholic Telegraph; Cath. Almanac, 1839, 1840; Shea, vol. iii, p. 653.

CHAPTER IX

BISHOP HUGHES AND THE SCHOOL QUESTION

THE EDUCATIONAL TREND

BISHOP HUGHES assumed charge of the diocese of New York during a period in which a profound change in the idea of public education, which had gradually been taking place in people's minds, was being given definite legal sanction in those States that were most advanced in matters educational.[1] This change involved the abolition of the denominational character of all State-supported schools. In Massachusetts the movement culminated in the "non-sectarian" system of education perfected and enforced by Horace Mann; while in New York the result was seen in the turning over of all the moneys appropriated by the State for popular education to the Public School Society and its undenominational schools. In colonial times, the State-supported schools in the several colonies had been denominational, and dogmatic religious instruction was given in them as a matter of course. The constitutions adopted by the States, after the Revolution, did not affect the character of the schools in this respect; but the gradual rise of dissentient religious bodies in the colonies and States, due to the influx of emigrants and other causes, brought about important changes which led to the establishment of a "non-sectarian"

[1] His consecration as coadjutor-bishop of New York took place Jan. 8, 1838.

system of schools. As long as there was homogeneity in religion, it was natural that the public school systems should reflect the prevailing religious teachings; but with the growth of dissentient denominations and religious indifferentism, and the disestablishment of the State-supported churches, there was a corresponding tendency toward complete separation of religious and secular teaching in the case of the young. For a considerable period, however, a compromise arrangement was tried, and schools of the various denominations were given support by the State.

CATHOLIC SCHOOLS AND THE STATE

In many places, Catholics shared, more or less, in the rights claimed and accorded other religious bodies in this respect. In the Middle Western States, Catholic teachers were sometimes paid out of the State funds, by arrangement with the local authorities, although the arrangement was usually not continued long. The same was done in some places in the east. In the town of Lowell, Mass., for a period of sixteen years, the Catholic schools were comprised within the public school system of the place and supported out of the common school funds. St. Peter's School, New York, in the year 1806, applied for and received an appropriation out of the funds raised by the State for the support of the common schools, and this appropriation was renewed from year to year. St. Patrick's School, which was opened in 1816, was accorded the same right, and, by an act of the legislature in April, 1820, the commissioners of the common school fund were empowered to pay to the trustees of the Roman Catholic Benevolent Society a proportion of the school fund for the support of the orphan asylum.[1] In the distribution of the school fund in New York City in the year 1822, St. Peter's, with 315 pupils, received $619.36; St. Patrick's, with 345 pupils, received $679.20; while the orphan asylum, with 32 inmates, received $62.72.[2] Other denominational schools in New York likewise received their due proportion. Non-denominational schools were under the direction of the Public School Society, which received and distributed the money for their support. All the schools in New York City at this time were thus under the direction of private associations, which acted as the agents of the State in the distribution of the common school fund. In 1824, however, through the efforts of the Public School Society, the grant to the denominational schools was discontinued, with the exception of the orphan asylums, and the distribution of the entire school fund was placed in the hands of the Public School Society.[3] Although professedly "non-sectarian," the schools of the society were in reality offensively Protestant. The teachers were almost exclusively Protestant, the Protestant Bible was read, some of the books used were sectarian in character, and the atmosphere of the schoolroom was, generally speaking, such as to constitute a menace to the faith of Catholic children.[4]

[1] Boese, Hist. of Public Education in N. Y., p. 98 seq.
[2] Ibid.
[3] N. Y. City Ed. Pamphlets, doc. no. 41; doc. no. 80, Report of Comm. on Arts and Sciences and Schools, p. 342.
[4] Works of the Most Rev. John Hughes, vol. i, p. 51 seq.

ORIGIN OF THE SCHOOL CONTROVERSY

The beginning of the great school controversy in New York may be dated from Governor Seward's message to the legislature on January 1, 1840, in which, acting on the advice of Dr. Nott, President of Union College, who was strongly in favor of denominational schools, he made the following recommendation :[1]

"The children of foreigners, found in great numbers in our populous cities and towns, and in the vicinity of our public works, are too often deprived of the advantages of our system of public education, in consequence of prejudices arising from difference of language or religion. It ought never to be forgotten that the public welfare is as deeply concerned in their education as in that of our own children. I do not hesitate, therefore, to recommend the establishment of schools in which they may be instructed by teachers speaking the same language with themselves, and professing the same faith. There would be no inequality in such a measure, since it happens from the force of circumstances, if not from choice, that the responsibilities of education are in most instances confided by us to native citizens, and occasions seldom offer for a trial of our magnanimity by committing that trust to persons differing from ourselves in language or religion. Since we have opened our country and all its fulness to the oppressed of every nation, we should evince wisdom equal to such generosity by qualifying their children for the high responsibilities of citizenship."[2]

[1]Clarke, Lives of Deceased Bishops, vol. ii, p. 98.
[2]N. Y. Assembly Documents, 1840, vol. i, p. 5.

FIRST PETITION TO THE ALDERMEN

Bishop Hughes was in Europe at the time, but the vicar-general, Father Power, a veteran champion of the cause of Catholic education, being informed by a friend in Albany that sentiment in the legislature was favorable, called a meeting of the trustees of all the Catholic churches of New York City. After a discussion of the matter, it was resolved to apply for a share of the common school fund, and a visit to Albany convinced the vicar-general that the application would be successful if it was pressed forward with Catholic unanimity.[1] A petition was drafted by representatives of the eight Catholic churches in the city, each of which maintained a free or charity school, the total attendance at the Catholic schools being given as about 3,000.[2] The petition was addressed to the common council, as charged by law with the distribution of the school fund, and was concurred in by the Scotch Presbyterian Church in New York City, and by the Hebrew Congregation in Crosby Street. Against it, remonstrances were made by the Public School Society, the Methodist Episcopal churches, the East Broome Street Baptist Church, the Dutch Reformed churches, the Reformed Presbyterian Church, and many citizens.[3] The petition was rejected by the aldermen, April 27. Father Power, regarding the battle as only well begun, organized a series of meetings in the

[1] N. Y. Freeman's Journal, July 25, 1840; Works of Bishop Hughes, vol. i, p. 41.
[2] Report of the Committee on Arts and Sciences and Schools, doc. no. 80, p. 357.
[3] Document no. 80.

cathedral school for the discussion of Catholic education, with the evident purpose of enlightening Catholic opinion on the subject and, at the same time, instructing and influencing the non-Catholic public. It was soon made evident that the Catholics of the city, a few politicians excepted, were united on the question,[1] and the fortnightly meetings and discussions brought about an increasing concentration of public attention upon the question.

BISHOP HUGHES' POSITION

Such was the condition of things confronting Bishop Hughes when he returned from Europe. Whether he regarded the time as ripe for the agitation of the question or not, Bishop Hughes realized that it was now too late to retreat, and with characteristic resolution and energy he at once threw himself into the fight and assumed the leadership of the Catholic forces. On July 20, the second day after his arrival, he appeared at the meeting in the cathedral school, and, in a masterful address, urged the agitation of the question, pointing out, on the one hand, that the result of the attempt to teach morality without religion must inevitably result in practical infidelity or indifference to religion, and, on the other, that the tendency of the public schools, as they were actually conducted, was to draw away the mind of the Catholic child from the religion of his parents. If in Catholic schools, he asked, the children received the same education in secular branches which they would get in the State schools, did Catholic schools

[1] See Truth Teller, vol. xvi, pp. 53, 62 seq.

not effect the same benefit to the State? And if, with morality, they also at proper times inculcated the principles of religion, would they not make the rising generations better citizens, more upright in their intercourse with their fellow-men, more mindful of the sacred relations of the married state, and more attentive to their social duties? Catholics should therefore be granted, he argued, "a fair and just proportion of the funds appropriated for the common schools, provided the Catholics will do with it the same thing that is done in the common schools, and leave no reason to complain that the system is not followed."[1] While laying down these fundamental principles of the Catholic position, Bishop Hughes was careful, at the same time, to point out that the movement was entirely non-partisan, and pleaded for a calm and fearless discussion of the questions involved, on the basis of constitutional rights, expressing his conviction of the readiness of the American people to do justice to Catholics in the matter, as soon as the justice of their claims was clearly apprehended. At a general meeting of the Catholics of the city, held a fortnight later, an address to the citizens of the city and State of New York was adopted, in which the above principles were set forth at length and explained.[2]

SECOND PETITION

During the months of August, September, and October, immense audiences gathered every two weeks in the basement of St. James' Church to lis-

[1] Works of Bishop Hughes, vol. i, p. 43 seq.
[2] Ibid., p. 56.

ten to the discussion of the question by Bishop Hughes. The Catholics of the city were aroused, and the public interest increased.[1] As the Revised Statutes of the State forbade the appropriation of the public moneys to "Incorporated *Religious* Societies," Bishop Hughes now made the point that it was not as a religious society that Catholics appealed for a portion of the school fund, but simply as citizens, and that, inasmuch as they could not conscientiously allow their children to attend the schools of the Public School Society, they had the right as citizens to have their children educated in schools and by teachers of their own selection, at the public expense, provided that no part of the public funds diverted to the support of their schools and teachers were employed for the teaching of the Catholic faith. In other words, the money was asked simply for the teaching of the *secular* branches in the Catholic schools.[2] How much Bishop Hughes was willing to concede in this direction, in deference to established laws and public sentiment, was shown when, in the petition to the board of aldermen, drafted under his direction September 21, for a reopening of the case before that body, he agreed to confine the teaching of religion to after-school hours, and to turn the "material organization" of Catholic schools over to the control of the board of aldermen or of the Public School Society, should the conditions of the law require this. A compromise-arrangement was thus in reality offered by the bishop, his proposition being as follows:

[1] See Freeman's Journal, 1840.
[2] Works of Bishop Hughes, vol. i, pp. 69, 87, 106.

"Your petitioners are willing to fulfil the conditions of the law so far as religious teaching is proscribed during school hours. In fine, your petitioners, to remove all objections, are willing that the material organization of their schools, and the disbursements of the funds allowed for them, shall be conducted, and made, by persons unconnected with the religion of your petitioners, even the Public School Society, if it should please your honorable body to appoint them for that purpose. The public may then be assured that the money will not be applied to the support of the Catholic religion."[1]

A new point was thus raised—one that had not been brought out in the previous petition to the board of aldermen or in the arguments before that body, and an entirely new practical proposition, of the nature of a compromise, presented, and Bishop Hughes felt confident of his ability to bring about a reversal of the former unfavorable decision.

THE DEBATE

The board of aldermen appointed Thursday and Friday, October 29 and 30, to hear the arguments. The interest of the general public in the question had, by this time, been thoroughly aroused, and dense crowds struggled for admission to the council chamber. Bishop Hughes spoke for the Catholics and was opposed by Theodore Sedgwick and Hiram Ketchum for the Public School Society, as well as by several ministers representing the Methodist Episcopal and the Presbyterian churches.[2] After dealing at length with

[1] Ibid., p. 106.
[2] Ibid., p. 125.

the arguments contained in the remonstrance of
the Public School Society, the bishop took up the
main questions as stated by his opponents, which
were:

"1. Have the common council of this city, under the existing laws relative to common schools in
the city of New York, a legal right to appropriate
any portion of the school fund to religious corporations?

"2. Would the exercise of such power be in
accordance with the spirit of the constitution, and
the nature of our government?"

THE CATHOLIC PROPOSITIONS

While agreeing with his opponents that, under
the existing laws, the school fund could not be
appropriated to *religious* corporations, Bishop
Hughes carefully drew the distinction which has
been noted above, and asserted that the Catholics
applied for the fund, not as a religious society, but
as citizens, and in precisely the same capacity in
which they were taxed for the fund. His position
on this point and his willingness to exclude from
the curriculum of the Catholic school any positive
and explicit teaching of the Catholic faith, during
the regular school hours, were made clearer by a
series of propositions which he presented to the
board after the debate, while the decision was
pending. In these propositions, which may appropriately be inserted here, Bishop Hughes reduced
to detailed practical form the general compromise-
proposition presented in the Catholic petition to
the board:

"There shall be reserved to the managers or trustees of these schools, respectively, the designation of the teachers to be appointed, who shall be subjected to the examination of a committee of the Public School Society, shall be fully qualified for the duties of their appointment, and of unexceptionable moral character; or in the event of the trustees or managers failing to present individuals for these situations of that description, then individuals having like qualifications of unexceptionable character, to be selected and appointed by the Public School Society, who shall be acceptable to the managers or trustees of the schools to which they shall be appointed; but no person to be continued as a teacher in either of the schools referred to against the wishes of the managers or trustees thereof.

"The school shall be open at all times to the inspection of any authorized agent or officer of the city or State government, with liberty to visit the same, and examine the books used therein, or the teachers, touching the course and system of instruction pursued in the schools, or in relation to any matters connected therewith.

"The undersigned are willing that, in the superintendence of their schools, every specified requirement of any and every law passed by the legislature of the State, or the ordinances of the common council, to guard against abuse in the matter of common school education, shall be rigidly enforced and exacted by the competent public authorities.

"As regards the organization of their schools, they are willing that they should be under the same police and regulations as those of the Public School Society—the same hours, the same order, the same exercises, even the same inspection.

"But the books to be used for exercises in learning to read or spell, in history, geography, and all such elementary knowledge as could have a tendency to operate on their hearts and minds, in reference to their religion, must be, so far as Catholic children are concerned, and no farther, such as they shall judge proper to put in their hands. But none of their dogmas, nothing against the creed of any other denomination, shall be introduced."[1]

On the second day of the debate, Bishop Hughes spoke for three hours and a half; but, unfortunately, the discussion was given a religious turn by some of the Protestant ministers who took part in it, and the bishop's speech was devoted chiefly to the refutation of time-worn calumnies against the Church. "Eight or nine hours," he said later on, in referring to the council's attitude, "were wasted in the discussion of a theological tenet, but not one half hour was given to the only question which the common council should have permitted to come before them, namely: Are the rights of this portion of the citizens violated or not? If so, are there in our hands the means to apply a remedy?"[2] It was easy to forecast the council's decision, which, when it was finally rendered, on January 12, 1841, was overwhelmingly against the petition of the Catholics, only one vote being registered in their favor.

BEFORE THE LEGISLATURE

It was now decided to carry the fight to the

[1] Works of Bishop Hughes, vol. i, p. 199 seq.; Clarke, op. cit., p. 102. It will be observed that the arrangement proposed by Bishop Hughes did not differ substantially from the famous "Faribault Plan" proposed by Archbishop Ireland some years ago, and approved by Rome in the decision "Tolarari potest."
[2] Works, p. 243; O'Gorman, Hist. of the Church in the U. S., p. 373.

legislature, and, a month later, at a meeting of
the Catholics in Carroll Hall, a committee was appointed to draft a memorial to that body. The
memorial was presented to the Hon. John C.
Spencer, Secretary of State and *ex officio* superintendent of public schools, who soon afterward
made a report to the legislature in which he recom-
mended such a change in the school system of New
York City as would greatly limit the powers of
the Public School Society and, perhaps, open a
way to Catholics to obtain what they asked.[1]
Governor Seward was still favorable to Catholic
schools, and high hopes were again entertained of
justice being done to Catholic interests. The fight
was now transferred to the legislative halls in
Albany.

The enemies of the Catholic claim were active,
and employed every means within their power to
overcome the advantage which the Catholics possessed before the legislature in the attitude of the
Governor and Secretary of State. As in the discussion before the common council, they sought
deliberately to arouse religious prejudice, and
stooped to calumny to accomplish this purpose.
The press of the metropolis, with a few honorable
exceptions, teemed with matter calculated to stir
up the spirit of sectarian hate. Meanwhile,
Bishop Hughes, calm and dignified but none the
less determined, continued his campaign for the
enlightenment of public sentiment on the question.
Mass-meetings of the Catholics were called, and
a series of addresses delivered by the bishop in
which the illogical and unfair position of the Pub-

[1] Ibid., p. 220 seq.; Brann, John Hughes, p. 77.

lic School Society was set in clear relief, and the soundness and justice of the Catholic position vindicated with an eloquence and ability that entitle these great speeches to a place among the masterpieces of American oratory. Against the system in vogue, with its discrimination against Catholics and others who were taxed for its support, he appealed to the American sense of fair play:

"It is asked, 'What system would be deemed just by the Catholics?' I answer, any system that will leave the various denominations each in full possession of its religious rights over the minds of its own children. If the children are to be educated promiscuously as at present, let religion in every shape and form be excluded. Let not the Protestant version of the Scriptures, Protestant forms of prayers, Protestant hymns, be forced on the children of Catholics, Jews, and others, as at present, in schools for the support of which their parents pay taxes as well as Presbyterians."

To the only logical solution of the question, if there is to be *any* religion taught in the public schools, in view of religious conditions in America, he pointed, in saying:

"There is another system which the Catholics would deem just and equal. It is that each denomination should prescribe the amount and quality *for its own children* of religious instruction which, consistently with the ends of the State in providing education, might be incorporated with it. This plan, if it were practicable, would, in my opinion, be much safer for the welfare and security of society."[1]

[1]Works of Bishop Hughes, vol. i, p. 293 seq.

There can be little doubt that, had the real issue been fought out on its merits at Albany, justice would have been rendered the Catholic petitioners; but the appeal to bigotry gained the day. Alarmed by the rising storm of religious prejudice, with the elections coming on in the fall, the State Senate, when the matter came to a vote during the summer, postponed a decision until the January following.

MADE A POLITICAL ISSUE

The battle-ground was thus changed again— this time to the arena of popular suffrage. The cry of "No Popery" was raised, and re-echoed from one end of the State to the other. In the metropolis especially, a spirit of malignant religious intolerance was in the air, and from pulpit and hustings, as well as through the press, a storm of denunciation and vituperation was launched against the Catholic Church and Bishop Hughes. Candidates for office were obliged to declare themselves on the question of separate Catholic schools. Bishop Hughes had from the beginning opposed all attempts to make the issue one of party politics, but, at the last moment, with the candidates of both parties pledged against his plan, he adopted the alternative of a Catholic party, and, at a mass-meeting of his people, held only four days before the election, candidates were nominated for the legislature who were pledged to the bishop's plan. It was too late to influence the result, but the comparatively large vote polled by the Catholic party had the effect of frightening the politicians and inducing a disposition in the legislature to compromise. Governor Seward, in his message in January, 1842, again brought the question to the attention of the legislature, and on April 9 a bill was passed which was the death-knell of the Public School Society, by the extension to New York City of the general State legislation for common schools.[1]

RESULTS OF THE CONTROVERSY

Bishop Hughes wisely recognized that nothing further was to be gained by continuing the controversy. He had been, as Bishop Kenrick put it, "fairly worsted" in his fight for justice for Catholic schools, and his defeat had a discouraging influence upon similar movements that were making in other parts of the country.[2] And yet, he had gained some great advantages. He had dislodged the Public School Society, a private corporation, from its monopoly of public education. He had roused the Catholic public the country over to a keen sense of the importance of the question of religious instruction in the school. He had convinced them that the attendance of Catholic children at the public schools, as then conducted, meant proximate danger to their faith, and the issue of the struggle made it plain that nothing in the way of a compromise was to be hoped for which would render the danger remote or remediable. The only alternative for Catholics was to establish and develop a system of schools of their

[1]Hughes, loc. cit., p. 242 seq.; Brann, Life of Bishop Hughes, p. 80 seq.; O'Gorman, op. cit., p. 374.
[2]Letter of Bishop Kenrick to Dr. Cullen, Mar. 28, 1843.

own, independent of State support and control.
To this task Bishop Hughes turned immediately
with all the ardor and energy that a great mind
is capable of bringing to the performance of a
great work, and throughout the rest of his life the
development of a Catholic system of education was
ever foremost among the great projects for which
he worked and planned. His educational principle
was:

"Let parochial schools be established and maintained everywhere; the days have come, and the
place, in which the school is more necessary than
the church."

And he carried out this principle in practice, saying to each new pastor he appointed:

"You must proceed upon the principle that, in
this age and country, the school is before the
church."[1]

HIGHER CATHOLIC EDUCATION

In the year 1839, a diocesan seminary had been
opened at Lafargeville, in Jefferson County, and
two years later the institution was removed to
Fordham, and a college for secular students established in connection with it. Father Andrew
Byrne was now sent to Ireland to secure Christian
Brothers to take charge of boys' schools, but, owing to the scarcity of teachers, his mission was for
the time being unsuccessful.[2] While in Europe,
however, Bishop Hughes had engaged the Ladies
of the Sacred Heart to send a colony of Sisters to

[1] Considine, Brief Chron. Account of the Ed. Institutions in
N. Y. City, pp. 18, 19.
[2] Clarke, Lives of Deceased Bishops, vol. ii, p. 265.

found an academy for the higher education of girls in the diocese, and in the year 1841, under the direction of Madame Elizabeth Gallitzin, a cousin of the famous prince-priest Demetrius Augustin Gallitzin, the Sisters established themselves at Manhattanville, from which place they gradually extended their work, founding schools and academies in many parts of the country.[1] In 1845 Bishop Hughes again crossed the ocean, for the express purpose of getting teachers for his growing system of academies and schools. In France, he succeeded in obtaining a number of Christian Brothers who, three years later, opened two schools for boys—St. Vincent de Paul's Academy in Canal Street, and De La Salle Academy on Second Street, near Second Avenue. In the year 1846, the college at Fordham was chartered as a university, and soon afterward it was transferred to the Jesuits. In 1847, the Jesuits also opened St. Francis Xavier College, on Sixteenth Street, in the church basement.[2]

PAROCHIAL SCHOOLS

While he was thus providing for higher and intermediate Catholic education, Bishop Hughes' efforts were not less fruitful in behalf of parochial schools. When in Europe, he secured a colony of Sisters of Mercy from Ireland for educational and hospital work. The Sisters of Charity were a strong body in the diocese, and in 1846 they were organized as a separate religious community.[3]

[1] Clarke, loc. cit., p. 110; Brann, op. cit., p. 87; Cath. Directory.
[2] Considine, op. cit.; Brann, ibid.; Clarke, ibid.
[3] See chap. vii, Sisters of Charity of Emmittsburg.

The number of Sisters in the new organization grew rapidly, and the community was able to furnish teachers to most of the schools that were being established. The number of schools also rapidly increased, the increase averaging more than one a year. Bishop Hughes' aggressive educational policy of "the school before the church" was, in fact, carried out literally. In the interval of twenty-three years between the debate before the common council and the time of his death, about thirty-eight new schools were established, and this, too, in the face of an immense diocesan debt, which at times involved the bishop in serious financial embarrassment. Before his death, it must have been a source of satisfaction to the great prelate to see that, as the fruit of his unsparing labors in behalf of Catholic education, the diocese could boast of several flourishing institutions of higher education for young men as well as several for young women, a number of academies for boys and also for girls, and a common parish school attached to nearly every church in New York City and its suburbs.[1]

[1]Considine, op. cit.

APPENDIX A

CURRICULUM OF ST. JOSEPH'S ACADEMY, CONDUCTED BY THE SISTERS OF CHARITY AT EMMITTSBURG (ABOUT 1813)[1]

Daily Program

8 A.M.　Opening of classes.
　　　　1st Class, Grammar, Parsing, Spelling, Reading.
　　　　2d Class, Grammar, Parsing, Spelling, Reading.
　　　　3d Class, beginning of Grammar, Reading, and Spelling.
　　　　4th Class, Spelling and Reading.

9.30 "　1st Class, Writing.
　　　　2d Class, Writing.
　　　　3d Class, Writing.
　　　　4th Class, Writing.

10.30 "　1st Class, Book-keeping.
　　　　2d Class, Ciphering.
　　　　3d Class, Ciphering.
　　　　4th Class, Ciphering.

11.30 "　Industrial Work and study. Part of the time to be employed by the pupils in "learning stitches," in sewing and mending, and part to be spent in preparing for the next classes; some allowed to give the entire hour to industrial work.

[1]The copy of this curriculum in the archives of St. Joseph's Academy is in the handwriting of the Rev. John Dubois, President of Mt. St. Mary's Seminary, Emmittsburg, who succeeded Father Dubourg as Ecclesiastical Superior of the Sisters of Charity, and who subsequently became bishop of New York.

12.45 P.M. Spiritual Exercises.

1   "   Dinner, followed by Recreation till 3 o'clock.

3   "   1st Class, History.

            2d Class, History, combined with Writing Exercises.

            3d Class, Spelling, Parsing, Reading.

            4th Class, Spelling and Reading.

4   "   1st Class, French twice a week; Geography three times a week.

            2d Class, French twice a week; Geography three times a week.

            3d Class, French.

            4th Class, French; the first principles of Grammar.

5   "   Recreation.

6.15 "   Study until Supper.

APPENDIX B

PROSPECTUS OF A CATHOLIC ACADEMY IN 1838[1]

(*Loretto Academy, Ky.*)

THE tutoresses of Loretto Academy, as well as those who at all times preside over the pupils, have been carefully selected from the most numerous community in the west, with a view not only to talent and learning but also to disposition and aptitude to fashion and habituate the young mind to what is useful, elegant, and proper. The French language is taught by French ladies; Painting by ladies who have long taught with reputation; Music by the pupils of the talented professor, Peterson; Dancing by Madame Blaique, who also has schools in Lexington, Louisville, and Cincinnati.

The branches taught are as follows: Reading, Writing, Arithmetic, English Grammar, Geography, with the use of Maps and Globes; History, Ancient and Modern, with Chronology and Mythology; Rhetoric and Composition, Botany, Optics, and the elements of Mechanics, Hydrostatics and Astronomy, Chemistry and Natural Philosophy, the French language, Needlework, plain and fancy; Marking, Lace and Bead Work, Drawing and Painting in water colors, Crayon Drawing, Painting on Satin and Velvet; Music, Vocal and on the Piano-Forte and Guitar, Dancing. Lessons and Exercises will be given in Polite Literature.

[1]From the advertisement of the Academy in the Catholic Advocate, Bardstown, Sept. 8, 1838.

Terms

Board and Washing, per session........$35 00
Tuition, in Reading, Writing, English
    Grammar, Plain Sewing and Mark-
    ing, per session.................. 6 00
Tuition, in Geography, with the use of
    Maps and Globes, Fancy Needle-
    work, Embroidery, Beading, Draw-
    ing and Painting, Rhetoric and His-
    tory, Botany and Philosophy, extra.. 4 00
Extra charge for Music and use of Pianos,
    per session..................... 15 00
Extra charge for Music on the Guitar.... 12 00
Extra charge for the French Language...   5 00
Extra charge for Dancing, per quarter... 10 00

The Academic year is divided into two sessions —the first commencing 1st September, and expiring 15th February; the second commencing 20th February, and expiring 1st of August.

APPENDIX C

Prospectus of a New York Private School in 1829

Besides the parochial schools, which were being multiplied rapidly about this time, there were also many private Catholic schools. School-teaching was always a favorite occupation for the better educated among the Irish and the German immigrants. The newspapers and periodicals of the time contain many notices of these schools. The following advertisement of a well-known New York school is characteristic of a fashion of setting forth the claims of educational institutions upon the patronage of the public which prevailed throughout the country, with non-Catholics as well as Catholics. It is taken from Truth Teller, New York City, Jan. 8, 1829.

CHRESTOMATHIC INSTITUTION
or
SEMINARY FOR GENERAL EDUCATION

No. 36 Cherry Street, a few doors from Franklin Square

P. S. Casserly, T.C.D., Principal

At a time when there are so many respectable seminaries for the education of youth in this city, many of them too conducted with judgment and success—it may seem intrusive to call on public patronage for the encouragement of one more. But without drawing any invidious comparisons, or seeking to depreciate the pretensions of others, by extolling his own, the subscriber trusts he now comes before a discerning public, with peculiar claims on its support. Born and educated in an academy of long standing, in his native land, carefully instructed in all the branches both of a Classical and an English education, in that solid and withal elegant manner, for which the old countries are so remarkable, constantly adding to his stock of acquirements, by perusing the best works on education, personally examining the different systems of Bell, Lancaster, Feinagle and Edgeworth, operate on each of these systems in his own seminary, over which he presided for many years, and added to this, having the paramount advantage of being practically and critically conversant with the Sizarship course of Trinity College, Dublin— allowedly the most difficult in Europe, Mr. C. may assert with confidence, that he can offer the enlightened citizens of New York an extensive course of useful as well as polite education, not surpassed by any in the United States. From all these varied advantages, from his intimate acquaintance with the best modes of education now followed in England and Ireland, from his long experience in the art of teaching—for it is an art —from that well-grounded confidence in his preceptorial capability, which a life-time's familiarity can alone bestow, and from the honorable testimonials which he has received from some of the most eminent literary characters, both in Europe and America, Mr. C. presumes to look for the fostering hand of the intelligent and enterprising emporium of the western world. The most undeviating attention shall be paid, by conciliatory monition, to inculcate habits of mental discipline, genteel deportment, strict propriety of conduct, and unremitting application. The best masters in the several departments are engaged; but the classes can, in no instance, be confided exclusively to assistants; as, consistently with his plan of teaching, they must be individually subjected to the personal examination and instruction of Mr. C. himself, whose interest and reputation are mainly dependent on the character of his establishment.

The location of the seminary is in a healthy and retired situation, free from the noise and interruption of public streets. The course of instruction is divided into two departments: the English, embracing spelling, reading, explanation, elocution, writing, arithmetic, English grammar, parsing, exercises, composition, history, geography, use of Globes and Maps, astronomy, book-keeping, mensuration, surveying, geometry, trigonometry, navigation, algebra, etc. The classical or collegiate, containing the Greek, Latin, French, Spanish, and Italian Languages, with constant reference to grammar, syntax, exercises, prosody, derivation and peculiarities.

APPENDIX D

STATISTICS OF THE CATHOLIC CHURCH IN THE UNITED STATES IN 1838 [1]

DIOCESES	Churches	Other Stations	Clergymen on the Missions	Clergymen otherwise Employed	Ecclesiastical Seminaries	Clerical Students	Colleges for Young Men	Female Religious Institutions	Female Academies	Charitable Institutions [2]
Baltimore....	61	10	44	28	3	63	4	3	8	12
Philadelphia..	63	8	43	1	1	12	0	0	1	7
New York....	38	12	50	0	0		0	0	2	5
Boston......	18	45	27	0	1		1	0	0	1
Detroit......	*12	*12	21		0		1	2	1	5
Cincinnati ...	24	16	24	3	1	9	1		1	2
Vincennes ...	10	40	20	2			1	1	1	
St. Louis....	29	46	31	28	2	32	2	9	9	3
Bardstown....	*23		25	22	2	25	2	6	9	1
Charleston...	12	34	14	1	1	7	1	2	2	1
Mobile......	*10		7	3			1	1	1	
New Orleans .	24		28					3	3	2
Natchez[3].....										
Nashville....										
Dubuque										
15	**334**	**223**	**334**	**88**	**11**	**148**	**15**	**27**	**38**	**39**

[1] From the Catholic Almanac for 1838. "The numbers marked with an asterisk (*) are not given as strictly exact, though it is believed they approximate to the truth, and are as accurate as could be ascertained from the statements forwarded to the editor from the several dioceses."

[2] Under the heading "Charitable Institutions," it was intended chiefly to designate orphan asylums. No attempt was made to ascertain the total number of Catholic schools. Taking the country as a whole, it must have contained, at this date, about 200 Catholic parish schools, exclusive of institutions of secondary-school and collegiate rank.

[3] The dioceses of Natchez, Nashville, and Dubuque had just been formed. In 1839, only 4 priests are reported as being in these three dioceses.

APPENDIX E

Bibliography

Documentary Sources

Original documents and records were consulted at the following places:

New Orleans, archives of the Ursuline Sisters, at the Ursuline Convent.

Annapolis, Maryland Will-books pertaining to the Colonial period, in the office of the Register of Wills.

Washington, manuscript records in the archives of Georgetown University.

Washington, records of the Visitation Convent, Georgetown.

Baltimore, original letters and documents, in the Cathedral archives.

Baltimore, archives of St. Mary's Seminary.

Notre Dame, Ind., original documents in the collection in Bishops' Memorial Hall.

Emmittsburg, Md., archives of the Mother-house of the Sisters of Charity.

Loretto, Nerinckx County, Ky., archives of the Mother-house of the Sisters of Loretto.

Early Catholic Newspapers

Among the early Catholic periodicals, the following were found to contain material of importance for the study of Catholic educational history in the United States. They are arranged chronologically, the date of the foundation of each being added.

United States Catholic Miscellany, Charleston, S. C., 1822.

Catholic Miscellany, London, Eng., 1822. Vol. I contains some valuable letters from Catholic missionaries in the United States.

Truth Teller, New York City, 1825, successor of the *Shamrock*.

The Jesuit, or *The Catholic Sentinel*, Boston, 1829.

The Metropolitan, a monthly, Baltimore, 1830.

The Catholic Telegraph, Cincinnati, 1831.

The Catholic Herald, Philadelphia, 1833.

New York Weekly Register and Catholic Diary, 1833; became merged in the *Freeman's Journal* in 1841.

The Catholic Advocate, Bardstown, Ky., 1836.

New York Freeman's Journal, 1840; absorbed the *Weekly Register* in 1841.

The Religious Cabinet, Baltimore, 1842. The next year the name was changed to *The United States Catholic Magazine*. Vols. I-VIII contain much valuable matter relating to the history of Catholic schools during the period of publication, as well as during and after the Colonial period.

Books, Pamphlets, etc.

General histories are not included in the following list, except their treatment of educational matters is such as to render them of special importance for the history of Catholic education. In the case of works that are rather rare, reference is given to the libraries in which they were used.

ALERDING, RT. REV. H. A History of the Catholic Church in the Diocese of Vincennes. 1883, pp. 636.

AMERICAN CATHOLIC QUARTERLY RESEARCHES. Philadelphia: Founded in 1884.

One of the most valuable sources of materials for early Catholic educational history.

ANNALES DE LA PROPAGATION DE LA FOI,
1823-1840.

Invaluable for the study of Catholic educational history.
Contains numerous letters from American priests and bishops
describing their work.

BALDWIN, JANE. The Maryland Calendar of
Wills. Baltimore: William C. Dulany Co.,
1901, pp. 219.

Contains abstracts of the wills made in the colony, 1635-85.

DE BARBEREY, MME. Elizabeth Seton et les com-
mencements de l'Eglise Catholique aux Etats-
Unis. Paris: 1881, 2 vols.

BAYLEY, RT. REV. JAMES ROOSEVELT. Memoirs
of the Rt. Rev. Simon Wm. Gabriel Bruté.
1876, pp. 261.

BAYLEY, RT. REV. JAMES ROOSEVELT. Sketch of
the Early History of the Catholic Church on
the Island of New York. 1870, pp. 242.

BENAVIDES, ALONZO DE. Memorial to the King
of Spain dated 1630, Madrid. Translated by
John Gilmary Shea and 25 copies published
in 1899, 31 pp., 8vo, Library of Congress.

BERTRAND. Bibliothèque sulpicienne ou Histoire
littéraire de la Compagnie de Saint-Sulpice.
Paris: A. Picard et fils, 1900, 2 vols.

BLACKMAR, FRANK W. Spanish Colonization in
the Southwest, Johns Hopkins University
Studies, vol. iv, 8th series, 1890, pp. 79.

BOESE, THOMAS. Public Education in the City of
New York, its history, condition, and statistics. An official report to the Board of Education, 1869, pp. 228.

BRANN, REV. HENRY J. Life of John Hughes.
New York: Benziger Bros., 1892, pp. 182.

BROWN, ELMER ELLSWORTH. The Making of
our Middle Schools. New York: Longmans,
Green & Co., 1903, pp. 547.

BROWNSON, S. A. Life of Demetrius A. Gallitzin. New York: Pustet & Co., 1873, pp. 444.

BURNING OF THE CONVENT, THE. A Narrative of the Destruction by a Mob of the Ursuline School, Charlestown, Mass. By one of the Pupils. Boston: 1877, pp. 198.

CATHEDRAL RECORDS, BALTIMORE. Catholic Mirror Publishing Co., 1906, pp. 115.

CATHOLIC DIRECTORY.

A rich mine of statistics and facts relating to the history of Catholic education in the United States. The first Directory was issued in 1817, under the title of *The Catholic Almanac,* and was very small. The second was issued in 1822, under the title of *The Laity's Directory.* Beginning with 1833, the Directory was published annually, and was gradually enlarged. A complete collection exists in the Riggs Library, Georgetown University, J. G. Shea Collection.

CLARKE, RICHARD H. Lives of the Deceased Bishops of the Catholic Church in the United States. New York: 3 vols., 1888.

(CLEWS) PARSONS, MRS. ELSIE WORTHINGTON. Educational Legislation and Administration of the Colonial Governments. New York: The Macmillan Co., 1899, pp. 524.

CLINCH, BRYAN J. California and its Missions. San Francisco: Whittaker & Ray Co., 2 vols., 8vo, 1904.

CONSIDINE, REV. M. J. A Brief Chronological Account of the Catholic Educational Institutions of the Archdiocese of New York. Benziger Bros., 1894, pp. 59.

COUES, ELLIOTT. On the Trail of a Spanish Pioneer—The Diary and Itinerary of Francis Garces, 1775-6. New York: Francis P. Harper, 2 vols., 8vo, 1900.

COX, I. J. Educational Efforts in San Fernando de Bexar (San Antonio). In *Texas Historical Association Quarterly,* 1902.

DAVIS, GEORGE LYNN-LACHLAN. The Day Star of American Freedom, or The Birth and Early Growth of Toleration in the Province of Maryland. New York: Charles Scribner, 1855, pp. 290.

A valuable compendium of information relating to early Maryland history, and drawn largely from documentary sources.

DE ANDREIS, VERY REV. FELIX, First Superior of the Congregation of the Mission in the United States. Sketches of his life. Pp. 276.

The edition of 1861 contains a valuable "Sketch of the Progress of the Catholic Religion in the United States, from the beginning of the century to the year 1860," which gives much educational information. This "Sketch" was omitted in the edition of 1900. References in the text are to the first edition.

DE COURCY, HENRY. The Catholic Church in the United States. 1856, pp. 591.

DE GOESBRIAND, RT. REV. L. Catholic Memoirs and Biographies of Vermont and New Hampshire. Burlington: 1886, pp. 166.

DEXTER, EDWIN GRANT. A History of Education in the United States. New York: The Macmillan Co., 1904, pp. 656.

DOCUMENT NO. 80, being a Report of the Committee on Arts and Sciences and Schools of the Board of Assistants (New York City), on the subject of appropriating a portion of the School Money to religious societies for the support of schools. New York: 1840, Georgetown University, Shea Collection.

DWINELLE, JOHN. Colonial History of the City of San Francisco. A Narrative Argument in the Circuit Court of the United States for the State of California, 1869, 8vo, pp. 369.

EDUCATION IN LOUISIANA IN FRENCH COLONIAL DAYS. By M. A. C., in *American Catholic Quarterly Review,* vol. xi, pp. 395-418, July, 1886.

EDUCATION IN NEW ORLEANS IN SPANISH COLONIAL DAYS. By M. A. C., in *American Catholic Quarterly Review,* vol. xii, pp. 253-277, April, 1887.

EGGLESTON, EDWARD. The Transit of Civilization from England to America in the Seventeenth Century. New York: D. Appleton & Co., 1901, pp. 344.

Chapter V consists of an extremely interesting study of the influences which went to make up early American schools and school systems. There are many references to first-hand sources of information.

ENGLAND, RT. REV. JOHN, Works of. 5 vols., 1849.

FARMER, SILAS. The History of Detroit and Michigan. 1884, pp. 998.

Contains a fair though brief sketch of the educational work of Father Richard.

FAY, EDWIN WHITFIELD. The History of Education in Louisiana. Printed as Circular of Information, no. 1, 1898, by United States Bureau of Education.

FINOTTI, REV. JOSEPH M. Bibliographia Catholica Americana, Part I, from 1784 to 1820, inclusive. New York: The Catholic Publication House, 1872, pp. 318.

Contains a list of the early catechisms printed in this country and references to several other works of an educational character.

FLINTHAM, LYDIA STIRLING. Sisters of Loretto. Pp. 16.

FOLEY, HENRY, S.J. Records of the English Province of the Society of Jesus. In eight series, with two additional volumes of General Statistics and Collectania. London: 1878.

GOLDEN BELLS IN CONVENT TOWERS. The Story of Father Samuel (Mazzuchelli) and Saint Clara (Sinsinawa, Wis.). 1904, pp. 127.

GORDY, J. P. Rise and Growth of the Normal School Idea in the United States. Circular of Information, no. 8, Bureau of Education, 1891, pp. 145.

GRIFFIN, MARTIN I. J. History of Bishop Egan. Philadelphia: 1903, pp. 256.

HAMMER, REV. P. BONIVENTURA. Eduard Dominik Fenwick, Der Apostel von Ohio. St. Louis: B. Herder, 1890, pp. 168.

HASSARD, JOHN R. G. Life of the Most Rev. John Hughes. New York: 1866, pp. 519.

HELPS, SIR ARTHUR. The Spanish Conquest in America. 4 vols., 1900.

HILL, REV. WALTER H., S.J. Historical Sketch of the St. Louis University. St. Louis: Patrick Fox, Publisher, 1879, pp. 160.

HISTORICAL RECORDS AND STUDIES. See *United States Catholic Historical Magazine.*

HISTORICAL SKETCHES OF THE CATHOLIC CHURCHES AND INSTITUTIONS OF PHILADELPHIA. A Parish Register and Book of Reference. Philadelphia: Daniel H. Maloney, Publisher.

HOUCK, REV. GEORGE F. The Church in Northern Ohio. New York: Benziger Bros., 1887, pp. 266.

HOWLETT, REV. WILLIAM J. Historical Tribute to St. Thomas Seminary, near Bardstown, Ky. New York: B. Herder, 1906, pp. 197.

HUGHES, RT. REV. JOHN, Works of. In 2 vols., 1864.

Vol. I contains his speeches and lectures on the school question.

JACKSON, HELEN HUNT. Father Junipero and the Mission Indians of California. Boston: Little, Brown & Co., 1902, pp. 159.

KATHOLISCHEN KIRCHEN UND INSTITUTE, DIE, IN CINCINNATI. Cincinnati: Catholic Publishing Association, 1889, pp. 195.

LAMBING, REV. A. A. A History of the Catholic Church in the Dioceses of Pittsburg and Allegheny. New York: Benziger Bros., 1880, pp. 531.

LATHROP, GEORGE PARSONS. A Story of Courage: Annals of the Georgetown Convent of the Visitation. 1895, pp. 380.

McCOY, REV. JOHN J. A History of the Catholic Church in the Diocese of Springfield. Boston: Hurd & Evarts Co., 1900, pp. 283.

McGIRR, JOHN E. Life of Rt. Rev. William Quarter, First Bishop of Chicago. New York: 1850, pp. 142.

McLAUGHLIN, ANDREW C. History of Higher Education in Michigan. Circular of Information, no. 4, 1891, Bureau of Education, pp. 179.

Gives an account of the organization of the Catholepistemiad, or University of Michigania.

MAES, RT. REV. CAMILLUS P. The Life of Rev. Charles Nerinckx. Cincinnati: Robert Clark & Co., 1880, pp. 619.

Contains an historical sketch of the origin and development of the Loretto sisterhood up to the date of publication.

MARTY, REV. MARTIN, O.S.B. Dr. Johann Martin Henni. New York: Benziger Bros., 1888, pp. 321.

MARYLAND HISTORICAL SOCIETY PUBLICATIONS. Number 7 contains the *Relatio Itineris* of Father White, and Annual Letters of the missionaries. Cf. also numbers 8, 9, 20.

NEW YORK CITY EDUCATION PAMPHLETS. A series of Reports and Papers dealing with Education in New York City. Teachers College Library, Columbia University.

Document no. 41 contains a report of the rise and development of the public school system of New York, 1869.

O'GORMAN, RT. REV. THOMAS. A History of the Roman Catholic Church in the United States. American Church History Series, 1895, pp. 515.

O'SHEA, JOHN J. The Two Kenricks. Philadelphia: John J. McVey, 1904, pp. 495.

PUTNAM, DANIEL. The Development of Primary and Secondary Education in Michigan. Ann Arbor: 1904, pp. 269.

RECORDS OF THE AMERICAN CATHOLIC HISTORICAL SOCIETY OF PHILADELPHIA, begun in 1884.

RÈGLEMENTS DES RELIGIEUSES URSULINES. Seconde Partie: Des Écolieres Externes. Paris: 1705, pp. 143-186.

RÈGLEMENTS DES RELIGIEUSES URSULINES de la Congrégation de Paris. Paris: 1860, pp. 190.

RELATION DU VOYAGE DES DAMES RELIGIEUSES URSULINES de Rouen a la Nouvelle-Orleans. With an introduction and notes by Gabriel Gravier. Paris: 1872. Congressional Library Print.

This is a precious work for the student of Catholic educational history. It consists chiefly of a series of five letters of Madeleine Hachard (Sister Stanislaus) to her parents in

France, the third being the "Relation" proper, or account of the voyage. There is also an appendix, consisting of several memoirs on the state of the Church in Louisiana, taken from the archives of the Minister of Marine, Paris.

RELATION DU VOYAGE DES PREMIÈRES UR-SULINES a Nouvelle-Orleans et de leur établissement en cette ville. Par le Rev. Mère St. Augustin de Tranchepain, Supérieure. New York: J. G. Shea, Cramoisy Press, 1859. Congressional Library.

This work consists of five letters. The first is Sister Stanislaus' account of the voyage, referred to above. The other four are Circular Letters, largely biographical in character, written on the occasions of the deaths of four Sisters in New Orleans, the last referring to the death and character of Mother Tranchepain.

RENSHAW, HENRY. The Louisiana Ursulines. A Lecture, constituting part 4, vol. ii, of the Publications of the Louisiana Historical Society. New Orleans: December, 1901.

In the appendix to this volume are given the articles of agreement between the "Company of the West" and the Ursulines.

REPORTS OF THE COMMISSIONER OF EDUCATION. Report for 1892-3 contains a conspectus of educational legislation in several of the English colonies.

RILEY, JOHN T. Collections and Recollections. Martinsburg: 1892-1902, 7 vols.

RILEY, JOHN T. Conewago, a Collection of Catholic Local History. Martinsburg: 1884, pp. 220.

RIVAUX, ABBÉ. Life of Mother St. John Fontbonne, Foundress and First Superior-General of the Congregation of the Sisters of St. Joseph. Translation. New York: Benziger Bros., 1887, pp. 295.

SADLIER, AGNES. Elizabeth Seton. New York: D. & J. Sadlier & Co., 1905, pp. 289.
SCHARF, J. THOMAS. The History of Maryland. 3 vols., 8vo. Baltimore: John B. Piett, 1879.
SETON, ELIZABETH. Memoir, Letters and Journal. Edited by the Rt. Rev. Robert Seton. 2 vols. New York: 1869.
SHEA, JOHN GILMARY. History of the Catholic Church in the United States. 4 vols.

This standard work is of great value for the study of Catholic educational history; contains much educational information, drawn largely from original sources, with frequent references.

SPALDING, MOST REV. M. J. Sketches of the Early Catholic Missions of Kentucky, from their Commencement in 1787 to the Jubilee of 1826-7. Louisville: 1844, pp. 308.

A most valuable record, drawn from original sources, of the foundation of the Church in Kentucky and the neighboring States.

SPALDING, MOST REV. M. J. Sketches of the Life, Times and Character of the Rt. Rev. Benedict Joseph Flaget, First Bishop of Louisville. Louisville: 1852, pp. 405.
SPALDING, RT. REV. J. L. The Life of the Most Rev. M. J. Spalding. New York: The Catholic Publication Society, 1873, pp. 460.
SPRING HILL COLLEGE, Mobile, Ala., 1830-1905. Mobile: 1906, pp. 221.
STEINER, BERNARD C. History of Education in Maryland. Circular of Information, no. 2, United States Bureau of Education, 1894.
TRAHEY, REV. JAMES J. The Brothers of Holy Cross. Notre Dame, Ind.: 1907, pp. 168.
UNITED STATES CATHOLIC HISTORICAL MAGAZINE, under the auspices of the United States

Catholic Historical Society, New York. Published as a quarterly from 1887 to 1892, later in the form of periodical volumes, called Historical Records and Studies.

Contains much in the way of historical data relating to the early schools.

UNIVERSITY OF NOTRE DAME DU LAC, Indiana, A Brief History of, from 1842 to 1892. Prepared for the Golden Jubilee. Pp. 256.

URSULINES IN LOUISIANA, THE. By the Author of "Leaves from the Annals of the Sisters of Mercy." New Orleans: Hyman Smith, 1886, pp. 38.

VAN DEN BROEK, FATHER, The Story of. Chicago: Ainsworth & Co., 1907, pp. 94.

VERWYST, REV. P. CHRYSOSTOMUS, O.F.M. Life and Labors of Bishop Baraga. Milwaukee: M. F. Wiltzius & Co., 1900, pp. 476.

VITANCURT, AUGUSTIN DE. Teatro Mexicano, including the Menalogio Franciscano. Congressional Library.

The latter section especially contains much information about the friars who labored in the New Mexican missions.

WALSH, RT. REV. LOUIS L. The Early Irish Catholic Schools of Lowell, Mass. Boston: Thomas A. Whalen & Co., 1901, pp. 20.

WALSH, RT. REV. LOUIS L. Historical Sketch of the Catholic Parochial Schools in the Archdiocese of Boston. 1901, pp. 16.

WEBB, BENJAMIN J. The Centenary of Catholicity in Kentucky. Louisville: 1884, pp. 580.

WHITE, REV. CHARLES I. Life of Mrs. Elizabeth A. Seton. New York: 1853, pp. 581.

WICKERSHAM, JAMES PYLE. A History of Education in Pennsylvania. Lancaster, Pa.: Inquirer Publishing Co., 1886, pp. 683.

WISCONSIN HISTORICAL COLLECTIONS.

Volume V contains a study of the early schools of Wisconsin, by W. C. Whitford, President of Milton College, pp. 320-351.

WOODSTOCK LETTERS, vols. i-xxv.

A large and important collection of materials relating to early American Catholic history.

INDEX

Jesuit schools and educational
influence, sources of information, 37; in Lower California, 52, 53; New Or-
leans, 67, 68; Kaskaskia
and Mackinaw, 86; Detroit,
87; Maryland, 89 seq.;
Colony of New York, 104;
Pennsylvania, 119 seq.;
Washington, D. C., 256;
Frederick, Md., 257; New
York, 267 seq., 376; Wor-
cester, Mass., 283; New
Hampshire, 284; Missouri,
304, 314; Arkansas, 319;
Kentucky, 324; Cincinnati,
329.

KANSAS, Osage Mission
School, 231, 235.
Kaskaskia, early schools, 86;
Visitation academy and
school, 309.
Kaukauna, Wis., 338.
Keily, Rev. Jeremiah, 261.
Kenrick, Rt. Rev. Francis
Patrick, at First Provincial
Council of Baltimore, 249;
as bishop of Philadelphia,
260 seq.; also 374.
Kentucky, first school, 175;
see Sisters of Loretto, Sis-
ters of Charity of Nazareth,
Sisters of St. Dominic,
Bardstown.
Kohlmann, Rev. Anthony,
S.J., 267, 268.
Kundeck, Rev. Joseph, edu-
cational work in Indiana,
353.

LABADIE, Monique (Mrs. Antoine Beaubien), teacher in
Father Richard's school,
Detroit, 183, 184, 197, 347.
La Croix, Mich., Indian
school, 346.
Ladies of the Sacred Heart,
educational work, 298, 306,
321, 375.
La Fourche, La., Lazarist
seminary, 303.
Lalor, Alice, Foundress of
Visitation Convent, George-
town, 169, 203.
Lancaster, Pa., earliest Cath-
olic school, 132; German
language used, 155; later
schools, 264.
Lancasterian System in
Catholic schools, compared
to Ursuline System of
dizainières, 77; introduced
into United States, 199;
New York, 269, 271; New
Orleans, 305.
L'Anse, Mich., 345.
La Pointe, Mich., 345.
La Salle, Ill., 314.
Las Casas, works for school
legislation for natives, 40.
Lazarists, or Congregation of
the Mission, educational
work, 298, 301 seq.
Lazuen, Rev. Fermin Francis,
educational work, 58 seq.
Leopoldinen-Stiftung, assist-
ance to schools, 251, 294.
Lexington, Ky., 242.
Little Rock, Ark., 235, 319.
Loras, Rt. Rev. Matthew,
first bishop of Dubuque, 318.

PRINTED BY BENZIGER BROTHERS, NEW YORK